The Making of Christian Communities in Late Antiquity and the Middle Ages

The Making of Christian Communities in Late Antiquity and the Middle Ages

Mark Williams

Anthem Press
London

This edition first published by Anthem Press 2005

Anthem Press is an imprint of
Wimbledon Publishing Company
PO Box 9779, London, SW19 7QA

Typeset by Mudra Typesetters, India
Printed in India

Contributors

The Making of
Christian Communities

Giles Constable is senior member in the School for Historical Studies,
the Institute for Advanced Study, Princeton. His publications include
The Letters of Peter the Venerable, *The Reformation of the Twelfth
Century*, and *Three Studies in Medieval Religious and Social Thought*.

Ásdis Egilsdóttir is Associate Professor of Medieval Icelandic
Literature in the University of Iceland. Her publications include works
on Icelandic hagiography and Christian poetry. Her standard edition
of *Biskupa sögur* (Bishops' Sagas), with an introduction and notes,
is due to appear in 2001.

E Rozanne Elder is a graduate of the University of Toronto's Centre
for Medieval Studies. She is currently Director of the Institute of
Cistercian Studies and Professor of History in Western Michigan
University and Editorial Director of Cistercian Publications, Inc.

C Stephen Jaeger is Professor in the Program of Medieval Studies at
the University of Illinois at Urbana-Champaign. He is the author of
numerous books and articles including *The Origins of Courtliness,
The Envy of Angels* and *Ennobling Love*.

James Marchand is Professor Emeritus of German, Linguistics and
Comparative Literature, and a member of the Center for Advanced
Study in the University of Illinois at Urbana-Champaign. He was
recently named one of the 2000 Outstanding Scholars of the Twentieth
Century by the International Biographical Centre, Cambridge,
England, for contributions to Medieval Studies, Linguistics and
Computer Studies.

Brian Patrick McGuire is Professor of History in the University of
Roskilde. He is the author of numerous books, including *Friendship*

and Community: The Monastic Experience, 350–1250, and *Brother and Lover: Aelred of Rievaulx,* and translator of *Jean Gerson: Early Works.*

Oliver Nicholson is Associate Professor in the Department of Classical and Near Eastern Studies and Director of the Center for Mediaeval Studies in the University of Minnesota. He is working on a study of the persecution of Christians in the Roman Empire and a monograph on Lactantius and also on the future Oxford Dictionary of Late Antiquity, of which he is the General Editor.

Fred Paxton is Brigida Pacchiani Ardenghi Professor of History in Connecticut College. He is the author of *Christianizing Death: The Creation of a Ritual Process in Early Medieval Europe* and *A Medieval Latin Death Ritual: The Customaries of Bernard and Ulrich of Cluny,* as well as numerous essays and articles on canon law, church history, health and mortality in Medieval Europe.

Father Chrysogonus Waddell, OCSO is a monk of Gethsemani Abbey, Kentucky. He is the author of *Narrative and Legislative Texts from Early Citeaux* and *Cistercian Lay Brothers: Twelfth-century Usages with Related Texts.*

Raymond Van Dam is Professor of History at the University of Michigan. His books include *Leadership and Community in Late Antique Gaul* (1985), *Saints and Their Miracles in Late Antique Gaul* (1993), and *Kingdom of Snow: Roman Rule and Greek Culture in Cappadocia* (2002). *Families and Friends in Late Roman Cappadocia* and *Becoming Christian: The Conversion of Roman Cappadocia* will be published in 2003.

Contents

Preface   ix

Introduction   1

Chapter 1. The Disruptive Impact of
    Christianity in Late Roman Cappadocia   7

  1. New Patterns of Behavior   9
  2. New Histories   15
  3. Lost Histories   19
  4. Mosoch the Founder   22

Chapter 2. Constantinople: Christian City,
    Christian Landscape   27

Chapter 3. Communities of the Living and the
    Dead in Late Antiquity and the Early
    Medieval West   49

Chapter 4. The Gothic Intellectual Community:
    The Theology of the *Skeireins*   63

Chapter 5. 'Seed-sowers of Peace': The Uses of
    Love and Friendship at Court and in
    the Kingdom of Charlemagne   77

Chapter 6. Scaldic Poetry and Early
    Christianity   93

Chapter 7. Heloise and the Abbey of the
  Paraclete   103

Chapter 8. Communities of Reform in
  the Province of Reims: The Benedictine
  'Chapter General' of 1131   117

  Background   118
  Present Questions   120
  The Abbots   121
  The Abbeys   122
  Abbots by Rank   122
    The Veteran Abbots   123
    The Middlers   123
    The Freshmen   123
    The Latecomers   124
    The Alumni   124
  Conclusions   127

Chapter 9. When Jesus Did the Dishes:
  The Transformation of Late Medieval
  Spirituality   131

St Joseph and his Family   133
Jean Gerson and the Renewal of
Theological Discourse   135
Gerson's *Josephina*: A New Spiritual Hero   139
The Meaning of Gerson's Devotion to St Joseph   148

Notes   153

Preface

Giles Constable

There were many types and layers of community, both secular and religious, in the ancient world. Starting with the family, to mention only the most obvious, the secular communities built up through the household, the town and the regions to the empire, which in theory embraced the entire *oikoumene*. Cutting across these communities were those of language, ethnic origins and occupation, which brought together people of diverse origins and background. The religious communities clustered around various temples and shrines sometimes coincided with broader regional and ethnic cults culminating in the cult of the emperor, to whom all inhabitants of the empire, including Jews and Christians, were expected to make sacrifices. The cult of the emperor survived the Christianization of the empire without radical transformation and was appropriated by the Christians because, according to Glen Bowersock, 'it succeeded in making multitudes of citizens in far-flung regions feel close to the power that controlled them.'[1] Together with Roman law, the imperial cult made the empire into a single vast community.

Into this complex hierarchy of overlapping communities Christianity acted at the same time as a solvent of traditional communities and as the creator of new ones. Jesus himself undermined the strength of the family when he promised everlasting life to 'everyone that both left home or brethren or sisters or father or mother or wife or children or lands for my name's sake'[2] and warned that one of His disciples must hate 'his father and mother and wife and children and brethren and sisters'.[3] The new type of Christian community was described in the Acts of the Apostles, which said that 'The multitude of believers had but one heart and one soul. Neither did any one say that aught of the things

he possessed was his own; but all things were common unto them.'[4]
These words were an inspiration not only for Christians during
persecutions but for religious communities after the recognition of
Christianity; they remained programmatic for monasteries throughout
the Middle Ages.[5] At least two of the articles in this volume, those by
Chrysogonus Waddell and E Rozanne Elder, are concerned with the
monastic sense of community in the twelfth century. The former examines the importance of the liturgy and a written rule in binding a community together and linking it to other traditions. The latter shows
how a regional group of abbots, many with a common background,
were united in their concern for monastic reform.

The other articles explore a wide variety of types and levels of Christian community in Late Antiquity and the Middle Ages. Several emphasize the importance of buildings, tombs, statues, relics, holy men,
processions, and other ceremonies – what Oliver Nicholson calls the
'Christian appropriation of the landscape'. The emperor continued to
be a focus of community, especially in the East and at times in the
West, where Charlemagne's court served as 'the originator and focal
point of friendship' and brought together like-minded men from all
over the Latin West. The 'community of love' embraced the dead as
well as the living: confraternities of prayer included not only members
of families (and *familia* in a broader sense) and of religious institutions, but also all baptized Christians, for the salvation of whose souls
prayers were offered. Beginning in the Carolingian period, many monasteries formed associations with other religious houses, and with lay
men and women outside their walls. In some respects these paralleled
guilds, which originated as societies designed to ensure proper burial
for their members and intercessory prayers after they died, as well as
mutual support in the present life.

Brian Stock has emphasized the importance of textual communities.[6]
They are represented here by the Gothic commentary on the Bible, which
showed a 'reverence for the Word' and linked the Goths to the broad
theological trends in the fourth century, and by the Icelanders, whose
poetry reflected their conversion to Christianity and the importance of
the ties between poets and patrons in Icelandic society. Another sort of
intellectual and spiritual community is shown in Brian McGuire's article on the new view of Joseph in the late Middle Ages. Each period
had its characteristic saints who represented shifting religious and social ideals and gathered followers and admirers who made up the pattern of communities.

The variety and richness of these articles thus point the way for a new approach to the concept and reality of community in Late Antiquity and the Middle Ages. These communities, such as those of the emperor and the Christian God, often overlapped and were a source of tension. The ideals of 'one heart and one soul', and of common property, remained strong on the local level but sometimes conflicted with the interests of other communities, including the parishes and dioceses, and even the papacy. Particular communities, such as groups of heretics and those on the borderlines of heresy, showed the divisive as well as the unifying force of the concept of community. Not all these aspects are studied in this volume, but it helps to open up an important and largely unexplored area of Christian history.

Giles Constable
Institute for Advanced Study, Princeton

Introduction

Mark Williams

The rise and spread of Christianity in the Roman and post-Roman world has been exhaustively studied on many different levels, political, legal, social, literary and religious. Christianity's displacement of various forms of polytheism has been heralded as a unique spiritual advance, as well as condemned as leading to the decline of the Roman empire. Amid these larger questions of empire-wide import, the basic question of how Christians of Late Antiquity and the early Middle Ages formed themselves into communities of believers has sometimes been lost from sight. Yet it was a question of which these Christians themselves were acutely – and sometimes acrimoniously – aware.

There were many sources of the debate among Christians on how they should order their communities. St Paul often commented on how his readers should relate both to one another and to those outside the Christian orbit. This was no trivial question for, as has been noted, Christianity was unique in being a spiritual system into which one could not be born (at least in principle), but which one had to choose to follow. As adherents of a religion with its origins both within Judaism and at the same time outside traditional polytheistic beliefs, Christians had almost no choice but to organize themselves into more or less separate communities; Christianity's survival as a faith depended upon this as much as upon any official or unofficial tolerance that Christians might have enjoyed. Once heresy became a problem, Christian leaders had to deal not just with the question of who was and who wasn't a Christian, but with what to do with those who had for some reason gone astray or even abandoned the true faith. Again, once Christianity became a legitimate and empire-wide faith of Rome, other problems of community-formation became pressing: what about those who might have embraced the faith for the wrong reasons? How did one decide that these were the wrong reasons? It cannot have been easy for the faith of the martyrs to become the faith of their former persecutors – on either side.

On the level of personal relationships, even, the coming of Christianity caused tensions that brought changes. In republican and imperial Rome the term *amicitia* had always had a broad range of meanings, from what we might today refer to as 'character friendship', in which the relationship is cemented by the virtues shown by each friend,[1] to 'benefit friendship', in which each maintains friendly relations with the other based upon the benefits that accrue to each side, to an 'alliance', in which the relationship of *amicitia* describes an agreement among businessmen or politicians or even families contemplating a dynastic marriage between their children. Of course, Cicero's *De amicitia* provides the theoretical framework which described these pagan Roman concepts of friendly relations between individuals and groups and upon which they ultimately came to depend; because of this, Cicero's essay and related works also provided for the early Christians exempla of the sorts of relationships which they hoped to emulate, if not surpass. For example, Aelred of Rievaulx's dialogue *De spiritali amicitia* assumes a Ciceronian starting point for its discussion of friendship, but Aelred and his interlocutors are eager to show how Christianity allowed and even demanded that true, spiritual friendship be extended to more than just a few people. This, Aelred claimed, proved the superiority of Christian over pagan friendships, since pagan antiquity could offer only a few pairs of paradigmatic friends, while Christians could point to innumerable martyrs who laid down their lives for their friends in the faith.[2] So even at the level of personal relationships, those foundations of larger community, we can discern a sometimes curious mixture of the old Roman and the new Christian, sometimes uneasily blended but still, despite the volatility, a formulation that endured and evolved during the Middle Ages.

So, for the Christians of Late Antiquity and the Middle Ages, the term 'Christian community' had a range of meanings, not all of them necessarily consistent. To ascetics like Jerome and John Cassian, the ideal of community had a clear and unambiguous meaning. Yet the pains Cassian takes in his *Institutes* and *Conferences* to commend this ideal to an audience of Gallo-Roman readers suggests that Cassian's works are at least as apologetic as they are ascetic; most visions of golden ages – and this is how Cassian viewed Egyptian monastics[3] – tend to be apologetic or even polemical. Moreover, Jerome's opinion of the secular clergy is positively hostile.[4] It is plain that Cassian and his allies in the Latin west faced an uphill battle in arguing for an ascetic conception of Christian community, especially since the heresy of Cassian's older contemporary Priscillian had been associated with extreme ascetic practices as well as with sorcery, sexual immorality and scriptural irregularity. (Interestingly, Christians were not above making charges against one another of almost precisely the sort that their own pagan adversaries had made against them before the Constantinian revolution.) Once monasticism had become more widely accepted in the Latin west of Late Antiquity and the early Middle Ages, attempts were constantly made by secular authorities to render monks less of a social threat than they were ordinarily perceived to be; thus, among other actions, a statute was enacted in 390 AD banning monks from cities and towns, probably with the aim of preventing them from taking part in theological debates in urban settings. Earlier, a letter of Valentinian I, Valens and Gratian forbade monks to seek legacies from widows.[5] The continued official efforts of secular authorities to control the activities of ascetics suggests a basic difference of opinion between them on the nature and province of Christian community.

To Christian aristocrats like Paulinus of Nola and Sulpicius Severus, to say nothing of men like Sidonius Apollinaris, the ideal of Christian community meant something else altogether from what it meant to monastic apologists, however much these men claimed to have been influenced by asceticism. Despite their apparent receptiveness to ascetic ideals, it would be hard to conceive of Christians who stood further from the ideals of Cassian's Egyptian exemplars than Paulinus and Sidonius. For example, Paulinus condemns one of the messengers of Sulpicius (a wretch named Marracinus) in his twenty-second epistle, outwardly for his failure to adopt both the outward and the inner trappings of monasticism, but the whole style of the letter suggests that Paulinus's censure arises originally as much from Paulinus's upper-class view of Marracinus's social climbing as from Paulinus's own Christian principles. Indeed, as Robert Bartlett has suggested,[6] the spread of Christianity in Europe was always associated with the spread of bishoprics loyal (though sometimes uneasily so) to the bishop of Rome and to the liturgy he represented. To the extent that these bishoprics were the purview of the aristocracy (however it was defined), they represented a continuation of types of Christian community that can be traced back to Roman ideas and ideals.[7] And if this lineage holds, then the tensions that existed among clerics, bishops and the papacy can trace their lineage back to the Roman world as well.

It is probably trivial to remark now on the tensions between continuity and change that marked the end of Antiquity and the beginning
of the Middle Ages, not least because such tensions mark every age and
every culture. Yet studies of these tensions and the communities that
both gave rise to them and endured them are instructive. It was such an
interest – or rather, a group of related interests – that gave rise to the
conference held at Calvin College in November 1998; the theme of the
conference was 'The Making of Christian Communities'. The essays in
this book are the result of that conference. Each of the authors whose
work is represented here addressed some aspect of Christian community; each ties in with the great themes of continuity and change that
forced Christians of all stripes at various times to confront their
assumptions about the things that drew them together as well as those
that drove them apart. For example, in the first paper, Raymond Van
Dam addresses the disruptive influence of Christianity in Cappadocia
during the later Roman empire. For the leading churchmen of the area,
including Basil of Caesarea, Christianization meant wrenching the
local histories of Cappadocia out of their original Roman contexts and
relocating them into different narratives of ecclesiastical and biblical
history. According to Van Dam's reading, the Christianization of
Cappadocia led not simply to tension with the pre-existing Roman
order, but even to subverting it.

Similarly, Oliver Nicholson's 'Constantinople: Christian Community,
Christian Landscape' contrasts the development of Christian culture at
Byzantium against the notions of divine protection of cities that underlay
much pagan devotion in late antiquity. Christian rejection of pagan claims
to divine protection led in many instances to persecution, but on the other
hand the idea of divine protection of a city by the Christian God lay at the
back of much of Constantinople's development as a Christian metropolis,
as well as behind larger changes in Mediterranean culture in general.

In 'Communities of the Living and the Dead in Late Antiquity and
the Early Middle Ages', Frederick Paxton explores the complexities of
relations between the living and the dead from the third to the tenth
centuries. The main sources of this complexity appear to have been
familial and social relations, which intruded upon what may seem at
first to be a relatively simple matter of spiritual relations within the
community of faith. The Church's response to these tensions involved
the creation of an ideal of community between the living and the dead,
mediated by the Church.

The Goths get their due as intellectuals and theologians in James

W Marchand's essay 'The Gothic Intellectual Community: The Theology of the *Skeireins*'. Though perhaps best known as missionaries to the other Germanic tribes, the Goths produced biblical translators and exegetes, not to mention Christian polemicists.[8] The fragmentary (and much mistreated) commentary on the gospel of John, the *Skeireins* can and should be taken as emblematic of the Goths' talents for exegesis and places them firmly in the mainstream of Biblical exegesis of the fourth century.

In 'Seed-Sowers of Peace: The Uses of Love and Friendship at the Court and in the Kingdom of Charlemagne', C Stephen Jaeger turns our attention to a more personal form of community between Christians. Although love and friendship were court ideals throughout the Middle Ages, these virtues were especially important at the court of Charlemagne. Jaeger analyses poems, letters, and other documents to show that friendship created community at the royal court and was adopted as a communal ideal throughout the kingdom. The focus of Jaeger's paper is on Alcuin, who called those engaged in the project of courtly friend- and peace-making 'seed-sowers of peace'.

The Calvin conference coincided roughly with the thousandth anniversary of the conversion of Iceland to Christianity. Ásdís Egilsdóttir commemorates the occasion in her paper 'Scaldic Poetry and Early Christianity'. Focusing upon a number of the key scaldic poets, Einar Skulason and Gamli the Canon, Egilsdóttir explores the tensions that arose as the newly arrived Christian religion influenced the intricate poetic diction of scaldic verse, which had its roots in pre-Christian myth.

Of the many religious communities founded in the twelfth century, one of the most remarkable was the abbey of the Paraclete (near Nogent), founded as a community of women religious in 1129 when Abælard, abbot of St-Gildas-de-Ruy in Brittany, invited Heloise and a group of nuns expelled from Argenteuil to found a religious community around an abandoned oratory. Chrysogonus Waddell OCSO explores the role of Heloise in his contribution 'Heloise and the Abbey of the Paraclete' by concentrating upon the monastic institutes for the abbey that were almost certainly composed by Heloise herself. The portrait of Heloise that emerges from Waddell's study is of a woman who is practical, free and independent in judgment, and innovative within a traditional monastic context.

In 'Communities of Reform in the Province of Reims: The Benedictine "Chapter General" of 1131', E Rozanne Elder explores the events surrounding the remarkable synod of 1131 in Reims, which involved Pope Innocent II, King Louis VI of France, Archbishop Reynaud of Reims, and over three hundred bishops and abbots of his province, along with courts and councillors. One aspect of this synod was a gathering of Benedictine abbots – perhaps as many as 21 of them – in chapter. This was 84 years before chapters general were mandated by the Fourth Lateran Council. What accounts for this seemingly extraordinary event? Traditional interpretations have pointed at the influence of Bernard of Clairvaux, whose Cistercian order used chapters general. However, Elder explores other possible motivations for this synod besides the influence of Bernard.

Jean Gerson, perhaps best known today as chancellor of the University of Paris, wrote poems and treatises about St Joseph as the father of Jesus. Brian Patrick McGuire examines Gerson's treatment of Joseph in 'When Jesus Did the Dishes: The Transformation of Late Medieval Spirituality'. Gerson treated St Joseph not as a virtually comic figure or even a fool who could not comprehend the Incarnation, but as a male spiritual figure of use to a church that suffered from an imbalance between female affective spirituality and male abstract pursuits. For Gerson, St Joseph represented a balanced, chaste virgin father who could be a focus for the renewal of religious life for contemporary secular clergy.

In closing, I wish to express my sincere gratitude to all of those who made the Christian Communities conference at Calvin College a possibility. The former director of the Calvin Center for Christian Scholarship, my colleague and friend Professor Ronald Wells, guided the application for funding from the very beginning and was the conference's indispensable mentor; his successor at the Center, Professor James Bratt, has taken up where Ron left off, providing encouragement as the papers have made their way at last into print. The support staff of the Calvin Center, Ms Donna Romanowski and Ms Amy Bergsma, have been ever-present though virtually unseen aids at every step along the way, from arranging food and accommodations for participants to wrestling with and ultimately reconciling papers in multiple formats as they arrived from the contributors. Finally, I am sure that I speak for all the contributors and participants in thanking Professor John Traupman, for undertaking to put forward this volume of papers, and to Tom Penn and the rest of the staff at Anthem Press, whose work has made this book better in every way.

Mark F Williams
Calvin College
Grand Rapids, Michigan
March, 2001

Chapter 1

The Disruptive Impact of Christianity in Late Roman Cappadocia

Raymond Van Dam

The successful spread of Christianity into the Roman empire has long been one of the most intriguing and most challenging of issues for ancient historians and patristics scholars. The challenge has always been to invent an explanation that is neither so generalized that it becomes historically meaningless, nor so precise that it has no relevance beyond a few specific examples. Modern studies of the rise of Christianity typically start at the beginning of the process by outlining the factors that distinguished Christianity from rival religious cults and that made Christian beliefs and behavior somehow more attractive, more acceptable, more desirable. In his *Mission and Expansion of Christianity in the First Three Centuries*, still an influential account a century after its publication, the great patristics scholar Adolf Harnack explained the success of Christianity in terms of a whole list of attributes, among them more aggressive proselytism, more attractive doctrines, more attractive institutions of charity and social assistance, and better organization. From the beginning Christianity 'possessed, nay, it was, everything that can possibly be considered as religion'.[1]

Such a triumphalist account is, of course, already wholly compromised. With our unavoidably retrospective viewpoint we historians are always one step behind, as we explain the obvious and account for the evident. At the time, both in the early Roman empire and well into Late Antiquity after the conversion of emperors, the eventual success of Christianity was not a necessary, nor even a predictable outcome. In the later fourth century men still ridiculed Christianity for its beliefs and its behavior. As Basil of Caesarea once preached about the end of the world and the regeneration of life through God's judgment, some in his audience 'let loose a loud guffaw'.[2] Only in retrospect does that mockery seem hollow. Christianity was furthermore not very widespread. The recent efforts to improve the standing of Christianity by claiming that by the early fourth century it was already prominent in Roman society are merely modern attempts to create a context that downplays the genuine surprise of the Emperor Constantine's decision to ally himself with Christianity.

During the fourth century Christianity was still not immediately acceptable, and it was still a cult with serious limitations. Its success, even with the patronage of emperors, was certainly not assured. One other factor also hinted at the difficulty of its spread. Often the practices and beliefs of Christianity conflicted with local traditions and conventional practices. Because of the writings of the three Cappadocian Fathers, Basil of Caesarea, Gregory of Nazianzus and Gregory of Nyssa, the region of Cappadocia (as well as the neighboring region of Pontus) is well enough documented during the fourth century to serve as a test case. Cappadocia is seemingly an odd selection as a test case, since in the history of the ancient classical world it had consistently been peripheral, on the geographical edges of the lowlands and coastal regions where great civilizations and cultures flourished, on the political margins of the great kingdoms and empires. In the highlands of central and eastern Asia Minor the spread of Greek culture and the imposition of Roman rule had not been all that successful or thorough. The determined survival of local customs and indigenous languages had undermined the possibility of cultural uniformity, and the lingering commonness of so-called bandits had highlighted the limitations of administrative totality. Well into Late Antiquity the outback of Cappadocia remained under-Hellenized and under-Romanized. This inability to introduce Greek culture or to impose effective imperial rule was a preview of the limited impact of Christianity in the region. Even with the support of emperors Christians could anticipate the survival of pagan cults and the appearance of variant forms of Christianity.

Nor were church leaders very adept at accommodating local customs and indigenous traditions. Because churchmen like the Cappadocian Fathers often preferred to confront native practices and beliefs, the spread of Christianity was thoroughly disruptive in local society. This chapter is a brief introduction to some of the consequences of this disruption in Cappadocia during the fourth century. Christian churchmen introduced new regulations about acceptable behavior, for instance regarding permissible marriages, and they imposed a new hierarchy of clerics and bishops who all served for life. These new standards conflicted with traditional patterns of marriage, and with the usual expectations of rapid turnover among most magistrates and priests (Section 1). Because churchmen had limited means of enforcement, they had to find a legitimation for this new morality and new hierarchy instead in the rhythms of history and the characteristics of the natural environment (Section 2). The intrusive impact of Christianity did not stop with introducing and then legitimating new behavior, however. These new histories and new legends themselves became disruptive, as they crowded out the old legends and myths that cities and families already used to explain their cults and their prominence (Section 3). In many cases all that remained by the later fourth century were disconnected fragments of these old legends. One such myth had apparently highlighted the original ancestor of all Cappadocians, the mysterious Mosoch the Founder (Section 4).

The issue here is not merely the rise of different fads in historical interpretation, a process with which modern historians are all too familiar. Instead, facts, content, data vanished wholesale. In order to introduce and justify new behavior and new expectations, communities had to imagine themselves differently. The rise of Christianity resulted in both the remembering of new, more relevant legends and the forgetting of old, outdated legends.[3]

1. New Patterns of Behavior

In the mid-370s Basil responded to a series of questions from another bishop about discipline and penance. Basil's replies took the form of a long series of chapters or canons, which in modern editions are numbered consecutively through three of his letters.[4] Most of these questions sought advice on the penalties for various sins and misdeeds. Since some of the questions mentioned specific cases and specific people, it is possible to assume that they were raising genuine issues of immediate concern for the pastoral duties of bishops. Several of these canons discussed the penalties for clerics who had committed sins, such as sexual misbehavior. The common penalty for such wayward clerics was the loss of their offices: 'the [previous ecclesiastical] canons order a single penalty to be applied to fallen [clerics], dismissal from their office'.[5] Basil suggested that clerics who took up arms against bandits should be deposed from their offices,[6] while priests who had unwittingly become involved in an 'illegal marriage' should be prevented from performing their clerical duties, although they could keep their offices.[7] He likewise suggested that priests and deacons who had expressed only an intention of sinning should be excluded from the celebration of the liturgy.[8]

Basil's comments introduce one of the most notable characteristics of the ecclesiastical hierachy that differentiated it from many pagan priesthoods, and from other hierarchical institutions in the Roman empire. This distinguishing characteristic was the lifetime tenure of bishops and clerics. When local aristocrats had served as priests in municipal or provincial cults, they had typically held their priesthoods for a year or so, and they had also often held priesthoods in different cults, sometimes concurrently. Their service as municipal magistrates also typically lasted only a year or two, although they might repeat their offices. The honorific inscriptions that cities or family members set up to honor these local aristocrats customarily commemorated not the length of their tenures as priests or magistrates, but the number of positions they had held and the number of times they had held them. In the early second century, for instance, Sebastopolis in Pontus honored the career of a local aristocrat who, in addition to having served for life as a priest in the imperial cult, had also held some municipal magistracies 'many times' and served as supervisor of the city's market 'even more often'.[9]

In the imperial administration a similar pattern of short tenures in office and long interruptions of retirement was common. Only the emperors had lifetime tenure, and only the emperors were even expected to hold their office for life. The normal pattern for imperial office-holders was to combine occasional service of a year or so in a sequence of increasingly more prestigious offices, punctuated by long periods of retirement. The career of Symmachus, one of the most notable of the senators at Rome during the mid- and later fourth century, was typical. Symmachus held four major offices, a governorship in Italy, a governorship in Africa, the prefecture of Rome, and a consulship in 391, each for about a year, each separated by intervals of six to ten years. The upper levels of the imperial administration hence accommodated many men through rapid turnover. At Rome, for instance, there were over one hundred known prefects of the city during the fourth century, some of whom held the office for only a few months. In 351 alone five men held the office. Among pagan priests, among municipal magistrates and among the top magistrates in the imperial administration, short tenures and rapid turnover were the normal state of affairs.

In contrast, within the ecclesiastical hierarchy the normal expectation was of lifetime tenures. Once men were ordained as clerics, they served for the remainder of their lives. They could move up within the hierarchy, eventually becoming deacons and priests and perhaps even bishops, but they could not drop out to hold secular offices or to resume a life of leisured retirement and then perhaps return for another stint as a cleric. Bishops were even more restricted, since they were supposed to remain attached for life to their particular sees and not transfer to another city. At least in theory, competent bishops at small sees could not move up to become bishops at larger sees.

Basil's comments about the discipline of clerics hence reflected the consequences of the imposition of this new pattern of lifetime tenures as clerics and bishops. Clerical service had to be associated with an irreproachable life. Because lifetime tenure for all clerics and the permanent attachment of bishops to their sees hampered the potential for promotion and upward advancement, it became all the more important both for the men who became bishops and for those who remained lesser clerics to agree that moral and spiritual qualities alone had been the differentiating factors. Lifetime tenure furthermore made it difficult to remove wayward clerics. If they misbehaved, it was not possible simply to wait for the end of their tenure and replace them. But by associating their penalties with personal misbehavior, Basil and other bishops could resort to disciplinary sanctions that included outright dismissal from office. A new pattern of lifetime office-holding led to new regulations, new sanctions, and new expectations.

A second set of examples of disruptive practices that the spread of Christianity introduced involved those predictably contentious topics, sex and violence. Several of Basil's responses discussed permissible marriages. Basil was particularly intent upon insisting that a man or a woman could not marry the sister or brother, respectively, of a first spouse, or that a man could not marry his brother's wife (that is, the same prohibited marriage from the opposite perspective). Such marriages were presumably among those that he classified as 'a union of forbidden kin', which were subject to the same penalty as adultery.[10] As elaboration upon his opinions Basil referred to another letter in which he had discussed such second marriages.[11] In that letter Basil had countered the possibility of marriage between in-laws with several different arguments. He directed one argument against the apparent endorsement of a fellow bishop by suggesting the possibility of forgery. A second argument was necessary to contradict the implication of Leviticus 18:18 that seemed to allow a man to marry his wife's sister after his wife's death. Basil countered by claiming that this legislation applied

only to 'those in the Law', that is, to Jews. Yet another argument highlighted definitions of kinship. Basil argued that because marriage made
husband and wife into 'one flesh', as Matthew 19:5–6 had described the
union, the wife's sister acquired kinship with the husband, and that
hence the husband could no more have a relationship with her than
with his own sister. And since 'the regulations about kinship are appli-
cable to both men and women', a woman could likewise not have a
relationship with her new 'brother', her husband's brother. He furthermore argued that a marriage between a man and his wife's sister
would cause too much turmoil for the man's children. The children
from his first marriage would be uncertain about his new wife, since
they would not know whether she would behave with the hostility of a
stepmother or the affection of an aunt, and the children from his second marriage would be uncertain whether they were the siblings or the
cousins of the children from his first marriage.

These were not effective arguments. Basil had to suggest that someone had impersonated the bishop in order to explain away his endorsement, he had to stretch his exegesis of the biblical passages to claim
that ties by marriage were similar to ties by blood, and he had to resort
to unflattering stereotypes about the hostility of stepmothers to claim
that they would be hostile to their new stepchildren. The primary weak-
ness of Basil's arguments, however, was that they seemed to take so
little account of actual practices. Within the senatorial aristocracy of
Rome during the late Republican and imperial periods, for instance,
high mortality rates and the demands of shifting political alliances had
made divorce and remarriage very common and created blended families that often included a step-parent and half-siblings. Among Roman
senators of the fourth century marriage between kin was still common.
Among non-aristocrats premature deaths would likewise have left surviving spouses who were still young enough to contemplate remarriage.
Since older men often married young women of a different generation,
it would have been common for a young stepmother to be about the
same age as her adult stepchildren, a likelihood that Basil seemed to
acknowledge by classifying the infatuation between men and their stepmothers as the equivalent of incest.[12] Remarriages were hence common,
and so was uncertainty over permissible relationships among step-rela-
tives, half-siblings and former relatives by marriage.

Basil also ignored the fact that strategies of marriage involved more
than simple definitions of permissible relationships, since apprehen-
sions about fiscal arrangements, dynastic succession and perpetuation

of the family name also entered the calculation. One concern involved dowries: marriage of a deceased wife's sister would presumably imply that a husband could continue using his first wife's dowry. Another concern involved the family legacy: marriage of a deceased husband's brother would prevent a woman from being forced into a disadvantageous marriage that might produce a competing set of heirs, or simply from being left unmarried. Within the Roman aristocracy such concerns about property and succession had sometimes led to marriages between first cousins, step-siblings and descendants of half-siblings. In Roman law restrictions on permissible marriages had focused much more on considerations of differences in rank and status than on ties by blood or marriage. In the end, Basil too seems to have recognized that he was facing a difficult fight in trying to restrict marriages between in-laws. At the conclusion of his letter he simply hoped that this 'sacrilegious practice' would remain where it was now common and not contaminate his own region.

Another practice to which Basil objected was the abduction of women, also known as bride theft. In one of his canons Basil insisted that a man who had abducted a woman who was already engaged to another man must return her to her fiancé. An abductor was also to return an unengaged woman, this time to parents or brothers or other relatives. The girl's guardians would then decide whether to return the girl to her abductor and accept the relationship as binding. An abductor who seized a married woman, however, was liable to the penalty for fornication.[13] Other responses added some nuances to these general regulations. A man who abducted a girl before marrying her could keep her as his wife, but was liable to the penalty for abduction.[14] An unmarried girl who willingly ran off with a man without her father's knowledge was herself liable to a penalty.[15] A widow who pretended that she had been abducted in order to remarry was liable only to the penalty for bigamy.[16]

In part Basil may have been reacting to this violent practice because the possibility of abduction had once threatened his own family. His own mother, when a young woman, had had to worry that one of her suitors might become so passionate over her beauty as to abduct her; so she had quickly married.[17] Basil's mother had been vulnerable because she was by then an orphan without parents to negotiate an engagement and marriage. The more common scenario, in traditional societies in which bride theft is still prevalent, is for marriage by abduction to function as a device to sidestep an engagement that parents or guardians have arranged for young girls. A rejected suitor might resort to abduction; so might an engaged fiancé who was fearful of another suitor. In order to seize the girl an abductor would typically gather supporters to help; in one of his canons Basil too conceded that some people provided assistance to abductors.[18] In another case Basil was indignant to learn that an entire village had sheltered an abductor and even fought to prevent the girl's rescue.[19] Sometimes the girl was a willing participant in her own abduction, since it gave her the opportunity effectively to choose her own husband; in that case the abduction was more of an elopement. Whether violent kidnapping or consensual abduction, the end result was the same: the disruption of arrangements that parents, and especially fathers and male guardians, had made to benefit their families and their communities. From the perspective of patriarchal figures of authority like bishops, bride theft was dangerously disruptive, and because it might even initiate feuds between families, it was also a challenge to the harmony of communities. With these canons Basil had rejected a common strategy employed by young people to impose their own preferences and instead decided in favor of the patriarchal authority of fathers and male guardians and the social stability inherent in arranged marriages.

From our vantage point it is all too easy to applaud these changes and locate them in a progressive theory of social transformation. Regulations about permissible degrees of marriage and the condemnation of the use of violence in abducting women seem to be markers of the progress of civilization, while the academics among us are all too aware of the benefits of lifetime tenure. Yet Basil's long and repeated discussions demonstrate that this new pattern of office-holding and these regulations about behavior were disruptive in traditional Cappadocian society. The newness or oddness of these patterns and preferences that Basil and other likeminded bishops wanted to introduce makes it difficult to understand how they might acquire wider normative authority.

Unlike emperors and imperial magistrates, bishops could not resort to threats of force. In support of their own preferences emperors often threatened the imposition of grievous penalties and punishments. When Diocletian and his fellow emperors had issued an edict against the practice of close-kin marriage, including marriage between in-laws, they had threatened whippings 'of appropriate severity'.[20] When Constantine had issued an edict that condemned bride theft and marriage by abduction, he had imposed tortures and penalties on the nurse for not being watchful enough, on the abductor and his partners, on the girl for not staying indoors, and even on the parents if they decided to accept the marriage.[21] Enforcement of imperial edicts was problematic throughout the provinces, however, and in outlying regions like Cappadocia and Pontus they were often probably not even promulgated. Even though the sanctions that Basil suggested in his canons were seemingly a bit more lenient, involving mere penance, exclusion from prayers, or excommunication, their acceptance and enforcement would be equally problematic. Imposing new, Christian expectations about patterns of office-holding and a new, Christian configuration of moral and immoral behavior required more than threats and penalties.

2. New Histories

A more comprehensive solution was to associate these new patterns with nature and history. In order to revise the present, bishops and other churchmen required new legends and new myths about the past. By publicizing new histories for cities and regions they could suggest that Christian patterns of behavior had long been characteristic of their communities, and by advertising new histories for families they could justify the prominence and lifetime tenures of the men who, like themselves, had become bishops and clerics. In addition to rewriting history, the Cappadocian Fathers reinterpreted the natural landscape to suggest that Christian morality was inherent even in the behavior of animals. The new patterns of Christian behavior that they promoted would then appear to be as permanent as the landscape and as timeless as history.

The Cappadocian Fathers rewrote the histories of their communities by stressing the roles of prominent individuals as founders in both Pontus and Cappadocia. For Pontus Gregory of Nyssa highlighted the career of Gregory Thaumaturgus and his importance in spreading Christianity. In his account Gregory Thaumaturgus had been a native of Pontus who studied overseas before returning to his homeland in the mid-third century. Upon becoming bishop of Neocaesarea he was remarkably successful in expanding Christianity. Gregory of Nyssa applauded his success with a graceful, even if highly implausible, compliment: when Gregory Thaumaturgus had arrived in Neocaesarea there were only seventeen Christians, but upon his death only seventeen pagans were left.[22]

The career of Gregory Thaumaturgus provided a history, a myth that located the spread of Christianity in Pontus to an era long before emperors had converted and begun to patronize Christians. Various cities could claim a connection to Gregory Thaumaturgus, including Amaseia, whose bishop had originally consecrated him, and Comana, for which Gregory Thaumaturgus selected a bishop. The city of Neocaesarea had certainly tied its reputation to the activities and teachings of their famous bishop, and over a century later its congregation claimed to be celebrating the liturgy exactly as they had received it from Gregory Thaumaturgus. The church that Gregory Thaumaturgus had constructed was a rock-solid warranty both for the veracity of the legends about him and for the significance of the Christian community at Neocaesarea.

For Cappadocia Gregory of Nyssa hinted at a legend about another founder. Gregory knew that early traditions had already suggested that Jesus' apostles had eventually scattered as missionaries to various regions and cities. So he claimed instead that the founder of Christianity in Cappadocia was the centurion who had glorified Jesus at the foot of the cross.[23] This was apparently the first reference to this centurion's role in the Christianization of Cappadocia. Later traditions would of course expand on this legend by naming the centurion as Longinus, identifying him as a native of Cappadocia and describing his martyrdom and subsequent cult at Caesarea. Eventually a shrine to this centurion was established in Cappadocia.

The legend about the centurion implied that Christianity in Cappadocia had an ancestry that went all the way back to the moment of Jesus' death. Gregory's brother Basil provided additional confirmation about the antiquity of local Christianity by arguing that Christian morality and theology were inherent in the region's natural landscape. In a series of sermons about the six days of creation Basil highlighted the moral implications of the flora and fauna. Birds in particular provided examples of proper and improper behavior. The cranes that kept watch at night, the storks that cared for their elderly and the crows that guarded the storks were all appropriate examples of vigilance, affection and hospitality. Basil furthermore used the example of the turtledove that remained alone after losing its mate as an argument that women should prefer the nobility of widowhood to a second marriage. He also made some theological deductions from the behavior of birds and insects. One was about the possibility of a virgin birth. Because a vulture could lay an egg without coupling, 'the history of birds' has indicated that it was 'not impossible or contrary to nature for a virgin to give birth while preserving her virginity immaculate'. Another theological implication concerned the transformation of the human body at the moment of resurrection. As an appropriate analogy Basil mentioned the metamorphosis of the Indian silkworm from a caterpillar into a flying insect.[24] In the minutest customs of birds and insects Basil was now able to find examples of proper morality and orthodox theology. This exegesis implied that the Christian lifestyle he was promoting was not new, since it had been inherent in nature from the very moment of creation.

These legends about the heroic founders of Christianity in Pontus and Cappadocia blended into a second type of legendary history that focused on the significance of particular families. Attachment to the legacy of Gregory Thaumaturgus directly benefited at least two prominent families in Pontus. The first person at Neocaesarea to offer lodging to Gregory Thaumaturgus was reputed to have been a local notable named Musonius. At the beginning of Basil's episcopacy a century later the bishop of Neocaesarea was likewise named Musonius, and it is likely that he was a descendant of this earlier Musonius. His ancestor's generosity seems to have boosted the standing of his family by associating its prominence with the introduction of Christianity under Gregory Thaumaturgus: 'the passage of time has transmitted to his descendants the memory of such a distinction'.[25] The other family from Pontus that benefited from its attachment to the legacy of Gregory Thaumaturgus was the family of Basil and Gregory of Nyssa. Although they made their ecclesiastical careers in Cappadocia, their family was from Pontus. The family's attachment to Gregory Thaumaturgus went back almost firsthand to the saint's life, since their paternal grandmother had memorized some of the saint's memorable sayings and passed them on directly to her grandchildren. When Gregory of Nyssa later collected some of these sayings and stories, he composed a *Life* of Gregory Thaumaturgus in which the saint's life became a model for his and his brother's lives. Long ago a local bishop had discerned with 'the power of prophecy' that Gregory Thaumaturgus was destined to become a bishop.[26] By implication, the sons of this family that was so devoted to the saint's memory were perhaps destined to become bishops themselves. In addition to Basil and Gregory of Nyssa, who became bishops in Cappadocia, their youngest brother Peter became bishop at Sebasteia, and the successor to Musonius as bishop of Neocaesarea was one of their relatives.

In Cappadocia the family of Gregory of Nazianzus produced a different sort of history. His family's history focused on his father's conversion to Christianity. Gregory the Elder had not suffered during the persecutions. Instead, he had quickly realized the implications of Constantine's patronage for bishops. Within a few years he had become bishop of Nazianzus, his hometown. In Gregory's estimation, because his father had inherited a church that was in ruins, he was himself now responsible for the expansion of the Christian community there. For forty-five years Gregory the Elder dominated his community as bishop. At Nazianzus he had effectively become the founder of Christianity, and the success of his long career seemed to be a guarantee of the continued success of the Christian community there. By reviving the Christian community Gregory the Elder had also revitalized the city. 'I am an ancient city afflicted by demons. Through Gregory's efforts I have been energized again.'[27] The history of the city had merged with the history of this family. After Gregory the Elder's death, the city waited almost a decade in the hope that his son Gregory would become bishop. Finally it settled for one of Gregory's relatives. A legend about the prominence of Gregory the Elder had made his son seem to be the only possible successor as bishop. The memorial that explicitly linked city and family was the new church that Gregory the Elder had begun and his son Gregory had completed.

The ecclesiastical hierarchy had created a new institutional structure and new expectations about service. Yet despite its claims about open recruitment and the importance of spiritual values for advancement, it had not freed itself from the traditional pressures of patronage and the conventional importance of wealth and ancestry. Most of the men who became bishops would otherwise have dominated their communities as local notables, municipal magistrates or priests, or they would have gone on to hold offices in the imperial administration. To explain their continuing prominence as bishops, to justify their lifetime tenures, churchmen provided a rationale that associated these men and their families with earlier legendary heroes of the spread of Christianity. With such heroic pedigrees no one could complain that these men might serve as bishops or clerics for life.

Churchmen likewise found a justification for the values of the new Christian lifestyle they promoted both in the weight of history and in a correspondence with nature. In their estimation, ancient history and the natural landscape had converged with the expectations of a new Christian society. With these sorts of warranties they could not be accused of having merely invented new legends and new interpretations. Once the natural environment was interpreted properly, once the past was understood correctly, the future would become apparent. Theirs was an old destiny. All they had done was remember the future.

3. Lost Histories

The most conspicuous relic of the memory of Gregory Thaumaturgus was the church he had built at Neocaesarea. Gregory of Nyssa was especially impressed that, more than a century after its construction, this church had survived a recent earthquake. 'When almost everything else was completely demolished, municipal buildings and private homes, everything in ruins, that church alone was unshaken, without any cracks.'[28] In contrast, other buildings, and the memories and legends they represented, were not as sturdy. To justify the disruption arising from the imposition of an ecclesiastical hierarchy and new regulations about proper behavior, churchmen throughout Pontus and Cappadocia had composed new legends about the rise of Christianity. But at the same time that these new legends explained and justified the new hierarchy and the new lifestyle, they were themselves disruptive. Once established, those new legends eclipsed older histories. The fourth century was not only a marvelously fertile period for the creation of new histories, it also marked the end of an earlier era when cities and families throughout the Greek world had carefully associated themselves with older legends about Greek myths and Roman history.

Strabo had been a contemporary of the first emperor, Augustus. His writings included the *Geography*, an extensive survey of regions, cities and temples in the Mediterranean world and Near East. As a native of Amaseia in Pontus he was deeply familiar with central and eastern Asia Minor. In his geographical survey Strabo liked to mention local stories and local myths. Everywhere he looked, he saw history and legends in the landscape and the monuments. Although he himself may not have been fully aware of the chronological details, the legends he recounted stretched back endlessly. For him, the epic poems of Homer were the starting point, and he often provided exegesis on verses from these sacred books. At one point he launched into a lengthy argument about whether Homer had mentioned some peoples from Pontus in the list of the allies of Troy, since their inclusion would indicate that the poet had certainly visited the coast of the Black Sea. Strabo also noted that the inhabitants of Pontus and Cappadocia still publicized legends that located their cities and shrines squarely in Greek mythology. Legends about Orestes were especially popular. Orestes was the son of the great king Agamemnon, the commander of the Greek forces during the Trojan War. Because Orestes eventually joined his sisters to avenge their father's murder by killing their own mother, classical Greek tragedians in particular had been entranced by the creative possibilities of the tensions within his dysfunctional family. According to legends current in Pontus and Cappadocia, at some point Orestes had traveled to central Asia Minor. At Comana Strabo discovered that people had already identified an indigenous deity named Ma with Enyo, a Greek goddess of war. They also claimed that Orestes and one of his sisters had introduced the cult in honor of this goddess, and that they had deposited at its shrine the 'hair of sorrow' from which the city had derived its name (*kome* is the Greek word for 'hair'). As Strabo commented of the people at another temple, 'they find an etymology for the name by presenting a myth'. Near Tyana was another shrine whose foundation locals also associated with a visit from Orestes. When Strabo visited, 'some people there kept repeating the same history about Orestes'.[29]

Legends about Alexander the Great were also widespread. In outlying regions Alexander's failure to visit was not a handicap, but rather an opportunity to provide suggestive links with other legends. Some people claimed that Alexander had mated with the queen of the Amazons, others that a mountain range in northern Armenia was in fact in India. In Pontus and Cappadocia stories about the regional kings who followed Alexander's conquests were also common. The most dominant were the Mithridatic kings in Pontus, and especially King Mithridates VI Eupator, who expanded his rule over much of eastern and central Asia Minor in the first half of the first century BC. Mithridates transformed both cities and the rural landscape through his construction projects. At Amaseia there were palaces, monuments, and royal tombs. At Cabeira he built a palace and a water mill. To demonstrate his mastery over wild beasts, and by implication over his subjects, Mithridates built a zoo to keep the animals alive for display and game parks for killing them. Throughout the countryside he built numerous garrisons.

Memories of King Mithridates and his dynasty survived for centuries. Three hundred years later Strabo's hometown of Amaseia still minted a coin that depicted the tomb of one of Mithridates' ancestors. But the coming of Roman rule to central and eastern Asia Minor devastated the countryside, left cities impoverished and ruined and undermined local ancestral traditions. The Roman general Pompey meddled on a grand scale. He pompously renamed many cities. Eupatoria, which King Mithridates Eupator had named after himself, now became Magnopolis, named after Pompey *Magnus*, Pompey the Great, and Cabeira, one of Mithridates' royal residences, now received the Greek name of Diospolis, 'City of Zeus'. Pompey also confiscated Mithridates' most precious treasures and deposited them on the Capitoline Hill in Rome. The imposition of a formal imperial administration did not end this destruction of local customs and traditions. Pompey reassigned regions from Mithridates' former kingdom in order to augment an existing province and to reward loyal partisans, and subsequent Roman administrators occasionally modified these territorial assignments and the standing of cities. The result for Pontus and Cappadocia would have been the same as the consequences for the region around Troy: 'because a different division of the region has been imposed under Roman rule, many people have already lost their languages and their names'.[30]

The renaming of cities, the realignment of regions and the theft of statues and monuments would have destroyed whatever etymological myths these cities and regions had previously developed about their names and titles and cults. Already when Strabo surveyed cities in Asia Minor he was sadly resigned to the great loss of past traditions. 'Tieium [a city on the coast of the Black Sea] is a small town that has nothing worthy of memory.'[31] Cities instead tried to accommodate the realities of Roman rule. In Cappadocia Caesarea assumed an imperial name during the reign of Augustus. Soon after the region was annexed as an imperial province, the city acquired a temple in honor of the imperial cult, and it eventually initiated a series of festivals in honor of emperors. In Pontus the royal city of Cabeira had already received the new Greek name of Diospolis from the Roman general Pompey. In the early first century AD the widow of the last Cappadocian king changed the city's name to Sebaste, a form of the Greek adjective corresponding to the emperor Augustus' name. By the end of the first century the name of the city had been changed once more, this time to Neocaesarea, the 'new foundation of Caesar'. The city's chief municipal cult kept pace with this process of cultural and political assimilation. First its local deity was identified with Zeus, the ruler of the Greek gods, and the city hosted a regional festival in honor of Zeus. Then statues of emperors were added to the sanctuary in order to link it with the imperial cult, and the city initiated games to honor the emperors. Both Caesarea and Neocaesarea now redefined themselves in terms of Greek culture and Roman rule.

Roman rule had encouraged the formation of new local customs and legends that replaced older traditions and that linked regions, cities and families with aspects of Greekness and Romanness. The rise of a Christian society during the fourth century in turn posed a similar challenge to these Greek and Roman legends. Although overshadowed and frequently obliterated, fragments of memories of older traditions nevertheless lingered in this Christian society. Pagan temples might become churches. At Comana, for instance, Christians transformed the shrines that the Greek hero Orestes was thought to have founded directly into churches, 'without making any changes at all in the structure'.[32] Pagan heroes seem likewise to have become Christian saints. In the same way that some local deities had once been identified with gods in the Greek or Roman pantheon, mythological founders and heroes were assimilated into a Christian civic liturgy. At Caesarea Bishop Basil celebrated the festivals of two rather obscure local saints, the centurion Gordius and the shepherd Mamas. In his commemorative panegyrics he hardly knew what to say about them. Since their names were apparently traditional indigenous names, perhaps he was simply trying to embellish some local traditions into full Christian cults. Basil and the metropolitan bishop of Tyana once feuded over the revenues from a shrine dedicated to 'the holy Orestes', located in the Taurus Mountains in southern Cappadocia. This St Orestes and his shrine are otherwise completely unknown. Perhaps it is not too fanciful to imagine that this saint's cult retained a memory of an earlier cult at Tyana that the locals once claimed had been founded by the Greek hero Orestes.

At Caesarea in Cappadocia stories about Basil would likewise modify or replace earlier legends. Gregory of Nazianzus once seems to have drawn upon a dim memory of an earlier legend, because when he described his friendship with Basil, he claimed that together they had exceeded Orestes and Pylades.[33] These two mythological heroes had been cousins, comrades-in-arms and paradigm examples of a close friendship. Orestes had also once been appropriated as a founder for cities and shrines in Cappadocia. According to Gregory, Basil had surpassed Orestes in his friendship; by implication, perhaps he had also replaced him as a founder at Caesarea. Myths about Basil had not just succeeded earlier myths, they had also updated and replaced them. Mythology conferred authority and respect. However new and disruptive were the disciplinary canons that Basil now proposed, people would respect them if at the same time they hailed him as a founder.

4. Mosoch the Founder

In the early fifth century Philostorgius wrote another ecclesiastical history. Philostorgius was a native of Cappadocia and grew up in the shadows of the great Cappadocian Fathers. Despite their prominence,

Philostorgius did not embrace their version of orthodox theology. Instead, he and his family accepted the doctrines of Eunomius, another Cappadocian theologian whom Basil and Gregory of Nyssa would personally discredit and vilify. Nor did Philostorgius remain in Cappadocia, since eventually he moved to Constantinople. In his ecclesiastical history Philostorgius was hence both ecumenical and local. He included many tidbits of odd information about biblical events and the Roman empire, and he was interested in legends about Cappadocia. When he mentioned Mazaca, the original name for the city that eventually became Caesarea, he noted that this name was derived from 'Mosoch, the founder of the Cappadocians'.[34]

Mosoch is an intriguing primal ancestor. His name suggests some sort of Semitic derivation, and his reputation as the founder of the Cappadocians seems to hint at a foundation legend for the region that was older than the adoption of Greek myths. Unfortunately he remains completely obscure. Philostorgius in fact knew so little about the legend that he could not match up the consonants and vowels in order to make sense of the postulated etymological link between the city's name of Mazaca and Mosoch's name. So he shrugged and invented a makeshift phonetic transfer: 'after the passage of time [the city] was called Mazaca through a swerving'. In the later Roman empire all that survived of whatever legends there may have been about Mosoch were his name, his reputation, and his obscure connection with the name of a city. The myth of Mosoch the Founder was a lost memory, a fragment of an abandoned past, a casualty of the adoption of Greek mythology or the imposition of Roman rule or the expansion of Christianity. In a Greek, Roman or Christian society, Mosoch the Founder had become meaningless.

Christian bishops like Basil had introduced new patterns of hierarchy and new expectations of behavior for local communities. Because those new patterns conflicted with established behavior and traditional expectations, churchmen reinterpreted both the natural landscape and history itself in order to link this new morality with much longer traditions. Even through they wrote in classicizing, Atticizing Greek, they did not locate their new interpretations in Greek myths and Roman history. Instead, they focused on biblical and Christian history. Their interpretations linked their communities with ecclesiastical history back to Jesus, with biblical history back into the Old Testament, and even with creation itself. Local legends that had situated communities in Greek and Roman history were hence lost. At best they remained curiosities, occasionally collected by ethnographers or historians.

A miniature version of this entire process was the change in names of Caesarea, Basil's episcopal see. The original name of the city had been Mazaca, somehow derived from the name of Mosoch the Founder. During the Hellenistic period the kings of Cappadocia had renamed the city with a respectable Greek name, Eusebeia, 'Piety'. This renaming presumably reflected their goal of introducing Greek culture and the amenities of a proper Greek city. At the end of the first century BC Archelaus, the last of the Cappadocian kings, had renamed the city again as Caesarea in order to honor the emperor Caesar Augustus. Archelaus himself was hailed as a 'founder',[35] and Caesarea became a proper city in the Roman empire. In the fourth century Bishop Basil founded a 'new city' in the suburbs of Caesarea that included a church, a clerical residence, a poorhouse and a hospital.[36] Rather than simply renaming Caesarea, Basil had founded a replacement settlement, a vatican outside the city's walls. The name for this new foundation was, not so surprisingly, 'Basilias', Basil's place.

Mazaca, Eusebeia, Caesarea, Basilias: each new name was an entire history in one word, and as a community changed its name and its cults, it changed its local history and its local legends. With each new name the city had also had to acknowledge a new founder or eponymous hero. Mosoch, a Hellenistic king of Cappadocia, a Roman emperor: the next member of this series was a Christian bishop. By the later fourth century Basil was hailed as the 'second founder and protector' and the 'guardian and patron of the community'.[37] Legends about him now defined his community.

Philostorgius deserves credit for breaking away from this powerful mythology about the significance of Basil. His curiosity was a valuable attribute, especially for a historian, since it made him inquisitive as well as critical. Reinforcing this inherent skepticism was a sense of grievance about the treatment of Eunomius. Basil and Gregory of Nyssa had reviled Eunomius and his theological doctrines; in contrast, Philostorgius made a pilgrimage to visit his hero in his retirement on a Cappadocian estate. Philostorgius then wrote his ecclesiastical history in part to defend Eunomius' reputation and to criticize Basil's behavior. As one later Byzantine reader noted with both horror and fascination, this history was a 'eulogy for heretics'.[38] Philostorgius was hence a heterodox Christian who wrote a heterodox history. He had clearly not followed the new orthodoxy either about theology or about history. Even when writing about his own homeland of Cappadocia and adjacent regions, he broke ranks. Gregory of Nyssa had rewritten the history of Pontus in order to highlight the significance of Gregory Thaumaturgus; Philostorgius seems not to have mentioned either Gregory Thaumaturgus or Gregory of Nyssa. Basil's supporters had not been reluctant to rearrange the past to correspond to their vision of a better future, and they had emphasized the significance of the Basilias for Caesarea and Basil's own reputation in Cappadocia. Philostorgius was simply a better historian than that. Realizing that the entire past was relevant for interpreting the present, he preferred to mention Mosoch the Founder and Mazaca, the region's original founder and the city's original name, even if the shards of their memories left him puzzled about the connections. Rather than wanting to forget old legends about Cappadocia, Philostorgius struggled to recollect and record them. He was still trying to remember the past.

Chapter 2

Constantinople: Christian City, Christian Landscape

Oliver Nicholson

In the year 446, when he was thirty-seven years old, Daniel, a monk from a village on the upper Euphrates, was elected abbot of his monastery.[1] 'Here you are, free at last,' he said to himself, 'do not be afraid, leave and fulfil your plan.' He went south and visited his hero, St Simeon the Stylite, standing on his column on a hillside in northern Syria. Simeon blessed him: 'The Lord of Glory will be your traveling companion.' He headed on towards Palestine and the Holy Places, to carry out his long-meditated plan to live there as a hermit.[2] On the way, he met an aged monk with long grizzled hair, who looked like Simeon. The old man warned Daniel against going any further towards Jerusalem: 'Verily, verily, verily – see I adjure you three times in the name of Christ – do not go there, but go to Byzantium. There you will see a second Jerusalem, the City of Constantine. There you will rejoice in the shrines of martyrs and imposing places of prayer, and should you wish to lead a contemplative life in a desert place in Thrace or in Pontus, the Lord will not leave you.'[3] The old man disappeared, but Daniel saw him again that night in a dream. He turned north towards Constantinople and settled a few miles outside the city as the old man had advised, by a bay on the European shore of the Bosporus.[4]

Daniel's mysterious counselor was not alone in thinking that Constantinople was a place particularly favored by the Christian God. It was a notion with a long future;[5] even as the Turkish army massed along the walls in the final fateful days of May 1453, there were those who hoped direct divine intervention would save the City.[6] This paper considers how it was that Constantinople became the God-protected City. It will concentrate in particular on two phases of this process. One will be the years following the initial foundation of the City on the site of the ancient town of Byzantium by Constantine the Great once he had become supreme ruler of the Roman Empire in 324. But first we will look at the era of Daniel the Stylite, the last years of the fourth and the whole of the fifth century, the years during which Constantinople developed the distinctive Christian character which it retained throughout the Middle Ages.

There is more here than a simple transformation of urban ideology. The development of Constantinople was part of a larger process of considerable complexity, the process by which Christianity came to occupy the commanding heights of the Divine Economy of the Roman Empire, and in doing so adapted itself to the new responsibilities which it had assumed in the time of Constantine. The conversion of the Roman Empire occurred at the level of the individual; its progress can be studied by counting those committed to Christianity and those who stood out against it.[7] But the conversion of the Empire was more than the sum of such individual commitments. It was a process involving the transformation of human habits and hopes, and of common patterns of behavior associated with them; it resulted in the formation of a distinctive Late Roman Christian civilization. Our consideration of Constantinople, therefore, should shed light on two current questions. First, what more was there to the conversion of the Roman Empire to Christianity than a change of heart on the part of numerous individuals; that is to say, how did a Christian civilization come into being in this city? And second, how did Christianity, a religion of the heart, become tied to particularities of place; how on earth, for a Christian, could a place become holy?[8] Constantinople was not, of course, a typical Late Roman city, and it is because it is not typical that it constitutes a particularly instructive example. It was from the start an imperial city and its imperial founder dedicated it at its inception to the God of the Christian martyrs.[9] In Constantinople, if anywhere, Christian emperors and the Christian faithful had a free hand to cooperate in creating a Christian civic community, to mould the landscape to make a Christian city.

The landscapes in which Christians found themselves in the fourth century were not secular or religiously neutral. Roman cities were religious communities because they were pathetically vulnerable to the forces of nature. They generally stored only one or two years' grain so they were never more than three bad harvests from famine.[10] From time immemorial they had survived the threats and vagaries of nature because they were under divine protection, protection assured to them by elaborate consecration of the urban geography and by a complex program of rituals. 'The Roman town, which is where Christianity first took root, was itself a sacred enclosure, marked off from its environment by a foundation rite which made the space enclosed by the town walls sacred, inviolable to defilement, equipped with gates for commerce with the outside world and for the elimination of pollution by the corpses of its dead.'[11] The civic calendar of a Roman city was determined by a seasonally reiterated round of sacrifices and festivals. A pagan explained: 'The reason we give the gods sacrifices and the other gifts is that, having become companionable after a fashion through our prayers, they may grant us good fortune and may avert evils from us... The gods are honored by these things...and if they have any recollection of offences committed by men, they disregard it, get rid of it, and renewing their friendship with us, once again become our patrons.'[12] Each festival had its appropriate location; the monuments and landscape of a Roman city and its surrounding countryside were intricately involved in the religious processes which prevented divine anger from bringing disaster upon the local economy.

The ancient city of Byzantium and the shores of the Bosporus were no exception; they were sacred landscapes punctuated by pagan temples and by places made holy by association with gods and heroes. A Byzantine mariner sailing down the Bosporus in the sixth century AD might use the lights in the dome of the Great Church of the Holy Wisdom as a guide to navigation.[13] In the centuries before Constantine a seaman's landmarks would have been monuments which commemorated the presence in the same waters of the very first ship known to Greek mythology, the *Argo* carrying Jason and his crew to collect the Golden Fleece from Colchis.[14] The bay of Sosthenion, above which Daniel was to have his pillar, for instance, was called Lasthenes, after one of the Megaran colonists who founded Byzantium; it had a temple of Amphiaraus which had been founded at the command of an oracle. All the way along the Bosporus were places set apart for the honor of Hecate, Apollo, Poseidon and other divinities; Jason and the Argonauts weave in and out of the aetiological myths and etymologies of local place names.[15] A poet of the reign of Nero contemplating a voyage across the open sea from Byzantium to Nicomedia might write lines commending his bark to Priapus and Apollo, worshipped on the further shore of the Propontis.[16] For Christian Byzantines the pagan monuments of the Bosporus and the stories associated with them were at best ancient history, at worst the work of demons; for those who lived by the Bosporus before the foundation of Constantinople, the associations which they thought existed between gods and heroes and the places along their shores were an integral aspect of the complex methods by which they ensured the continuing safety and success of their communities.

The transformation of religious geography brought about by Christianity in the maritime approaches to Constantinople can be seen occurring in the era of Daniel the Stylite; indeed the stylite himself had a hand in it. When Daniel first came to the Bosporus he settled not on a pillar but in an abandoned pagan temple, where he did battle with the demons who infested the place and who had, so claimed the disciple who wrote his life, long constituted a danger to shipping in the swift and difficult currents of the Bosporus.[17] In 460, after nine years in his temple, Daniel began to live on top of a column on a high and windy hill-top above the bay of Sosthenion, emulating deliberately the *ascesis* of St Simeon.[18] One admirer wrote verses which encapsulate the paradoxes at the center of the man's angelic life and had the poem carved on the column:

> Midway between earth and sky a man stands;
> Winds blow all about, he is not bothered...
> He lives on hunger for heavenly food
> And thirst for immaterial things
> Proclaiming the Son of a Virgin Mother.[19]

Disciples gathered round Daniel – one of whom wrote the *Life* from which we know about him. He lived on a succession of ever taller pillars on his windswept hill overlooking the Bosporus till 493, when he died at the age of 84.[20]

Daniel's column and the monastic community around it were far from being the only Christian landmarks for shipping passing between the Black Sea and the harbors of Constantinople in the middle of the fifth century. Near his demon-infested temple was a community with a church dedicated to St Michael, whose members gave Daniel a far from friendly welcome in the early stages of his stay.[21] Close to Constantinople also on the European side of the Bosporus was another sanctuary of the Archangel Michael.[22] Not far from Daniel but on the Asiatic side of the Bosporus was the large monastery of the Akoimetoi, the Sleepless Ones, whose 300 monks operated a shift system to sustain the Perpetual Adoration of God after the manner of the Sleepless Angels. The Akoimetoi was constantly tapped for monks to man new monasteries in the City.[23] It was indeed in the early years of Daniel's time by the Bosporus that the most famous of Constantinople's urban monasteries was founded, that of St John Studios, whose burnt-out church still stands in the southwest of the city, one of Constantinople's oldest surviving monuments.[24]

During the fifth century monks and monasteries became a powerful force in the formation of a distinctive Christian landscape in and around the City of Constantinople. Daniel doing battle with the demons in his temple had been preceded in the previous generation by Hypatius who had told his monks: 'Consider your calling, brethren; it is to an angelic company that you have been recruited...if during the short course of your lives, you fight and by the grace of Christ you triumph over the artifices of the Enemy...you will become even better than the angels.'[25] Hypatius's own triumph over demons included cures for the possessed, and various confrontations with pagan divinities when he traveled into the hinterland. On one occasion, three days' journey away from the Bosporus, he encountered a household of 40 idol-worshippers, one of whom had been beaten and thrown out by his companions because he wished to become Christian. Hypatius healed his sores and he lived for 30 years as a monk. His erstwhile companions did not last a year: they were taken by the anger of God, some died, their house was destroyed.[26] On another occasion the country people warned Hypatius not to walk along a certain road, for fear of meeting the goddess Artemis. But 'the righteous man has the confidence of a lion'. Hypatius actually met the goddess, ten times taller than a man, riding on wild boars (*potnia theron*). He made the sign of the Cross, the boars fled with a loud scream and the saint passed safely on his way.[27] Monks were instrumental in breaking the associations of individual places with unchristian powers and also in endowing places – not necessarily the same ones – with a Christian aura. But monks in Constantinople and its surroundings were more a feature of the fifth century than of the fourth. The biographer of Hypatius could claim that when his hero came to the city around 400 AD there was only one monastery in the area, that of St Isaac, which was founded around 380.[28] The Christian character given to the city and its surroundings specifically by monks dates from late in the century after Constantine.[29]

The settlement of monks in and around the city at the end of the fourth century and in the fifth century coincides in fact with the earliest evidence we have of another aspect of Christian public life in Constantinople: religious processions through the streets. It was not simply that people went to church, the church came to them; words of a Patriarch of Antioch might equally be applied to Constantinople: 'the whole city has become a church for us'.[30] There is, though, a problem in studying these processions. The evidence for Christian devotional use of the city streets in the fifth century does not record the normal practice of the church: the processions which are mentioned in our sources are those which have some particular historical significance. We are reduced not so much to making bricks without straw as to making them only with a few drinking straws. For instance, we know that in the last decade of the fourth century adherents of the Arian heresy were forbidden to celebrate the Liturgy within the city. Accordingly on every feast day, Saturday and Sunday they would gather in the porticoes and proceed out beyond the city walls to celebrate the Liturgy in the suburbs, chanting psalms with suitably Arian antiphons and responses as they went. John Chrysostom, after becoming Patriarch of Constantinople in 398, was determined to trump this devotional display and organized orthodox parades, embellished with silver processional crosses given by the empress and enlivened by appropriate antiphonal singing. Needless to say, there was fighting and it was the misfortune of the Arians that a stone, alas too well-aimed, happened to hit on the forehead an imperial eunuch who was conducting the orthodox chants. The Arian processions were stopped by an imperial order, though the orthodox continued to sing in the streets into the fifth century.[31]

In the Middle Ages religious processions through the streets of the city involving the court, the clergy or both formed a regular part of Byzantine life. Such processions marked church festivals and the feasts of saints. They also commemorated the deliverance of the city from a number of historical earthquakes. During one of these earthquakes 'no one dared to remain at home, but all fled outside the city, chanting litanies day and night; for there was great peril, such as there had not been from the beginning of time'.[32] The earliest record of emperor and people praying together in public after an earthquake comes from the year 396;[33] the earliest to be commemorated in after years with annual litanies and processions date from the middle years of the fifth century.[34] Such observances reinforce the impression that it was in those years that the city was acquiring its distinctive Christian traditions.

Regular processions claimed the streets for Christ. Processions accompanying the transfer of relics of the saints to shrines in and around the city left a more tangible Christian mark on the landscape. In the first year that John Chrysostom was Patriarch of Constantinople, the empress accompanied a crowd carrying the relics of a martyr out to the church at Drypia, nine miles west of the city, along the Marmara coast. The procession, says Chrysostom, emptied the city; its torches as they were carried through the night formed a moving river of fire.[35] No doubt ceremonies had attended the earlier transfer of relics of St Andrew,

St Luke and St Timothy to the Holy Apostles at Constantinople in 356–7, the first known case of a long-distance translation of relics.[36] But it is in the course of the last decade of the fourth century and the early fifth century that Constantinople, its hinterland and the shores of the Marmara and Bosporus came to be dotted with shrines of the saints, such as St John the Baptist at the Hebdomon and St Isaac the monk nearby.[37] The remains of the prophet Samuel arrived in 406, and were conducted to their new home by an enthusiastic procession which stretched, says St Jerome, all the way back to the Jewish sage's former resting-place in Palestine; the praetorian prefect and the prefect of the city were present; the emperor led the way.[38] Similarly, some years ater, the hand of St Stephen was ceremoniously installed, while in 438 the relics of John Chrysostom himself were brought back from the depths of Cappadocia, where he had died in exile.[39] In the fifth century it came to be believed that fragments of the True Cross found by Constantine's mother were lodged in his statue on top of the Porphyry Column at the center of the Forum of Constantine. The story is unlikely to be true; it tells us more about the fifth century than about the time of Constantine.[40]

The process by which signs of Christianity – monks, processions, relics – came to be integrated into the landscape of Constantinople and its surroundings from the very end of the fourth century onwards coincides with a significant change in the relationship of the city with its ruler. Constantinople had been founded by Constantine as an imperial city, dominated by the emperor and his officials. From the last decade of the fourth century onwards it became the permanent imperial residence. The Emperor Theodosius I, who died in 395, was the last emperor until Heraclius in the early seventh century to go himself with his army on campaigns. His son (395–408) set an example which lasted for over two centuries by not stirring from Constantinople:

> The Emperor Arcadius
> Stayed within a ten-mile radius.
> It was rather laborious
> For the Emperor Honorius.

Imperial immobility had large consequences for Constantinople. The hippodrome, for instance, acquired fresh significance as a political arena. It had long been a familiar political fact that emperors were obliged to confront the crowd of the city where they were residing when they attended public festivals.[41] From the end of the fourth century onwards, it was specifically the hippodrome crowd of Constantinople which had the freedom to chant its praise or blame of the emperor and his policies. In the early sixth century a newly chosen emperor would be brought up the spiral stair from the Great Palace to the imperial box in the hippodrome to be exhibited to the assembled people of the city for their acclamation.[42]

It was not merely the permanent presence of the emperor which changed Constantinople; it was also the permanent presence of his court. For the bishops assembled across the Bosporus at the Council of Chalcedon in 451, Constantinople was the city made honorable not only by the emperor but also by the senate.[43] An ordinary Roman city was dominated by its resident grandees, the local landowners who constituted its city council and controlled the local food supply, even to the inconvenience of a visiting emperor.[44] By contrast the Senate of Constantinople was from its inception the imperial court seen in a different aspect.[45] From the end of the fourth century onwards this court found a permanent home in a single city. The process parallels the way that in the twelfth century the functions of English government eventually came to rest in one place; the Angevin Court of the Exchequer 'could be held in any considerable town', but the treatise which describes in detail the way it worked was written by a civil servant who clearly felt most at home staring out of an upstairs window across the Thames at Westminster.[46] The archives of the central administration at Constantinople were stored in vaults under the hippodrome; they extended back to the generation before that in which the emperors came to rest permanently in the city, that is to say to the generation which would have provided the most accessible precedents for the late fourth century.[47] It was the next generation of Byzantine bureaucrats, that which populated the court at Constantinople in the fifth century, which codified Roman law in the *Theodosian Code*.[48] Some senators of this generation, such as the generals Aspar and Ardabur, who gave valuable vessels to the Church of the Anastasis in the mid-fifth century, were distinguished military figures.[49] But those who served in a civilian capacity were learned men, chosen for their aptitude at civilized and literary pursuits; in the memorable phrase of Fr Gervase Matthew, the Byzantine civil service 'possessed some of the close-knit texture of a good Late Victorian club'.[50] This articulate class was integral to the development of the customs and institutions of the imperial city.

Constantinople, then, enjoyed the patronage not only of the emperor, but also of the expansive *noblesse de robe* which worked for him. The importance of these courtiers is well illustrated by the *Life of Daniel*. The erection of Daniel's first pillar was paid for by Marcus, an admirer who had sailed out to see him; Marcus was a silentiary, one of a select corps of imperial attendants who maintained silence in the emperor's consistory and often shared his confidence.[51] The land on which it was decided to erect the column belonged to one Gelanius, the chamberlain in charge of the imperial food and drink, and he objected to the trespass. Having complained to the emperor and the Patriarch and got nowhere, Gelanius came out to confront the saint. He was greeted with a hailstorm which ruined the ripe grapes of his vineyard. Eventually, the two made a deal, both speaking in their native Syriac so that bystanders would not understand. Daniel came a few steps down from his pillar, Gelanius rushed forward, shouting, 'Go back to your home and your way of life and pray for me,' and honor was satisfied on both sides.[52] The admirer who decorated Daniel's column with a poem in honor of his paradoxical way of life was Cyrus, who had been prefect of the city and praetorian prefect both at the same time. Indeed he became so popular with the people that court intrigue unseated him – on accusations of paganism. He was obliged to be consecrated a bishop and was sent off to a provincial see which allegedly had already killed four bishops. It says something for his political skill that he was able to survive and retire to Constantinople.[53]

It is true that not all the mandarins of the imperial service were keen Christians. One has only to think of the *comes* Zosimus, an official of the fisc who as late as the last years of the fifth century composed a history bitterly blaming Christianity and Constantine for everything which had gone wrong in the Empire over the past two centuries.[54] But Christianity was as much a part of the culture of the Byzantine bureaucracy as classical Greek literature. Even a prefect of the city keen to revive Olympic Games in the city of Chalcedon across the Bosporus – to the fury of St Hypatius – was required by imperial edict to burn the books of the 'nefarious and sacrilegious' heretic Nestorius, so that his followers might not 'misuse the name of Christians'.[55] In the fifth century the God-loving emperor and the resident Byzantine bureaucracy came to dominate Constantinople, and whatever the views of individuals, it was Christian practice which held the city together.

Fifth-century Constantinople seems the very model of a Christian imperial city. But that does not necessarily mean that all its elements were present when the city was first founded by Constantine in 324 and dedicated by him in 330. It is possible that in its earliest years Constantinople was a city no less Christian and imperial, but Christian and imperial in different ways. Such gradations of change were often smoothed over in Byzantine accounts of the early history of Constantinople. Byzantines valued continuity; the development of the Christian imperial city at the mouth of the Bosporus is presented as an easy transition. A story from the sixth-century chronicle of John Malalas illustrates the point. It concerns a temple, perhaps of Attis, at Sosthenion, near the pillar of Daniel. The Emperor Constantine, says the chronicle, looked carefully at the cult statue when he came to the temple and thought it looked like an angel dressed in the habit of a Christian monk. He prayed in the place and slept there in order to determine which power was present; he had a dream, as a result of which he dedicated the place to the archangel Michael.[56] The story represents Constantine not merely as a Christian emperor, but as a Christian emperor similar in tastes and habits to the devout potentates of early Byzantium. A similar preoccupation with continuity is to be found in fragments of a history written in the early years of the sixth century by Hesychius of Miletus. This comprehensive work spanned world history in six sections from the time of Bel to the early sixth century, each section being inaugurated by a significant event. The final segment started with Constantine's dedication of Constantinople 362 years after the start of the reign of Augustus. The surviving fragments provide a circumstantial account of the history of the city of Byzantium and its surroundings, treating, as did Malalas, the local myths as ancient history. In the context of a *longue durée* shaped by a mathematically minded providence, the foundation of the Christian imperial city is made to appear part of a smooth and continuous evolution.[57]

To understand the religious and political character of Constantinople in its earliest years it is necessary to step behind such Byzantine antiquaries. Constantinople was the most important and last-founded of a series of imperial cities frequented by emperors during most of the third and fourth centuries. By the time of Constantine, emperors had long since ceased to live at Rome, except for Gallienus (died 268), because he liked it and was prepared to allow the Levant and Gaul to be run by usurpers, and Maxentius (306–12), because he had no choice, being surrounded by competing potentates.[58] The reason was simple. Since the early third century the Empire had been obliged to defend itself regularly on three fronts, the Rhine in Germany, the Danube in the

North Balkans and the Persian Front, which ran through modern Eastern Turkey and Syria. Emperors were to be found on the move between these fronts or stationed in cities within easy reach of them. A number of imperial cities rose to prominence, many of them along the great roads which linked Antioch in Syria (convenient for the Persian Front) to Nicomedia in Northwestern Asia Minor, crossed the Bosporus and went through Serdica (modern Sofia in Bulgaria), Naissus (Nish) and Sirmium (Mitroviča) in Serbia, entering Italy at Aquileia at the head of the Adriatic before crossing Northern Italy to Milan and then the Alps to Arles in Provence, Trier in the Rhineland and eventually York. It is a constant surprise how much Late Antique history happened along this road. It was the outward route taken by the earliest pilgrim to the Holy Land to record his journey, the Bordeaux Pilgrim of 333; leading churchmen, such as Gregory of Nazianzus relegated from Constantinople to Sasima in the fourth century, or Theodore of Mopsuestia in the fifth century, held bishoprics in cities sited along it.[59] Some cities on the road saw the births of emperors (Constantine at Nish and Valentinian I at Cibalae), others their deaths (Maximinus Daia at Tarsus and Constantius II at Mopsucrene just beyond Tarsus, south of the Cilician Gates).[60]

With the reassertion of relative military security after the accession of Diocletian (at Nicomedia) in 284 and its consolidation by the creation of a Tetrarchy in 293, many of these cities were provided with monuments appropriate for an imperial residence. The Christian apologist Lactantius, no admirer of Diocletian, complained about the emperor's lust for building, his *libido aedificandi*: 'here a law court, here a mint, here a weapons factory, here a house for his wife, here for his daughter... It was thus that he was always raving trying to make Nicomedia the equal of Rome'.[61] There is a family resemblance between these imperial cities. All, except the retirement palace of Diocletian at Split and Galerius' rural residence at Romulianum, were grafted on beside existing cities. Many have residences with sea or river frontages; the palaces regularly enjoyed direct access to the city hippodrome, a political as well as a sporting space; mostly they had mints, and some had mausoleums to receive the remains of emperors.[62]

Diocletian and his senior colleague Maximian abdicated, at Nicomedia and Milan respectively, on May 1, 305, and were succeeded by their two junior colleagues and two fresh junior emperors. This new Tetrarchy soon crumbled into bloody civil war. At one point seven emperors contended for mastery.[63] From this tangled conflict

Constantine, first proclaimed as an emperor by his father's troops at York in 306, emerged in 324 as the ultimate victor. The principal points in Constantine's progress stand out. In 312 a victory just outside Rome, the Battle of the Milvian Bridge, made him master of everything west of the Balkans and enabled him to make an alliance with Licinius, who was able to bring down the last of the emperors responsible for the Great Persecution of the Christians. Licinius subsequently became superfluous to Constantine's plans. An attack on him – down the road which crossed the North Balkans – in 316–17 ended in stalemate at Cibalae, but in 324 a combined naval and military operation incorporating a siege of Byzantium enabled Constantine to eliminate his last rival: 'Having the power of this God as ally, beginning from the shores of Ocean I have raised up the whole world step by step with sure hopes of salvation, so that all those things which under the slavery of such great tyrants yielded to daily disasters and had come near to vanishing, have enjoyed the general restoration of right, and have revived like a patient after treatment.'[64]

The new master of the East might have chosen to maintain Nicomedia, the favored residence of the Tetrarchs and also of Licinius, as his principal city. The choice not to do so was swift and deliberate, too swift for us to give any credence to the charming later story that Constantine actually planned to build his new city at Troy.[65] One may suggest reasons for the choice of Byzantium. It was, for one thing, a strategic spot. In the classical Greek period the grain which came from the Black Sea to feed Athens and other Greek cities had been obliged to pass by Byzantium.[66] As every Russian and British diplomat of the nineteenth century knew, the Straits at Constantinople control access from the Black Sea to the warm water ports of the Mediterranean. But in Late Antiquity, its strategic importance ran the other way. It commanded the shores where Europe comes closest to Asia. An army marching between the Danube Frontier – along the line of the Orient Express – and the East would need to cross the Straits, and a force in Byzantium could deny it that crossing. This had made it a key point in recent civil wars, not only in Constantine's war against Licinius of 324 but further back in the war between Septimius Severus and Pescennius Niger in 193–6, when the city had sustained a three-year siege.[67]

For all its strategic importance, however, Byzantium had never been a great city. This was for a simple reason; it was an extremely difficult place to provision. The water supply had always been fraught with difficulty; water, water everywhere nor any drop to drink.[68] Equally, despite the fact that it had lands on both sides of the Sea of Marmara, Byzantium lacked the sort of broad fertile plain which made great cities out of places like Antioch and Ephesus.[69] In the pre-Roman period it lived largely off levies on trade passing through the Straits to the cities around the Black Sea which were obliged to import their wine and olive oil, two of the three staples of the Mediterranean diet: 'the Byzantines dwell in a place most fortunate as regards the sea...but as regards land most unsuitable'.[70] Ancient Byzantium covered little more than the tip of the peninsula now occupied by Stambul. Stray classical tombstones have been found near Hagia Sophia and Sirkeçi Station; a substantial concentration, indicating the presence of the principal cemetery, was near Beyazit Square.[71] These tombs, on the Second Hill of mediaeval Constantinople, would have been outside the walls of ancient Byzantium. This was not a large city.[72]

These defects Constantine turned to his benefit. He planned for a vast area to be enclosed by the walls of the city; it tripled, even quadrupled in size.[73] And he arranged for its people to be fed not from local produce but by grain imported by sea from Egypt.[74] This arrangement was essential for the growth of the city. The importance of the regular shipments from Alexandria is illustrated by an incident which occurred little more than ten years after the city's foundation. The theological enemies of Athanasius the Patriarch of Alexandria had been trying, with only limited success, to influence the emperor against him. Eventually they averred that Athanasius had been using magical means to control the winds which would prevent the sailing of the grain fleet for Constantinople. Athanasius was in exile before you could say 'the Father is not greater than the Son'.[75]

For the grain fleet was about more than food. To provision his city Constantine did not need to rely on the favour of local gods, who might need to be placated with appropriate fertility rites. Equally, he did not need to rely on local grandees. Drastic shortages could occur when the acts of an emperor did not please the large landowners of the city where he happened to be residing. Julian the Apostate, resident in Antioch with a large army during the winter of 362–3, wanted to lower the price of food. He was warned by the local notables that this often led to shortages, but persisted in his policy for the sake of popularity and was rewarded by a severe shortage in a time when there was known to be plenty in store.[76] Constantinople, unlike Antioch or Nicomedia, was not a provincial capital of ancient prosperity. Constantine could control it because he could control its food supply; he was not at the mercy of its local councillors and their public gods. The pagan historian who wrote in 500 AD that Constantine settled in Constantinople because he could not endure being blasphemed against by everyone was a shrewd observer.[77]

Constantine's city was unusual in the closeness of control exerted over it by the emperors. It was unusual also in being a city which was not held together by the observance of public rites in honor of civic gods. Paganism at the time of the foundation of Constantinople was not the object of mere antiquarian interest it was to become by the sixth century; it was still a living force and at its core was the practice of public sacrifice. The gods of a classical city were something more than totems, symbols of communal unity; they were the forces of Nature whose co-operation was essential for the survival of a city. Normality was sustained by the correct sacrifices being offered at the appropriate times: too much sacrifice might produce a rush of divine favour which it would be impossible to sustain, neglect brought divine anger and disaster.[78] Civic religion did not center on ideas or articulate belief. Such explanations as were necessary were provided not by theology but by myth, 'socially pervasive truths of low cognitive value'.[79] Christians would point out that their religion was odd precisely because it supplied a rational account of its practices; it brought together ideas and acts, sapientia and religio, in an unprecedented manner.[80] The core of ancient paganism was ritual action: rem, facias rem. It was precisely because Christians had refused to offer even the simplest sacrifice that they had been subjected to a sustained persecution which in the eastern half of the Roman Empire had lasted a full decade from 303 to 313.[81]

Constantine's first act on succeeding his father in the imperial power at York in 306 had been to stop the persecution of Christians in his dominions.[82] At some point in his reign, presumably after his conquest of the East in 324, Constantine actually made blood sacrifice illegal. The law in which he did this is known only from a reference in legislation by his son; the text does not survive.[83] But Constantine's hatred for the practice of sacrifice runs like a leitmotif through other legislation. 'The good people of Umbria may build a temple of the imperial cult provided there is no filthiness of polluting sacrifice performed in it.'[84] 'Foul sacrifices' had contaminated Mamre in the Holy Land.[85] If public buildings are struck by lightning, the normal rites may be performed to ascertain what the sign portends, and private individuals may perform the same procedures, provided that they abstain from sacrifice.[86] Imperial administrators were specifically forbidden to engage in pagan worship while performing their public duties. Only a single generation had passed since Christians were being executed for trying to prevent provincial governors from inaugurating official business with sacrifice.[87]

Constantine's loathing for 'sacrilegious abominations' was reflected in the public practice of his new city.[88] Constantinople did not witness the rites and processions normal in other cities; Constantine, his biographer avers, saw fit to purge Constantinople of all idol-worship, 'so that nowhere in it appeared those images of the supposed gods which are worshipped in temples, nor altars foul with bloody slaughter, nor sacrifice offered as holocaust in fire, nor feasts of demons...'[89] Such absence of pagan observance in the City's public life did not make each of its inhabitants automatically Christian. In the generation after Constantine, there were notable citizens who did not profess the Christian faith and yet spoke well of the city;[90] the apostate emperor Julian was noted for his affection for the place of his birth.[91] But the presence of individual non-Christians is irrelevant in assessing the unpagan character of Constantinople's public life. This was a community which was not ordered around a cycle of pagan civic ritual; it had no means of allaying the anger of the Gods, it dared to risk its survival in the face of the capricious forces of nature.[92] The reason that the Christians had been persecuted, according to one of their principal opponents, was precisely that 'such wilfulness had invaded those same Christians and such great folly had taken possession of them, that they did not follow those things set up by the ancients...they made up for themselves laws to observe, just as it pleased them and in accordance with their own whim'.[93] To such a devotee of 'the old laws and the public discipline of the Romans' the civic life of Constantinople would have seemed profoundly irresponsible; as late as 500 AD pagans were puzzled that despite its rashness the city seemed to enjoy an obvious success and prosperity.[94]

The absence of normal pagan cult may be illustrated by the celebrations which early Byzantine sources say were held to celebrate the birthday of the city every May 11 and which they claim were inaugurated by Constantine to mark the anniversary of his foundation.[95] It is not possible to be sure that this celebration was begun by Constantine or that it was performed in the early days of the city's existence; the sources were written considerably later. They describe a procession in which a gilded wooden image of Constantine, standing on a carriage and escorted by soldiers wearing cloaks and carrying candles, was borne into the hippodrome and brought to rest opposite the imperial box, where the emperor of the day would rise from his seat and bow down before it. The statue bore in its hand an image of the Tyche, the Good

Fortune of the City. The elements strikingly absent from this ceremony are sacrifice and statues of real gods. Constantine could be deemed human. The Fortune of the City was not a god in the same way as was Poseidon, the father of Byzas; she fell into that 'wide no-man's land between explicit pagan worship and uncompromising Christian rejection of all its trappings and associations' which was characteristic of the early fourth century.[96] Some Christians might find Fortune inoffensive, and others could object; a bishop might bluster against the city's Fortune as an instance of idolatry or he might appease Christians who had participated in celebrations of the civic totem because 'we know she is no god'.[97] The course of events at Caesarea of Cappadocia is instructive. By the year 362 there was only one temple in the city in working order, the temple of the Tyche. In that year Eupsychius, a local Christian notary, protested against the neopagan policies of the emperor, Julian the Apostate, by destroying this shrine as well. Christians in Caesarea in the early fourth century had drawn the line in one place; Eupsychius, impelled by disgust, had drawn it in another.[98] It may be that the birthday ceremony of Constantinople underwent a similar if less violent evolution; one writer says that the procession continued to be held in his own time in the sixth century, but another, writing later, says that Theodosius the Great abolished it in the late fourth century.[99] Early Byzantine traditions about the time of Constantine, as we have seen, entangle historical fact with wishful thinking, but if this ceremony is accurately described it fits well our image of a City whose principal public ceremonies lacked solid pagan content.

The monuments of Constantine's city tell a story similar to that of its ceremonies. The old acropolis of Byzantium with its three temples was dwarfed by the new conurbation where such structures were, so far as is known, conspicuously absent.[100] Constantine, it is true, is said to have built a pair of temples associated with the tutelary powers of the cities of Rome and Byzantium. One housed a statue of Rhea, Mother of the Gods, associated with Jason and the Argonauts, the other a representation of the Fortuna of Rome.[101] These buildings are described as temples by a keen pagan of c. 500 AD; they may in fact have been no more than alcoves in a portico. There is no record of a cult being offered there, except by Julian the Apostate, and the pairing of the local goddess with the Fortuna of Rome suggests that she was being presented as a civic totem rather than as a part of the local pantheon.[102] It is also possible that the image of Rhea was associated with a statue of Constantine's mother, the Empress Helena.[103] If this is so, it would provide a parallel to the Great Statue of the emperor himself that stood on the Porphyry Column in the center of the Forum of Constantine till it fell in 1106, and which is persistently associated in the sources with Apollo and the Sun.[104] It may even be that a 'transfer of religious value onto his own person' by Constantine in erecting these statues was inspired by an account of the pagan gods put forth by one of the emperor's Christian associates and was therefore meant to cut them down to size, not accord them an ecumenical courtesy. Lactantius, appointed by Constantine as tutor to his son, had demythologized the gods by arguing that they were simply ancient rulers whom their doting subjects had mistakenly deified after they had died.[105] Constantine could simply have been reversing the process, transforming divinities back into princes.

Whatever idea inspired him to erect them, these statues were not the only ancient images to decorate the city of Constantine. The emperor dedicated Constantinople 'having stripped almost all the other cities naked', remarked a chronicler.[106] The public places of the city were liberally bedizened with pagan statues divorced from their original context and function.[107] Constantine built a hippodrome at his new residence like those of other Tetrarchic cities – or rather enlarged an existing one.[108] The central reservation of the racecourse was embellished with sculpture brought from all over the Mediterranean world, including the Serpent Column, cast in bronze eight centuries before and dedicated at Delphi, which is still there.[109] The council chamber of the new Senate House was decorated with statues of the Muses brought in from Mount Helicon; before its doors stood the statue of Zeus from the oracular shrine at Dodona and Athena from the island of Lindos.[110] A pagan senator might flatter the oratorical achievements of his colleagues by referring to their place of assembly as a temple of the Muses, but any honor offered to the statues was entirely rhetorical.[111] No sacrifices were offered on the sacred tripod brought from Delphi. Like icons in a museum which never get kissed, these images had been lifted out of their ritual context: they were merely art.

The evidence for overtly Christian monuments and observances in Constantine's city, on the other hand, while not copious, is striking for its novelty. It is true that we look in vain for great church buildings like those Constantine gave to the church at Rome. Nothing is known of the city's first cathedral, Hagia Eirene.[112] The first Great Church of the Holy Wisdom was not consecrated until 360.[113] It seems that the Holy Apostles in its earliest form was an imperial mausoleum, comparable to the Rotunda of Galerius at Thessalonica, though an imperial mausoleum equipped with an altar for offering the bloodless sacrifice of the Christian Eucharist.[114] Constantine positioned Christian emblems at strategic spots: a cross high on the frontage of the imperial palace and representations at fountains in public squares of the Good Shepherd and of Daniel, whose survival in the lion's den had made him a model for persecuted Christians.[115] Indeed the emperor dedicated his city, says Eusebius, to the God of the martyrs,[116] and chose May 11 330, the anniversary of the death of the martyr St Mocius, a local victim of the Great Persecution, to perform the dedication. The basilica dedicated to St Mocius is not attested before the fifth century, but there was already by 359 a shrine later associated with St Acacius, allegedly a military martyr of the Great Persecution.[117] To judge by its monuments the city of Constantine was not that of Daniel the Stylite, with its Christian public processions and calendar customs, but the novelty of their presence, added to the unprecedented absence of civic cult designed to ensure the co-operation of the forces of nature, made it a distinctively Christian place.

For the Christianity of Constantine's court was a novel phenomenon. Many people, Stoics and Platonists among them, had long believed that in the end there was a single divinity which holds all things together, but they were not concerned with the worship of so remote a being: they called upon the god who was effective for the job at hand, whether the protection of a city's crops or the victory of an emperor's army. The appropriate response to the One God could only be a philosophic silence.[118] Christians asserted the existence of a single God and were quite willing to compare him to the Sun, 'one and alone, of perfect majesty and might and splendor'.[119] But they claimed also to know how to offer him practical honor; Christianity was not only wisdom, *sapientia*, but also worship, *religio*: 'where is *sapientia* joined with *religio*? There indeed where One God is worshipped, where all life and action are referred to a single head and a single purpose, there, in the end, where the teachers of wisdom are the same as the priests of God'.[120] The worship of the Most High God rendered redundant all other worship. If lesser beings were in opposition to God then worship of them was erroneous; if they were God's subordinates it was otiose.[121] Christians claimed that they had the means to supersede the public cults of cities, which is why theirs could never be one of the private observances which existed alongside civic religion. If there was a 'vacuum of holiness' in Constantine's city, it was more a consequence than an intention of its foundation.[122] The absence of pagan worship was in itself something distinctively Christian.

Where pre-Christian religion did obtrude, as with Constantine's pagan statues, it served the purposes of the new city in ways which recall the incorporation of pagan features into the Christian view of the world adumbrated in the *Divine Institutes* of Constantine's courtier, the rhetorician Lactantius. Sculpture from Delphi and Dodona adorned Constantinople. Lactantius had taken utterances from oracles, edited them and used them as Christian testimonies. He justified his citations by explaining that the powers behind oracles were once agents of God but had left his service, so their prophecies were to be trusted when they retailed knowledge obtained from their previous employer.[123] We have already seen how Lactantius could incorporate the gods into a Christian account of world history by claiming that they were ancient rulers mistakenly divinized.[124] Similarly his prophecy of the Last Times incorporates poetic prophecy of a Golden Age, but entirely on Christian terms; Vergil's poetry is quoted to describe a millennium of plenty to be enjoyed only by Christians.[125] This is not syncretism, nor is it pandering to residual paganism; it is the ruthless reinterpretation of the familiar in a fresh and Christian light.[126] Pagan elements in the *Institutes* serve a Christian purpose; the old city of Byzantium was dwarfed by what Constantine built beside it.[127]

Lactantius also discourages us from using buildings as a measure of Christianity. Solomon had built a temple for God and a city which he had named Jerusalem after himself, but 'the dwelling which he erected did not result from faith, as does the Church, which is the true temple of God constituted not by walls but by the heart and faith of men who believe in him and are called the faithful'.[128] Lactantius applied to Christian worship of the Most High God a passage where Seneca had expounded the way a Stoic ought to honor the greatest of all powers: 'for him there should not be built up into the heavens temples on the crowded crags, he should be consecrated in the hearts of each one of us'.[129] Persecutors who destroyed church buildings were wasting their time, 'for the true temple of God is among men'.[130] Lactantius rejected the notion that places might be holy in the sense that the pagan temples were holy, set apart as places where the gods were peculiarly present to their worshippers. But at the same time he asserted that particular places had a special function in the *Dispositio Summi Dei*, God's overall plan for the world.[131] The world would not come to an end while the City of Rome lasted.[132] Similarly the final millennium of prosperity for the righteous will be inaugurated with the foundation of a 'holy city' in the middle of the earth, where God its founder will dwell with the righteous as they rule.[133] More important, he had a sense of the relation of God to the world as a whole, conceived not as an agglomeration of particular holy places but as a single entity entirely created by God, not out of pre-existing raw material, but out of nothing.[134]

Domini est terra et plenitudo ejus. In a world wholly the handiwork of a single divinity, all things could be assimilated to the universal explanations supplied by Christianity: the pagan gods as historical characters and their myths as garbled versions of their earthly deeds, the oracles as inventions of forces in rebellion against God, the Roman Empire as one of the four world empires whose rise and fall had been predicted by in the Book of Daniel.[135] Locating holiness was not therefore a matter of delineating individual places sacred to particular gods and guarding them against ritual pollution.[136] It was more a matter of amplifying the obvious, of illustrating the importance of a place in the plans of the Christian God by eliminating the accretions of generations of demonic activity – as at the temple on the site of the Holy Sepulchre – or by transforming the familiar by giving it a Christian interpretation. Constantine, it is said, marked out the boundaries of Constantinople in the manner customary for the founding of a city, but he said as he did so that he was led onwards by a power whose presence was not part of the traditional ritual.[137] Customary ceremonial practice was thereby given an interpretation which might link it to a larger sense of the providence of the Christian God.

Christian appropriation of the landscape involved subtle and profound changes in patterns of habit, and 'a far from negligible proportion of human action follows recognized patterns'.[138] But it was not, despite the pious wishes of later Byzantine chroniclers, a matter of easy continuity. The spirit of authentic Christianity did not simply succumb to syncretism with stubborn pagan survivals; there was no straightforward transfer of power. Visitors to Daniel the Stylite's column by the Bosporus sailed through a landscape which was marked, interpreted and protected by sacred rites. So had Dionysus of Byzantium when he thought himself following in the wake of the good ship *Argo*, of Jason, Hercules and their crew. But in between, Daniel in his old pagan temple overlooking the Bosporus had to do battle with demons. And Constantine's city had been founded at the culmination of a generation's bitter dispute between pagans and Christians over the proper performance of public religion, a mythopoeic trauma which in the persons of the martyrs provided Christians with heroes for more than a millennium.[139] The development of Constantinople as a Christian imperial city in the fourth and fifth centuries was the history of a new community finding fresh ways of coming to terms with the landscape in which it lived. But it was also a part of the long and sometimes violent process by which the Roman Empire became Christian. If Christians of the age of Constantine really thought that soon 'almost everybody would in future belong to God, once the polytheistic madness had been removed', they were optimists.[140] But the emperor's new city did at least demonstrate to those Romans prepared to take notice that civic life was possible without the protection of the gods, a risk which by the Roman way of thinking only a Christian was equipped to take.[141]

Chapter 3

Communities of the Living and the Dead in Late Antiquity and the Early Medieval West

Frederick S Paxton

Third-century Christians belonged to multiple communities. All were, of course, members of families. Most were also members of households in urban quarters of some common linguistic, economic or social identity. Most men were imperial citizens. Still a minority in the empire, Christians nonetheless comprised a significant and growing group. There were about 30,000 in Rome around the year 250, served by some 155 clerics.[1] Their religious lives centered on their local church, but a web of textual and human connections, reaching outwards in space and backwards in time, linked them in various ways to other Christian communities. They gathered for worship in private homes, which had often by then evolved into architectural hybrids known as a 'house-churches' (*domus ecclesiae*). The only extant remains of such buildings lie at Dura-Europos, a Syrian city on the west bank of the Euphrates destroyed by Sassanian Persia in the year 256. The *domus ecclesiae* at Dura lay in the shadow of the western walls, not far from a synagogue and a mithraeum.[2] Archaeological analysis has revealed that, around the year 240, the owners of a private home joined two rooms off its atrium to make a large assembly hall, and converted another smaller room into a baptistery.[3] Similar arrangements must have existed in many places across the Roman empire in the mid-third century, but the Dura remains are a unique glimpse at the concrete shape of Christian communities when the historical record begins to be anchored in archaeological data as well as texts.[4] I will return to them.

Ideally, the totality of local churches comprised a single Christian community tied together through common belief and shared apostolic traditions. In reality, there was just as likely to be conflict both within and between congregations, and some were simply going their own way. Local churches had distinct personalities, as is evident from the rich growth of Christian variants that sprouted wherever gospels, apocalypses, apostolic letters and acts traveled. As a result, a stream of writings, expressing a wide range of belief about the meaning of Jesus's life and death, competed for attention and authority, usually by associating themselves with the names of his companions.[5] A hierarchical church order led by bishops, which had first emerged in Alexandria in the later second century, continually gained ground in the third. Its organization and inclusiveness gave it an edge over its non-hierarchical competitors, especially the multitude of communities commonly, if misleadingly, grouped as gnostics who had dominated the church in the mid-second century.[6] Nevertheless, the traditions that we call catholic and orthodox emerged only after centuries of highly contested give-and-take between varying visions of Christian belief and practice.

These realities did not only affect relations within living communities, for to be a Christian meant also to be part of another, unseen, group – the community of the dead. The living could be uncertain of the exact condition, location and status of the dead, but, as Robert Markus has observed, 'about the fellowship of the dead and the living in the community of the faithful there was never any doubt'.[7] Whether orthodox or heretic, no Christian imagined his or her religion in purely this-worldly terms. Christianity, in any understanding, focused squarely on death. This did not mean that everyone agreed on what the death and resurrection of Jesus meant. Conceptions could differ widely, from the docetist reduction to pure spirit, to the almost obsessive patristic concern with carnality that Caroline Bynum has so brilliantly illuminated.[8] Nevertheless, Jesus's death remained central, as did the promise of resurrection that it entailed.

Ideally, as well, the living and the dead formed a single Christian community. If I may borrow Patrick Geary's felicitous description of the early medieval scene, the dead were simply another 'age group'.[9] Since this was the case, there needed to be clear means of transition and clear points of contact between them. And since the community of the faithful was defined as much by whom it excluded as by its members, how to die so as to be counted among the blessed, and who, once dead, had unquestionably done so were bound to be issues of contention as much as communion.

This essay approaches the communities of the living and the dead between the second and the tenth centuries on more or less these terms. It addresses ritual activities like baptism and deathbed communion – and attitudes towards death and dying – but its central theme is the tension between the desire of the living to maintain family and social distinctions, both in this world and the next, and the Christian ideal of a single community of the faithful spanning them both. It does not attempt to be comprehensive – the subject is too vast and the material too rich. It will have succeeded if it manages to present a general introduction to the topic and indicate the directions in which ongoing programs of research seem to be headed.[10]

In any society, images of the communities of the living and the dead tend to mirror, and even to construct, one another. From the early Christian point of view, the dead, like the living, were strictly divided between those who had and had not been baptized into Christ. Around the year 405, Augustine of Hippo had to intercede in a local dispute between a bishop and a wealthy family whose son had died a catechumen. The family wanted him buried among the baptized in or near a church. Augustine supported the local bishop's position. Since the boy had not been baptized, he could not be buried in the places 'where the holy mysteries were celebrated'.[11] A further division separated the baptized who died 'out of communion' from those who did not. The most troublesome of the former were those who had denied their faith during persecution. The question of the status of the lapsed (*lapsi*), as they were known, was a burning issue from the middle of the third century through the Council of Nicaea in 325, which settled things only for the majority. In the wake of the Decian persecution of 250, the schismatic papal pretender Novatian refused communion to *lapsi*. In the fourth century, the North African Donatist and Meletian schismatics took the same rigorist position. All sides in these debates were committed to episcopal and clerical authority, and the schisms had as much to do with politics as with belief, but the refusal to extend reconciliation to *lapsi* rested upon respect for those who had made the ultimate sacrifice of martyrdom.[12] The intensity of the arguments may have derived in part from the fear that those whose status at death was uncertain might return as ghosts to plague the living.[13] It certainly derived from opposing visions of community. The schismatics were unified in their commitment to an exclusive 'Church of the martyrs', while the majority opted for inclusiveness and forgiveness for the lapsed, especially at death. The mainstream position was so inclusive, in fact, that it could encompass even those baptized by schismatics like Novatian.[14] One thing united both sides, however – the shared conviction that baptism and communion were *the* signs of membership in the community of the faithful, living and dead.

While reading John Van Engen's recent work on baptism and Christian identity in Late Antiquity, I was struck by a reference to Ambrose of Milan's *De sacramentis*, a series of daily talks by the bishop to a group going through the rites of initiation and their first experience of communion.[15] After covering each stage of the ritual leading up to the immersion, Ambrose stopped to consider the meaning of baptism itself. Having sinned, men and women were condemned to die, and to return to the earth from which they had been made. Baptism was invented as a way that the living could die and be revived. 'That is why,' he said, 'the baptismal font is like a grave.'[16]

What did he mean? Archaeological remains of early fonts and baptisteries are difficult to interpret. The earliest fonts do seem to have been rectangular, and might or might not have been modeled on sarcophagi; similarly, early remains of baptisteries are often but not always indistinguishable from mausolea.[17] The oldest more or less completely preserved baptistery is from the Christian 'house-church' at Dura-Europos.[18] After its discovery by an expedition from Yale University in the 1930s, some observers argued that the canopied structure at the west end of the northwest room, which bore a strong resemblance to tomb structures in the Roman catacombs, must have been a martyr's grave.[19] It has since been definitively identified as a font, but ambiguities remain. In fact, the exact relationship between early Christian baptismal architecture and the cult of the dead is an open question. There is evidence from the middle of the fourth century onwards of baptisteries attached to martyria in extra-urban cemetery complexes, and, from the fifth, of the presence of relics and altars in or associated with them.[20] Paul-Albert Février does not think that that attests to a 'formal connection' between baptism and the cult of the dead, but less formal possibilities remain.[21] There is no evidence for the existence of an altar in the large assembly hall at Dura and some for the use of the baptistery for the eucharist and for an understanding of baptism as a ritual death.[22] A canon of an episcopal synod held at Auxerre between 561 and 605 prohibiting burial in baptisteries was certainly directed against the practice, however rare.[23] More to the point, Ambrose had erected his baptistery at Milan in exact imitation of an imperial mausoleum there, which, like Diocletian's mausoleum across the Adriatic at Split, was octagonal in shape.[24] In Ambrose's system of Christian symbolism, eight-sidedness evoked the resurrection of Christ 'on the eighth day of the Passion'.[25] Thus, Ambrose's audience would doubtlessly have understood the bishop's allusion in a manner appropriate to the symbolism and mood of late fourth-century ecclesiology.[26] The font was like a grave in the way the baptistery at Milan was like an imperial mausoleum. Each was a way-station on a triumphant passage through death to resurrection and eternal life.

The significance of baptism in the life and death of Late Antique Christians can hardly be overestimated. The span of a Christian biography stretched from rebirth in baptism to a second rebirth in death, to final resurrection. God would see to the last transition. As for the others, baptism may initially have sufficed for both. Especially in the fourth and early fifth centuries, baptism was taken so seriously that it was put off as long as possible, and often performed at the deathbed and even over corpses.[27] Little attention was paid to the deaths of baptized Christians in good standing, which in ordinary cases occurred within a domestic setting with minimal ritual accompaniment.[28] What attention there was, was fixed on those whose death in martyrdom most clearly ensured a successful passage directly to paradise and full membership with the blessed community of the saints.[29] For the ordinary dead, the sign of their baptism, and the fact of their good standing among living Christians, was usually enough for them confidently to expect some share in the martyrs' glory, either immediately after death or at the resurrection which, while still to come, had not yet receded into the unknowable future.[30] In the Late Antique Church, baptism was not just an initiation into a living community, but a ritual of death and resurrection linking the recipient to Christian communities both living and dead. Christians were the younger siblings of Paul's Christ – 'the firstborn from the dead'.[31] Marked by baptism for salvation, they could await death with confident expectation and even anticipation of the resurrection to follow.

The conversion of Constantine of course enhanced the confidence of the baptized. Freed from the fear of tortured death in martyrdom, most Christians of the next couple of generations enjoyed a peaceful coexistence with their non-Christian neighbors. They had no need to struggle with them. The acceptance of baptism, the scriptural canon and the authority of priests and bishops virtually assured salvation after death. Differences between Catholics and Arians or Donatists loomed larger than those between Christians and the followers of traditional religion. It was enough to keep oneself free from the taint of idolatrous sacrifice. Participation in other forms of civic and cultural life did not trouble the consciences of clergy or laity.[32] The Roman Church, for example, had had its own cemeteries for over 150 years when certain Christian families chose to be buried with non-Christians in the catacomb on the Via Latina.[33] Even in the late fourth century, Christian families and congregations celebrated the anniversaries of the dead, whether ordinary people or blessed martyrs, just as their non-Christian neighbors did, with graveside feasts and song.[34]

Bishop Ambrose tried to redirect the cult practices of his congregations towards the dead – he forbade memorial feasts at the tomb, for example, out of concern for propriety and fear of drunkenness – but he did not try to alter their sense of the meaning of a Christian death.[35] Quite the contrary. As Eric Rebillard has shown in a recent study of pastoral responses to death and dying in the fourth and fifth centuries, Ambrose represented the most optimistic strain of Christian triumphalism when it came to his attitude towards death.[36] He urged baptized Christians to look forward to it with joy, arguing that life is a kind of death and death the beginning of a new life. Death marked the end of sin. It signaled entry into immortality and paradise. Philosophers contemplated it daily; ascetics prepared for it daily. Actual death was a mere formality. Not to welcome it would show a lack of faith.

When Ambrose preached in that manner, however, he was showing his age. Rebillard shows that some of Augustine's younger contemporaries, but above all Augustine himself, took up the opposite view. Baptism did not guarantee salvation; the effects of Adam's sin were not so easily mastered. Too much confidence in one's own salvation smacked of the proud claims of Donatists or Pelagians. Baptism simply 'launched a Christian on a lifelong process of convalescence'.[37] In such circumstances, the proper response to death could only be fear – fear of one's own sinfulness, and of God's inscrutable judgment.[38]

Rebillard's research on these matters adds to a growing consensus among scholars of Late Antiquity that the half-century from c. 380 to c. 430 marked a watershed between ancient and medieval Christianity in the West. The process of Christianization had reached the point where many felt the need for a new definition of what it meant to be a Christian.[39] One response was to suggest that the only real Christians were ascetics. In the decades before and after the year 400 debate raged over the meaning and status of asceticism in Christianity. The community was in danger of splintering along a divide between ordinary men and women and an elite cadre of perfected Christian ascetics. Augustine, not least because of his experience with Manichaeism, recognized the danger. He argued against overestimating the importance of asceticism in the Church and took up the cause of 'Christian mediocrity'.[40] In a world where

Christianity was the majority religion, religion must serve the majority, and that meant taking into account the limited ambitions and small sins of ordinary men and women. It meant that there needed to be a way for them to be as fully Christian as the most accomplished ascetic. There was, but at a price. Ordinary Christians would have to reimagine their own past as tainted by too much contact with paganism. They would have to give up the cozy relationships they had had with their non-Christian neighbors as well as a whole range of practices that previous generations had not found problematic.[41] They would have to submit their whole lives to the intense scrutiny of religious specialists. The ascetic movement was domesticated, but at the expense of some of the triumphant optimism of the imperial Church.

This less triumphant and more penitential Christianity, in which anxiety over death was heightened by fear of God's judgment, demanded, according to Rebillard, a pastoral response to death. It got it in the form of communion known as *viaticum*, which only began to be a normal part of the deathbed experience after the middle of the fifth century.[42] As a corollary to this argument, Rebillard rejects the possibility of any previous ritual around Christian deathbeds, including even the regular reception of a final communion, which he thinks emerged slowly in the fifth and sixth centuries as an extension of the *viaticum* granted to penitents at death. In particular, he concludes that the Roman death *ordo* used by Carolingian liturgists in the eighth and ninth centuries is neither authentically Roman nor ancient.[43] But then what is it? If it is a Frankish invention of the seventh or eighth centuries, it is a decidedly peculiar one. For almost everything about it – its psalmody, prayers and symbolic representations of the meaning of a Christian death – is in perfect accord with the attitudes expressed by Ambrose of Milan. It is, in the main, a ritual of triumphant expectation of salvation.[44] It does not call deathbed communion a *viaticum*, but rather 'a defender and advocate in the resurrection of the just'.[45] Similarly, it does not present communion as a provision for the soul's journey to the other world, but rather as an eschatological sign of membership in the community of the saved.[46] The question needs more work, but, if anything, Rebillard's research actually supports the notion that *ordo* 49 is a product of the confidence in salvation through baptism of the ancient Church.[47]

For Rebillard, such confidence was general up to the end of the fourth century, but it receded rapidly thereafter, more or less disappearing by the middle of the fifth century. I am not so sure. I will return to this argument in my conclusion, but would first like to draw attention to the fact that, however much more anxious the moment of death and difficult the transition to the other world may have been in the post-Augustinian West, the community of the living was not without its own resources.[48]

Not least of these was the cult of the saints. It has been twenty years since Peter Brown published his Haskell lectures on 'its rise and function in Latin Christianity'.[49] They remain a powerful contribution, bringing together central aspects of the changing relationship between the living and the dead in the critical period before and after the year 400: devotion to the cult of martyrs; the desire to be buried near them; their re-imagining as intimate human companions, advocates for their friends and clients at the court of a distant God; and the status of their bodily relics as proof of the Christian victory over decay and dissolution.[50]

The late Charles Pietri rightly criticized Brown for obscuring the normal religious structures of late antique Christianity in which the 'very special dead' had their place.[51] The regular liturgy and sacraments of the Church always provided the central points of contact between the human and the divine, and Brown's argument ignored them entirely. But Pietri missed the point in taking Brown to task for his arguments about 'the privatization of the holy'. In my reading, Brown does not claim that the cult of the saints developed in the private realm, or that martyrs' shrines were originally private places, but that, since the cult of the dead had always been a family affair in the Mediterranean world, it could not become public and communal without coming into conflict with deeply rooted patterns of behavior.

Even in the Christian catacombs outside Rome, well-to-do families had their own *cubicula*.[52] After the Peace of the Church, while the clerical ranks drew many, like Augustine, from outside the aristocracy, wealthy and powerful lay and clerical elites quickly developed nonetheless. I have already mentioned the impact of imperial mausolea on the architecture of baptisteries. Starting with Constantine, Christian emperors set the tone for the display of status in the afterlife by building their tombs in close proximity to martyrs' shrines and commissioning lavish sarcophagi. One has only to look at the gorgeous sarcophagi made for people like the urban perfect of Rome and Christian neophyte Junius Bassus, who died in 359, to see how aristocratic elites imitated such lavishness.[53] Such men expected to exercise power and influence as Christians in pretty much the same ways their pre-Christian forefathers had done.[54] They could resist the demands of bishops if they regarded them as disruptive to their basic patterns of life and rule. And it was their way of Christian living that bishops like Ambrose and Augustine told them they had to change. They were to curtail their funerary and anniversary feasts, which had always been as much about wealth and display as about piety. Their control over largesse was to be rechanneled through the treasuries of the bishops.[55] It was *their* private graves and *their* cult of the dead that needed to be drawn into the public realm.[56] They could not demand burial for their families in opposition to standard practice, as we saw in the case of the dead catechumen. They would not be allowed to appropriate the relics of the martyrs for their own use, and they would have to redirect the wealth previously lavished on the cult of the dead to the care of the poor.[57] The degree to which this episcopal effort succeeded marked a clear victory for the larger Christian community, but the battle had to be fought in each succeeding generation.

The key to victory may have been the cult of relics, for by integrating the saints into the cathedral centers within the walls of Late Antique cities, bishops appropriated their power to the service of the whole church community, blocking some of the centripetal forces that might otherwise have gathered around cult sites in the extra-urban cemeteries, where family and social status had freer play. Once this was accomplished, however, competition often moved inside the walls. Recent research on martyr cults in fifth- and sixth-century Rome, for example, has shown how clerical and lay elites on the one hand, and papal parties on the other, established local identities and asserted claims to authority by forging connections with particular saints.[58] Moreover, the practice of *ad sanctos* burial invited competition that ended up replicating social hierarchies, lay and ecclesiastical, in accordance with proximity to the graves of the holy dead.[59]

The cult of relics is also the key to the collapse of the borders that had kept the living and the dead segregated in their own cities – *polis* and *necropolis* – for millennia. As radical as was the Christian break with polytheistic and Jewish attitudes towards the dead, Christian families never questioned the ancient custom of burial outside the city walls. The first sign of change came when Constantius brought relics of the bodies of the apostles Andrew and Luke to Constantinople in 357.[60] Not long afterwards Ambrose had the bodies of two martyrs translated to a tomb beneath the altar of his new basilica outside Milan, a tomb that he had originally built for himself.[61] That was in 385. The next year, the Emperor Theodosius decreed that no buried body might be transferred to another place and that no one was to cut up or divide the bodies of the martyrs, or sell them.[62] That did not stop Ambrose, though – or almost anyone else for that matter. In 393–4 he brought relics of Bolognese martyrs back to Milan and in 396 sent portions of all of these to Bishop Victricius in Rouen, on the English Channel, where the bishop arranged a triumphant procession into the city in their honor.[63] Victricius' words of celebration at the arrival of the relics survive: 'See how great a part of the heavenly army deigns to visit our city; our habitation is now among a legion of saints and the renowned powers of the heavens.'[64] Over the course of the fifth century urban space was progressively Christianized as churches moved closer to city centers and were linked through common relics to suburban shrines and sanctuaries. This process went hand in hand with the Christianization of time as the feasts of the saints both inside and outside the walls began to eclipse the secular celebrations of antiquity.[65]

Nevertheless, at the end of the fifth century, outside of Africa, whose cities and rural villages may have witnessed a very early disappearance of ancient barriers, most of the dead still lay in their suburban cemetery sanctuaries, their presence in the cities of the living limited to a few holy relics.[66] There may have been exceptions (although not in the East, where intramural burials never caught on).[67] A 1985 excavation in Poitiers, for example, uncovered a palaeo-Christian cemetery in the intramural episcopal complex that can be securely dated to the second half of the fourth century.[68] It contained 34 graves and a total of 45 skeletons, half of which were of children. It does not seem to have been in use for very long and was quite clearly abandoned around the year 380, when regular interments presumably moved back to suburban cemeteries.[69] What does it mean? Was it an emergency response to an outbreak of disease in the Christian quarter of the city? Was the site, in a more or less uninhabited part of the city, not considered to lie under the ancient prohibition? Did someone object to the burials? There is no way of knowing.

In any case, the tide was turning. The physical merging of the communities of the living and the dead in western Christendom, whereby most graves clustered in or around urban and rural churches, proceeded steadily after the year 500. Essentially complete by the end of the first Christian millennium, it would remain the case across Europe throughout the Middle Ages and long afterwards.[70] The bishop of Poitiers may simply have jumped the gun. Towards the middle of the sixth century, Bishop Caesarius of Arles lined the intramural church of St Mary in his sister's convent with stone sarcophagi for the nuns and for his own burial.[71] Starting in the later sixth century, bishops were regularly laid to rest in their cathedral churches in the city centers.[72]

Simultaneously, outside the walls, monastic and other church complexes in the ancient cemeteries were often becoming the cores of new communities. As for the general population, the best evidence comes from early medieval archaeologists working in the territories of Merovingian Francia. Their findings involve not just the dissolution of barriers between the living and the dead, but also those between Romans and barbarians, and clerics and laity.

Along the northwestern continental borders of the Empire, in the fourth and fifth centuries, a new type of burial ground emerged – the so-called 'row-grave' cemeteries, in which bodies were laid out in regular lines of common orientation in fields some distance from human habitation.[73] Their occupants came from the mixed population of Gallo-Romans and free Germans, or 'Franks', that had been coming together in the borderlands for some time. The Franks had not buried their dead with grave goods in their ancestral homelands and seem to have picked up the habit from the locals.[74] As Frankish kings consolidated their power in the sixth century with the help of a warrior aristocracy, grave goods became more abundant and more opulent – signs of personal and family status. While the kings began to have themselves buried in churches outside the Gallo-Roman cities, their warriors began to dominate the field cemeteries where their graves became centers of familial and client burials. In the seventh century, the warrior aristocracy began to establish cemeteries, complete with mortuary chapels, on their family estates, sometimes converting their ancestors after the fact by placing a chapel over a pre-Christian mound burial.[75] They also founded rural monasteries, both as final resting places for their families and as sources of prayer for the good of their souls. These diverse arrangements persisted together until about the year 700, when the open-field cemeteries were abandoned, people stopped including grave goods in burials, and epitaphs began to disappear.[76]

These changes were followed, in the middle of the eighth century, by the disappearance of tomb decoration, and a growing lack of concern for spatial organization in cemeteries.[77] The significance of these changes has been much debated. Bailey Young has argued for the influence of new devotional forms among the aristocracy that stressed penance and humility.[78] Bonnie Effros has argued that the expression of family status was moving away from the funeral itself, where the richness of grave goods would be most evident, towards above-ground markers of status, and towards ritual commemoration – the prayers of monks, nuns, clerics and even the laity – which was beginning, in her words, to 'outweigh the importance of both grave goods and the external appearance of Christian graves', in a culture more focused on words than on objects.[79] The latter point is undoubtedly true, and trumps the first, since by the Carolingian period nearly all tombs had become anonymous.[80] What remained were the increasingly sophisticated ecclesiastical rituals and forms of commemoration through the liturgy.[81] Families were finally giving over control of their dead to the Church.

One of the most striking, but often overlooked, features of this whole process is the active role taken by the laity. The decision of a Frankish king to have himself buried in a particular place could bring fame to a church of otherwise little importance.[82] The new religious foundations and family chapels established by Frankish aristocrats became the core of the parish system within which local people would live and die for centuries. It was primarily these aristocrats who requested the new votive masses for their relatives, which became so popular from this time on. They were prime instigators of the complex system of exchange between the living and the dead outlined by Patrick Geary in a seminal article.[83] Early medieval families did not simply succumb to ecclesiastical pressure to accept Christian burial in accordance with traditional patterns. They realized that ecclesiastical institutions could preserve their continuity in an uncertain world, ensure their commemoration among the living, and become repositories of people and property that would strengthen the family both here on earth and in the hereafter. Ecclesiastics, in turn, used their expertise and creativity to continually foster the involvement of the laity in the founding and support of Church institutions by providing an ever-expanding supply of exchange mechanisms between the living and the dead.

The necessity of caring for souls in an afterlife that was becoming a much more active place was also critical. In two lectures delivered at Yale in October 1996 exploring this theme, Peter Brown linked the end of the ancient imperial order with the disappearance of notions of judicial amnesty.[84] Salvation could no longer be imagined as a dramatic act of imperial munificence. Moreover, as Christianity spread to places like Ireland, with its lack of central authority and yet highly refined legal system, Augustine's conception of life as a constant struggle with sin, as revised by thinkers like Gregory the Great, was extended into the afterlife. As a result, the Latin West took on a peculiar cast which saw 'the reduction of all experience, of history, politics and the social order quite as much as the destiny of individual souls, to two universal explanatory principles, sin and repentance'.[85]

In spite of his praise for Eric Rebillard, with which he began the first lecture, Peter Brown's argument effectively extends the period of transition between the baptismal religion of ancient Christianity and the penitential Christianity of the Middle Ages from the middle of the fifth century to the end of the seventh.[86] The most recent work on death, dying and the dead in the Carolingian world, by Cécile Treffort, pushes the definitive break forward another hundred years to the turn of the ninth century.[87] Her description of the Carolingian attitude to death and the afterlife is in perfect accord with Brown's: she sees everywhere a deep sense of sin and need for penance – but not until the turn of the ninth century. Who is right? In a way, they all are. The change that Rebillard first identified occurred over the whole of the five hundred years separating Ambrose from Charlemagne. It occurred, however, at a tempo precisely marked by the slow elaboration of penitential rituals around death, new forms of commemoration, and conceptions of purgation in the afterlife.[88] For every increase in the centrality of sin and the importance of penance in the life, and afterlife, of a Christian, there was a corresponding response, by the laity as much as by the clergy, that served to mitigate the gloom and reassert or reinvent the lines of communication between the living and the dead.[89]

Sin and penance were not foreign to the sensibilities of antique Christians; nor was triumphant optimism to those of their early medieval descendants. How else can we explain the postponement of baptism in the fourth and fifth centuries, which clearly derived from the fear of the consequences of sin following the ritual cleansing and the desire to optimize its power as a rite of passage? Or the confident expectation of salvation expressed in late seventh- and eighth-century epitaphs and sarcophagi such as those from the Merovingian abbey of Jouarre?[90] Above all, how can we explain the incorporation of the old Roman death ritual, with its echoes of ancient Christian attitudes, into the Carolingian ritual synthesis around death and burial? In the end, the distinction between 'ancient and medieval Christianities' may be too sharply drawn.[91] For all their acceptance of sin and the need for forgiveness, both in this world and the next, Carolingian Christians could afford to relive some of the optimism of late Roman imperial Christians in the face of death. Penitential attitudes towards death had an important place in Carolingian Christianity, and there is no question that clerics had begun to take over from the family the business of overseeing the death and burial of all members of the community.[92] It is also true that the tensions between different groups among the living continued to be played out in struggles over the dead, a phenomenon that can clearly be seen in the decrees of ninth-century church councils over burial rights.[93] The success of the Carolingian Church in propagating new forms of ritual behavior around death and dying did not mean that they had achieved, once and for all, the ideal of one community of the faithful, living and dead. It is, however, a striking example of the perennial attempt to turn that ideal into reality. In any case, the fact that the community that the living envisioned having with the dead always reflected that ancient Christian ideal, as well as the real paradoxes and tensions of the familial, political and social world in which they lived, is precisely what makes the investigation of either of them so revealing of the other.

Chapter 4

The Gothic Intellectual Community: The Theology of the *Skeireins*

James W Marchand

My topic is eight leaves of a text called by its first editor, Massmann, *Skeireins aiwaggeljons þairh Iohannen* (Interpretation of the Gospel according to John; see Figure 1).[1] Massmann borrowed the word *skeireins*, an abstract formed on the basis of the verb *skeirjan* (to explain), itself based on the adjective *skeirs* (clear) from 1 Corinthians 12:10.[2] I mention this, not to be finicky, but because occasionally it is said that Massmann invented the word, and false etymologies are occasionally given.[3] Massmann's title has stuck, so we will be discussing the *Skeireins* 'Interpretation (of the Gospel of St. John)'. The name is, of course, not without importance for a treatment of the text. Castiglione and Mai called it *Homilia*, which would give a different cast to our interpretation.

These eight leaves have undergone all the misfortunes a manuscript could, mostly at the hands of scholars. When found by Angelo Mai, they had already been torn from their original manuscript, so that no two leaves follow one another; they had been washed and scraped, and the original Gothic had been written over with Latin texts, the fate of all Gothic manuscripts except the Codex Argenteus. In his zeal to decipher them, Angelo Mai smeared or rather soaked them with nut-gall, a common practice in the day.[4] As is known, this treatment renders manuscripts fairly illegible to the next reader.[5]

To compound the felony Ehrle, in his zeal to protect the now damaged Vatican leaves, smeared them with gelatin (glycerine), thus rendering them impervious to ultra-violet rays, our best method of making them available to modern readers. A worse fate awaited them at the hands of philologists, however. In his admittedly incomplete count made about 1950, Bennett found that, in a text of 800 lines, averaging 13 letters per line, over 1,500 emendations had been proposed.[6] In Cromhout's edition alone, 940 words are deleted.[7] In my discussion, I shall simply follow the manuscript readings as far as possible, so as to avoid interpreting modern interpretations.

It is, however, in the matter of source criticism and what can only be called *Parallelenjägerei* (chasing after parallels) that the greatest crimes have been committed, and one has only to look at the sources and parallels cited by Dietrich,[8] the latest editor to deal intensively with such things, to see how far one can go, where parallels such as *anagkêi theikêi* (by divine power) are cited (here as parallel to *waldufnja gudiskamma* (by divine authority), though the parallel text cited, by Theodor of Herakleia, has *exousiâi theikêi* (by divine power). Nowadays, by the use of the *Thesaurus Linguae Graecae* database, one could find many examples of 'by divine power'.[9] A parallel Dietrich does not cite, for example, is *koinos pantôn Sôtêr* (common Saviour of all), from Athanasius, *De incarnatione*, par. 21. This is a perfect analogue for *gamains allaize nasjands* (la 6) (note the word order). So frequently, the understanding of the text is impaired by failure to place it in its context, leading inevitably to an impoverished reading. George P Landow's remark on the failure to embed earlier literature in its ambience is particularly appropriate here:

> Although it is a commonplace that we have lost the intimate knowledge of the Bible which characterized literate people of the last century, we have yet to perceive the full implications of our loss. In the Victorian period – to go back no further – any person who could read, whether or not he was a believer, was likely to recognize scriptural allusions. Equally important, he was also likely to recognize allusions to typological interpretations of the scriptures. When we modern readers fail to make such once common recognitions we deprive many Victorian works of a large part of their context. Having thus impoverished them, we then find ourselves in a situation comparable to that of the reader trying to understand a poem in a foreign language after someone has gone through his dictionary deleting important words. Ignorant of typology, we under-read and misread many Victorian works, and the danger is that the greater the work, the more our ignorance will distort and inevitably reduce it.[10]

My intention is to discuss only two leaves (I and III) of the *Skeireins*, with the intention of placing the work in context – which in this case largely comprises patristic exegesis – in an attempt to understand it and to situate it in its place in history, to read it as a fourth or fifth-century text.

It may be cause for surprise that I am writing on the *Skeireins* in a book devoted to 'The Making of Christian Communities'. I am, however, using 'community' in the way in which it is most commonly used in the present-day media, and discussing the Gothic intellectual community. This in itself will probably cause still more surprise, for we do not usually use the word 'intellectual' when speaking of Goths;[11] nor did one in the fourth century, where it was common to say such things as *krazein hôs Gotthôn* (shout like a Goth). This is, however, one of the most striking aspects of the Goths, namely, the rapidity with which they learned the intellectual fare of their day, patristic exegesis. St Jerome, in his famous letter to Sunnia and Frithila, two Goths who challenged his translation of Psalms in a number of passages, and whose corrections he occasionally accepted, said trenchantly (my translation):

> To My Beloved Brethren Sunnia and Fretela and to the others who are serving the Lord with you, Jerome.
>   1. Truly these apostolic and prophetic words have been fulfilled in you: 'Their sound hath gone forth into all the earth, and their words unto the ends of the world (Ps 18.5; Rom 10.18)'. Who would have believed that the barbarous language of the Goths would seek after the Hebrew truth (*Hebraica veritas*), and that, while the Greeks are indolent and contentious, very Germany would scrutinize the words of the Holy Spirit? 'In very deed I perceive that God is not a respecter of persons; But in every nation, he that feareth him and worketh justice is acceptable to him (Acts 10.34–35)'. The hands up to now hard from wielding the sword, and the fingers more fitting to handle the bow are softened to using the pen, and warlike hearts are turned to Christian gentleness. Now we also see the prophecy of Isaiah fulfilled in deed: 'and they shall turn their swords into ploughshares and their spears into sickles (Isaiah 2:4)'.

Or as Ch S Revillout remarked, as quoted by Scardigli: '*Les Goths en théologie comme en tout le reste montraient une intelligence prompte et facile, une remarquable aptitude.*'[12] If the sometimes exaggerated reports of the Roman historians, in particular Jordanes, are to be believed, they also had a strong reverence for the Word. In spite of occasional detractors, it can be said that the translation of the Greek Bible into Gothic by

Wulfila, who devised an alphabet for the purpose,[13] for those who wish to look closely, is a grand witness to the intellectual and spiritual force of the Apostle of the Goths. The translation of the Lord's Prayer alone, with its careful disambiguation of the Greek *basileia*, not always followed by more modern translators, reveals Wulfila's sensitive treatment of his material. He deserved the universal respect and honor tendered him; also worth remembering is his foster son, Auxentius, whose eloquence even impressed Ambrose, who disputed with him.

The history of the Goths, although occasionally murky and moot in individual details, is pretty much an open book. The authorities vie with each other in relating this history, and we have been fortunate to have such authorities as Gibbon, Thompson and Bury to relate it to us. We know that the Goths emigrated from Scandinavia around 1 AD, and I for one am willing to accept Oxenstierna's argument that it was from Västergötland.[14] They landed at the mouth of the Vistula, perhaps leaving us the name Danzig, moved south in various ways, finally appearing in Roman history in or about the year 247. We may be able to trace them back as far as 350 BC. Gothic archaeology is somewhat difficult to follow, but this picture seems fairly clear. For the fourth and fifth centuries, the picture is very clear, and we can follow the political history of the Goths easily, with the problem of their spread being somewhat difficult.[15]

The religious and intellectual history of the Goths is another matter, however. The historians seem to devote little time to such matters, and our first, perhaps even our major, problem is the discovery of sources.[16] This frequently takes us far afield, into languages such as Russian, Bulgarian, Romanian and Hungarian, and into archaeology and philology, areas which both historians of religion and Gothic specialists are often ill-equipped to explore.

We know that Wulfila's forefathers (*progonoi*) came from the village of Sadagolthina at the foot of Mount Parnassus (on which see now Salaville[17]), and that they were captured by the Goths upon raids during the years 267–269. They were Christians and converted at least some of their captors. We know a lot about Wulfila from the Church historians Socrates, Sozomen, Theodoret and Philostorgius, all available in ready translation, and from the report by his foster-son, Auxentius, who disputed with Ambrose, as reported in the latter's *De fide*, in a manuscript of which it is embedded.[18]

The history of the study of the 'theology' of the *Skeireins* is quickly told. The first editor, Massmann, whose services to scholarship were outstanding, got us off on the wrong foot. He did what any scholar might well have done: he searched for fourth-century commentaries on the Gospel of John and found Balthasar Corderius, *Catena Patrum graecorum in S Joannem ex antiquissimo graeco codice nunc primam in lucem edita* (Antwerp, 1630), not at all a bad choice, given Corderius's well-known care. On this he then based his source study, and came to the conclusion that the major source for the *Skeireins* was Theodorus of Heraclea's *Hermeneia*, even basing the name *Skeireins* on this work, as noted above. He ignored other commentaries on John not contained in Corderius, such as those of Chrysostom, Origen, Cyril of Alexandria and Theodore of Mopsuestia, as well as the rest of Greek and Latin patristics, which discussed the matters discussed by the skeireinist, often with reference to John, since the Goth was Arian, and these commentators were not.[19] That this left us with a skewed picture is natural, and Massmann went even further. In listing his parallels, he listed floscules which had nothing more to do with the *Skeireins* than the use of the same words. As I pointed out above, with our present tools we can often find Massmann's 'sources' in literally hundreds of works, and, of course, we have a better work on the *catenae* than that of Corderius in Reuss.[20] The century followed Massmann, however, being crowned by Dietrich's *Quellenuntersuchung* (Source Criticism) with its '*Parallelen aus der theologischen Tradition*', although Streitberg tried to reduce Dietrich's list.[21] He cites Ammonius, Cyril, Theodorus of Heraclea and Hahn's *Bibliothek der Symbole* (Breslau, 1897). Jellinek saw that this was no way to do source criticism.[22] He had already been (in 1891) the first to point out the influence of Ransom Theory, which he attributed to Irenaeus, at least as the remote source.[23] He seems not to realize that Ransom Theory was held by almost all fourth-century theologians.

Bennett, with little comment, eschews references to patristic exegesis almost entirely: 'On these topics the present edition has nothing either new or original to offer, and there would be little to gain in reproducing the extensive material that is already available.'[24] This is pretty much where things stand at the moment, though a glance through the MLA online bibliography reveals a number of articles which touch on the skeireinist's theology, as does Mossé's. *Bibliographia gotica*.[25]

Let us begin with leaf III of the *Skeireins*, which reads, with an interlinear translation:

> Sk 3a:1 ... managa wesun jainar:
> '... many were there;

Sk 3a:2 þaruh qemun jah daupidai wesun:
  and they came there and were baptized.
Sk 3a:4 ni nauhþanuh galagiþs was in karkarai Iohannes:
  John was not yet cast into prison.'
Sk 3a:7 þatuh þan qiþands aiwaggelista ataugida:
  By saying that the evangelist revealed
Sk 3a:10 ei so garehsns bi ina nehva andja was:
  that the plan concerning him (John) was near its end
Sk 3a:12 þairh Herodes birunain:
  through the scheming of Herod.
Sk 3a:14 akei faur þata at bajoþum daupjandam: jah
  ainhvaþarammeh seina anafilhandam daupein:
But that before this, both of them baptizing and
  each handing down his own baptism,
Sk 3a:19 miþ sis misso sik andrunnun:
  they disputed with each other,
Sk 3a:21 sumai ni kunnandans hvaþar skuldedi maiza:
  some not knowing which was to be the greater.
Sk 3a:24 þaþroh þan warþ sokeins us siponjam Iohannes miþ
  Iudaium bi swiknein:
Concerning this then arose a question between John's disciples with
  the Jews concerning purification,
Sk 3b:4 in þizei ju jah leikis hraineino inmaidiþs was sidus:
  because of the fact that now the custom of bodily cleansings
  had been changed,
Sk 3b:6 jah so bi guþ. hrainei anabudana was:
  and the cleansing by God had been commanded.
Sk 3b:8 ni þanaseiþs judaiwiskom: ufarranneinim jah sinteinom
  daupeinim brukjan usdaujaina:
No longer should they endeavor to use the sprinklings and daily
  bathings of the Jews.
Sk 3b:13 ak Iohanne hausjandans þamma faurrinnandin aiwaggeljon:
  but listening to John, the precursor in the Gospel.
Sk 3b:17 wasuh þan jah frauja þo ahmeinon anafilhands daupein
  For then the Lord was also handing down the spiritual baptism,
Sk 3b:20 eiþan garaihtaba warþ bi swiknein sokeins gawagida:
  so that properly was a question moved concerning purification.
Sk 3b:23 unte witoþ þize unfaurweisane missadede ainaizos witoþ
  raidida:
  For the Law concerning one of the sins of unwitting people

Sk 3c:1 azgon kalbons gabrannidaizos utana bibaurgeinais:
    the ash of a heifer burned outside the camp
Sk 3c:5 afaruh þan þo in wato wairpandans hrain:
    and after that casting it into clean water,
Sk 3c:7 jah hwssopon jah wullai raudai ufartrusnjandans:
    and sprinkling with it hyssop and red wool,
Sk 3c:10 swaswe gadob þans ufar miton munandane:
    as was fitting for those thinking without intent.
Sk 3c:13 iþ Iohannes idreigos daupein merida:
    But John was preaching a baptism of repentance,
Sk 3c:15 jah missadede aflet þaim ainfalþaba gawandjandam gahaihait:
    and promised the forgiveness of sins for those simply reforming,
Sk 3c:19 iþ fraujins. at afleta frawaurhte jah fragift weihis ahmins:
    but as to the Lord, [He promised] forgiveness of sins and the
    gift of the Holy Spirit,
Sk 3c:22 jah fragibands im þatei sunjus þiudangardjos wairþaina:
    and granting them that they might become sons of the Kingdom.
Sk 3d:1 swaei sijai daupeins Iohannes ana midumai twaddje ligandei.
    So that the baptism of John was lying in the middle of the two,
Sk 3d:5 ufarþeihandei raihtis witodis hrainein:
    going beyond, to be sure, the cleansing of the Law,
Sk 3d:7 iþ minnizei filaus aiwaggeljons daupeinai:
    but less by far than the Gospel's baptism.
Sk 3d:10 inuh þis bairhtaba uns laiseiþ qiþands:
    Concerning this he openly teaches us, saying:
Sk 3d:13 aþþan ik in watin izwis daupja:
    I indeed baptize you in water,
Sk 3d:14 iþ sa afar mis gagganda: swinþoza mis ist
    but he who comes after me is mightier than I,
Sk 3d:17 þizei ik ni im wairþs anahnewands: andbindau skaudaraip
skohis is:
    of whom I am not worthy that, kneeling, I might unbind the
    latchet of his shoe.
Sk 3d:21 sah þan izwis daupeiþ in ahmin weihamma:
    He then will baptize you in the Holy Spirit.
Sk 3d:25 bi garehsnai nu ...
    Concerning the plan now ...

Jellinek said that this leaf contained the most difficult passage in the
Skeireins. The problem lies to a great extent with us rather than with

the text. It is important to notice that the 'Red Heifer' of this treatment comes from the *Hebrews* rather than from *Numbers*, since it is often maintained that the Goths, as Arians, did not have the book of *Hebrews*. Massmann, who saw that part of the text had to be from *Hebrews*, nevertheless maintained that the skeireinist had also had recourse to the passage from *Numbers*, since 'outside the camp' is mentioned, and *Hebrews* does not mention it, according to him, and in this he is followed by later authorities, even Dietrich. This is, of course, based on a misreading of the *Hebrews*, where the Red Heifer is being presented as the type of Christ. Of course, as Jellinek said, we cannot expect Germanists to know about typology, since Schwietering and Curtius had not yet come along. But one might expect them to read the text; cf. *Hebrews* 13:11: 'For the bodies...are burned without the camp, wherefore Jesus also, that he might sanctify the people with his own blood, suffered without the gate.' We will encounter this failure to read the record over and over again. It is important also to note the typology, for it is often maintained that the Goths, as Antiochian critics, did not use typology and allegory.

Bennett, the only critic to treat the Red Heifer page extensively, could make little sense out of it and consulted a modern rabbi as to the rite of the Red Heifer.[26] This practice, whatever one thinks about a modern rabbi, has little to recommend it. The Jewish rite of the Red Heifer is treated thoroughly, for example, in Bonsirven, and Maimonides has written a famous treatise on it.[27] Nevertheless, we must insist again with Massmann and Dietrich that it is the Red Heifer of *Hebrews* which is intended. On it and sprinkling, see the article on *rhantizô* and *rhantismos* in the *Theological Dictionary of the New Testament*. This article or the one in Hastings on the 'Red Heifer' will suffice to indicate the nature of the Red Heifer rite in Judaism. On the Red Heifer as a type of Christ, the fourth and fifth century exegetes offer a great deal of evidence. To show how easy it is nowadays to do what Jellinek was recommending, I downloaded the Ante- and Post-Nicene fathers from the Christian Classics Ethereal Library site (http://ccel.org) and searched through them with a browser (so-called GREP utility) for 'heifer'. This brought in a number of patristic parallels: *The Letter of Barnabas* (I.142); Chrysostom, *On the Statutes* (1st Ser. 9, 440 ff.); Jerome, who in *Lives of Illustrious Men*, chapter LVII (p. 374) mentions that Trypho wrote a treatise on the Red Heifer; and the following passage from Theodoret's *Dialogues*: 'The image of the archetype is very distinctly exhibited by the lamb slain in Egypt, and by the red heifer burned without the camp, and moreover it is referred to by the Apostle in the *Epistle to the Hebrews*, where he writes "Wherefore Jesus also that he might sanctify the people with his own blood, suffered without the gate".'[28] Other parallels include Athanasius, *Letter XIV on Easter* (p. 542); Cyril of Jerusalem, *Catechetical Lectures*, lecture XIII (p. 91); Gregory Nazianzen, *Oration on Holy Baptism* (p. 363); Basil, *Letter* CCLXV (p. 304); Ambrose, *Of the Holy Spirit*, Book 1, Chap. VIII (p. 106; not a close parallel). The importance of all this is to show that the skeireinist *is* using the book of *Hebrews*, that he does use typology, and that he is simply in the mainstream. This does not require much of a knowledge of the Fathers, but it does require some reading in the Ante- and Post-Nicene fathers, and some ingenuity. If you have access to the *Thesaurus Linguae Graecae*, you can simply type in *damal* (for *damalis, damaleôs*), and you can find many more. Or, in the *Patrologia Latina*, type in *vacca* or even *vacca rufa*. This will prove that the skeireinist is offering us nothing new. There is no need to look for sources; indeed, sources merely cloud the issue; there are no sources. The skeireinist's treatment of the Red Heifer is standard fare.

This bring us to the final leaf and the *pièce de résistance*, Leaf I:

Sk 1a:1 nist saei fraþjai aiþþau sokjai guþ:
    'There is none who understands or seeks God

Sk 1a:2 allai uswandidedun:
    All have turned away

Sk 1a:4 samana unbrukjai waurþun:
    together they have become useless'

Sk 1a:6 jah ju uf dauþaus atdrusun stauai:
    and already they have fallen under the judgment of death

Sk 1a:8 inuh þis qam gamains allaize nasjands:
    For this then there came a common savior of all

Sk 1a:10 allaize frawaurhtins afhrainjan:
    to cleanse away the sins of all

Sk 1a:12 ni ibna nih galeiks unsarai garaihtein:
    neither equal nor similar to our justice,

Sk 1a:15 ak silba garaihtei wisands:
    but himself being justice

Sk 1a:17 ei gasaljands sik faur uns:
    that, giving himself for us

Sk 1a:18 hunsl jas sauþ guda:
    'an offering and a sacrifice to God'

Sk 1a:19 þizos manasedais gawaurhtedi uslunein:
he might work the redemption of this world.

Sk 1a:22 þata nu gasaihvands Iohannes
John now seeing this:

Sk 1a:24 þo sei ustauhana habaida wairþan fram fraujin garehsn
The plan which was to be carried out by the Lord,

Sk 1b:2 miþ sunjai qaþ:
with truth did say:

Sk 1b:3 sai sa ist wiþrus gudis.
Behold, this is the Lamb of God

Sk 1b:4 saei afnimiþ frawaurht þizos manasedais:
Who taketh away the sin of this world.

Sk 1b:6 mahtedi sweþauh jah inu mans leik. waldufnja þataine
gudiskamma, galausjan allans us diabulaus anamahtai:
He could have, to be sure, even without (assuming) the body of man,
by divine authority alone, released all from the tyranny of the devil.

Sk 1b:12 akei was kunnands þatei swaleikamma waldufnja mahtais
seinaizos nauþs ustaiknida wesi:
But he was aware that by such authority
the need for his power would be shown.

Sk 1b:17 jan ni þanaseiþs fastaida garaihteins garehsns:
and that no longer the plan of justice would be kept,

Sk 1b:20 ak nauþai gawaurhtedi manne ganist:
but that by force he would have worked the salvation of men.

Sk 1b:22 jabai auk diabulau fram anastodeinai nih nauþjandin ak
uslutondin mannan:
For, if the devil from the beginning (had worked) not by forcing, but
by deluding man,

Sk 1c:1 jah þairh liugn gahvatjandin ufargaggan anabusn:
and by lie persuading him to transgress the commandment,

Sk 1c:4 þatuh wesi wiþra þata gadob:
that would be against propriety

Sk 1c:5 ei frauja qimands mahtai gudiskai: jah waldufnja þana
galausidedi:
if the Lord, coming with divine power, also with authority
had released him,

Sk 1c:9 jah nauþai du gagudein gawandidedi:
and by necessity converted him to godliness.

Sk 1c:11 nei auk þuhtedi þau in garaihteins gaaggwein ufargaggan:
For then would He not seem in the constraint of justice to transgress

Sk 1c:14 þo faura ju us anastodeinai garaidon garehsn:
the plan already ordained from the beginning?

Sk 1c:16 gadob nu was mais þans swesamma wiljin ufhausjandans
diabulau: du ufargaggan anabusn gudis:
now it was more fitting those of their own will listening
to the devil, to transgress the commandment of God,

Sk 1c:22 þanzuh aftra swesamma wiljin gaqissans wairþan nasjandis
laiseinai:
those again by their own will to become assenters to the
teaching of the Savior

Sk 1d:1 jah frakunnan unselein þis faurþis uslutondins ins:
and to despise the wickedness of the one who previously had
deceived them,

Sk 1d:5 iþ sunjos kunþi du aftraanastodeinai þize in guda usmete
gasatjan:
but to establish a knowledge of the truth for the resurrection
of the way of life in God

Sk 1d:9 inuh þis nu jah leik mans andnam:
For this reason, then, he took on even the body of man,

Sk 1d:11 ei laisareis uns wairþai þizos du guda garaihteins:
that He might become for us a teacher of justice according to God.

Sk 1d:14 swa auk skulda du galeikon seinai frodein:
For thus He would be in conformity with His Wisdom

Sk 1d:17 jah mans aftra galaþon waurdam jah waurstwam jah spilla
wairþan aiwaggeljons usmete:
and invite man again by word and deed to become a
proclaimer of the way of life of the Gospel

Sk 1d:22 iþ in þizei nu witodis gaaggwei ni þatain gawandeins...
but since now the restriction of the law not only conversion.

Before we look at this leaf, however, we need to ask what the fourth
century thought of salvation, as Jellinek did in his 'Zur Skeireins'.
Jellinek is the only Gothic specialist to treat the theology of our leaf.
One can understand his surprise at finding that W Krafft, a theologian,
had missed the fact that the leaf deals with Ransom Theory.
Unfortunately, Jellinek was not familiar with patristics, so he could
only cite a passage from Irenaeus he found in F Chr. Baur's *Die
christliche Lehre von der Versöhnung*, a weak reed to lean upon. Modern
interpreters, such as Hastings Rashdall and Jean Rivière, are in a much
better position, with a number of excellent books on the Atonement. [29]

It is easy, however, to fabricate one's own history, for the theory of the redemption known by its designation by Ambrose as the *pia fraus* was until Anselm not just the prevailing theory, but the only theory of the Redemption. It may shock us as it did Rashdall, who continually calls it 'monstrous, horrible', and seeks over and over again to find it overthrown, and we may wish with Russell to be able to say: 'The idea of the trick faded, decisively rejected in the West by Augustine and in the East by Chrysostom.'[30] But both Augustine and Chrysostom are stout proponents of the 'trick', as was also Martin Luther. Leo the Great summed up the *pia fraus* for his day:

> For though the true mercy of God had infinitely many schemes to hand for the restoration of mankind, it chose that particular design which put in force for destroying the devil's work, not the efficacy of might but the dictates of justice. 134. And so it was no new counsel, no tardy pity whereby GOD took thought for men: but from the constitution of the world He ordained one and the same Cause of Salvation for all. For the grace of GOD, by which the whole body of the saints is ever justified, was augmented, not begun, when Christ was born: and this mystery of GOD's great love, wherewith the whole world is now filled, was so effectively presignified that those who believed that promise obtained no less than they, who were the actual recipients.
>
> 142. He was able to bring about solely by the power of His Godhead; so as to rescue the creature that was made in the image of God from the yoke of his cruel oppressor. But because the devil had not shown himself so violent in his attack on the first man as to bring him over to his side without the consent of His free will, man's voluntary sin and hostile desires had to be destroyed in such wise that the standard of justice should not stand in the way of the gift of Grace. And therefore in the general ruin of the entire human race there was but one remedy in the secret of the Divine plan which could succor the fallen, and that was that one of the sons of Adam should be born free and innocent of original transgression, to prevail for the rest both by His example and His merits.[31]

We see this same presentation over and over again, by all the fathers; in fact a simple search for *esca* and *hamus* in the *Patrologia Latina*, or for *delear,* 'bait', and *agkistron,* 'fishhook', in the *Thesaurus Linguae Graecae,* will yield a multitude of materials, for the fathers loved to put the *pia fraus* into terms of the bait of Christ's body on the hook of the cross. To cite just one example, from an anonymous fourth-century source found in *PG* 61.753–4 (my translation):

It is not from fear or horror of death that I say the words: 'Father, if it is possible, let this chalice pass from me (Mt. 26, 39)'. I am rather speaking here a word of hidden secrecy.

This word is a bait for the devil; with these words I must lure him to the hook. The devil saw me do many miracles, as I with a bare touch of the hand cured sicknesses, how I with one word drove out legions of demons, how a sign of my hand with the quickness of a winnowing fan smoothed the sores of the lepers, how I with voice alone made the knees of the crippled firm, how I rebuked wind and sea and how everything obeyed me trembling. By such deeds he had to notice that I am God's Son, and had to consider that my death on the cross signified his demise, that my descent into the lower regions would break his iron bolts and burst his brazen gates (cf. Ps. 23.7–10). Considering these things, he flees and hesitates to erect the precious cross, the sign of victory. What am I then to do? Like an experienced fisher I act cowardly, pretend to have fear of death and say: 'Father, if it is possible, let this chalice pass from me'. Such words of hesitation are supposed to cause him to believe that I am only a fearful human being and would like to escape death, and are supposed to urge him to erect against me, as he sees it, the secret made of wood, the cross, in the midst of the earth. I have to counter him with cunning, like an experienced fisher; I have to bear everything for the sake of the life of all. For since he from the beginning on aimed with cunning for the damnation of Adam, so will I all the more practice cleverness for the salvation of all. With seductive words he seduced Adam, with divine words the betrayer will be fooled. When the fisher throws the hook into the sea, but does not bait it and does not present the worm as fleeing by jerking it back now and again with his hand, the fish do not attack it. I have clothed the hook of My divinity with the worm of my body. Hidden in the bait of My body, I let the hook down into the depths of this life. If the worm does not twist like a worm, then the one who is to be caught does not approach the hook. And so I have to act like a worm. 'I am a worm and no man' (Ps 21.7), so that he will attack and bite on the hook and will be drawn out by

Me, and then will be fulfilled the passage in Job (40.20): 'You will draw out the dragon with a hook'. I act like a human being who is fearful and flees death. I will say: 'My soul is troubled unto death (Mt. 26.38)'. I will say: 'Father, if it is possible, let this chalice pass from me.' And when that one hears this word, then he will silently rejoice and be glad. For he is always alive to opportunities to work against Me. When he hears: 'Father, if it is possible, let this chalice pass from me,' he will rejoice, and what will he say? 'Hah! This One also is a human being! I swallowed Abraham, Isaac, Jacob, the patriarchs and the prophets. I will swallow This One, too. Just look! He is cowardly like a human being, He IS a human being, I will swallow Him.'

Those who are familiar with the famous miniature of Herrad of Landsperg will recognize the picture, so well treated by Zellinger.[32]

One of the most problematic things about 'medieval man' is the fact of his belief in what St Thomas called *epieikeia* (fittingness); this is what the skeireinist means by *pata gadob*. It would have been contrary to *epieikeia, justitia,* for God to save man by divine power; it was fit and proper for him to redeem mankind by a contrary trick: 'We need to remember how the first Adam was cast out of paradise into the desert, in order to think of how the Second Adam will return from the desert… Thus, the hunger of the Lord is a pious trick *(pia fraus).*'[33] St Augustine insisted over and over that this must be done properly: '*Non potentia Dei, sed iustitia superandus est* (scil. *diabolus)*' (the devil is to be conquered not by the power of God, but by *epieikeia,* 'rightness').[34]

Space does not permit me to go into *garehsns* and the various translations of it. It is obvious that it is Greek *oikonomia,* the plan of salvation which God proposed for mankind before all time, a commonplace of fourth and fifth century theology, as also later. Suffice it to say that I must disagree with my hero, Jellinek, who says, concerning the scheme of salvation presented on Leaf I: '*Von der allgemeinen theologischen Ansicht der Zeit weicht also der Skeireinist entschieden ab* (The skeireinist thus definitely departs from the common theory)'.[35] There is nothing new or startling in the theology of the *Skeireins*; it is just common fourth and fifth-century fare, where there is scarcely a theologian who does not espouse it. It may seem surprising from a nineteenth-century standpoint, but it is just the same old hat to the fourth century. The Goths may have advanced intellectually, but in theology they conformed.

Chapter 5

'Seed-sowers of Peace': The Uses of Love and Friendship at Court and in the Kingdom of Charlemagne

C Stephen Jaeger

The mix of intimacy and utility in my subtitle would have surprised no educated person in Late Antiquity and the Middle Ages. The inner tension of the phrase is the same as in Foucault's 'uses of pleasure',[1] and it is meant to occupy the same zone of friction where the private contends with the practical. Love and friendship were useful. Some comments on the 'utility' of love by Georges Duby in his book *France in the Middle Ages* bring it to a particular historical context – though not the one at issue in this study. Duby called the courtly love of the twelfth century 'a political weapon for the territorial princes whose money underpinned the courts'. That is saying a lot; and there is more: 'Courtly love also proved an extremely effective means of strengthening the State. In fact, it was so influential that no study of the progressive rationalization of power can afford to ignore it, although at this period it is only documented in literary works...'[2] These are sweeping statements, tossed off with magisterial neglect of both analysis and documentation. But their implied confidence that others can produce the documentation for Orphic claims seems to me justified. They also are startling for taking a literary phenomenon as airy and fantasy-bound as courtly love into the historian's realm of interest. But if Duby is right that courtly love is both an instrument of power and a vital moving force in the 'progressive rationalization of power', then historians of politics would do well to read more troubadour lyric and romances than they are accustomed to.

And yet studies of medieval government have successfully ignored the alliance of love and power for most of its history. So have literary studies. Far from crediting the social and political uses of courtly love, scholars of literature have tended in recent years to assign it to the realm of literary fantasy and to deny it any other form of real existence.[3] If Duby is right, then we need a radical change in the way we look at the integrating of emotion and power. Gert Althoff's studies of 'Friendships and Pacts' point in this direction, though he largely denies an affective side to the 'friendships' which seal treaties of peace and reconciliation.[4] Now there are two interesting studies by a young German scholar, Klaus Van Eickels, of princes sleeping together as a gesture of reconciliation.[5] The recent collection of essays edited by Barbara Rosenwein, *Anger's Past*,[6] shows how useful and rich for historians the study of that emotion can be.

The same is true of love and friendship. As an ideal code of behavior, they have many uses.[7] High among them is the creation of stable community. Alcuin of York, tutor, advisor and close friend of Charlemagne, used the language of peace and friendship as an instrument of peace-making in the kingdom. His dealings with King Aethelred of Northumbria show him at work in this capacity.

The last decade of the eighth century brought misery in many forms to Alcuin's Northumbrian homeland. In 790 the city of York experienced a rain of blood, so says the Anglo-Saxon chronicler, who also recorded other prodigies over the land in 793: immense whirlwinds, flashes of lightning and fiery dragons swept across the skies. In April 793 Vikings raided Lindisfarne, pillaging and destroying the community, the cornerstone of the English church.[8]

Alcuin watched the accession of King Aethelred to the throne in 790 with uneasy feelings. Under Aethelred's predecessor Aelfwald, a 'just and pious' king, morals had already begun to degenerate in the northern kingdom.[9] When Aelfwald was killed in a conspiracy, Aethelred advanced 'from a prison cell to a royal throne, from misery to majesty'.[10] Things deteriorated still further. What good could be expected from a man who cut his hair and beard like a pagan, who along with his nobles dressed and ate immoderately while 'Lazarus dies of hunger at the city gate'.[11] In late 790 Alcuin wrote to his friend, Abbot Adalhard of Corbey, expressing his uneasiness with the new king.[12] He indicates that he has sent admonitions to Aethelred and his supporters and has enlisted the help of 'certain nobles against injustice'.[13] Alcuin now enjoins Adalhard to take up or continue with him a mission of peace-making throughout Christendom: '*Pacis enim seminatores simus inter populos Christianos* (Let us be seed-sowers of peace among Christian peoples)'.[14]

Of Alcuin's writings to King Aethelred himself two letters from 793 have survived.[15] They give us a clear view of how Alcuin prosecuted his mission of peace and justice. The letters are stern admonitions to the new king and his nobles. Let us see how he speaks to these men whom he regards as violent and immoral and holds responsible for the degeneration of his 'most beautiful fatherland':

> Mindful of the sweetest love I bear for you, O brothers and fathers, men worthy of honor in Christ the Lord... I work, O dearest of companions, incessantly...to enjoin on you...the things that pertain to the well-being of this earthly fatherland and the beatitude of the heavenly... What is charity towards a friend, if it hides those things useful to the friend?[16]

The body of the letter is a harsh reprimand for their immoral ways. The Viking attack is a deserved punishment for fornication, avarice, rapine and false judgments, crimes for which entire peoples were destroyed in the Old Testament. It ends by returning to the themes of love and peace:

> Let there be a unifying peace and charity among you... Above all, have the charity of God in your hearts, and show the same charity in observance of his laws. Love him as your father so that he will defend you as his sons.[17]

The other letter of Alcuin to Aethelred has more the tone of a tract on the duties of a prince and the vices to be avoided, and the salutation is much sweetened:

> To his most excellent son King Aethelred and to his sweetest friends Prince Osbald and Duke Osberht and to all his friends in fraternal love, Alcuin...
> The delights of sacred love have often compelled me to admonish you to respect the ancient friendship, the salvation of your souls, the truth of the faith, and the concord of peace which you ought to preserve among you, because that friendship which can be abandoned never was true. A true friend is long sought, rarely found, kept with difficulty. Seeking you I have found friends. I shall keep you as friends, nor shall I abandon those whom I have begun to love.[18]

Alcuin finds a brief sermon on friendship useful to pacify and recall the nobles to order. The significant linking of friendship, salvation, the faith and peace restates, or at least applies the terms of, his seed-sowing mission. Yet whatever good his admonitions may have done in the short run, eventually succession and rule by violence prevailed. Aethelred was assassinated, supposedly in a conspiracy of his own lords, in 796.

The two letters show us Alcuin at work making peace, bringing harmony and concord, throwing up spiritual bulwarks against Vikings and moral degeneracy. The seeds sown were love and friendship, its language indistinguishable from that of the letters and poems he wrote in other affairs. He wrote often to clerical and monastic communities urging on them the *jus amicitiae*. The language of his peace-making efforts does not distinguish monastic, clerical and worldly communities. The *communio caritatis* applies to all alike. One example can stand here for many. In a letter addressed 'to various fathers', he writes:

> Let letters frequently pursue those whom loyal charity always pursues, because there is some refreshment for the one who loves when he explains the fervor of his seething mind in words or letters. For words are given to show forth truth, so that what the heart conceives truthfully, the tongue will express without deceit; and so that one brother will infuse his heart into the heart of another and thus create unanimity of souls in whom there is a community of charity.[19]

Souls barren of charity are dead, he goes on, because to be empty of love is to be deprived of the image of divine goodness within. Mutual love marked the disciples of Christ (John 13.35) and the same should hold true of brothers living a communal life. Alcuin conceived friendship not as a rule imposed on a community, but as a force of charity flowing from the breast of the lover and peacemaker. The lessons he enjoins on his corresponders are enforced by love, not by law. The social mission of love-making as Alcuin represents it operates by bodily radiation and charismatic force. Its effectiveness depends on the authority of the individual who loves.

One of the most interesting documents on Alcuin the peacemaker is a letter he wrote to Charlemagne, who was away on a campaign against the Saxons in the summer of 798.[20] Alcuin is responding to a letter of the king, now lost, that requests a musical composition from his tutor and favorite, one which will calm the battle rage of his troops when in camp. Alcuin writes in response a long letter, which answers the king's queries about points of astronomy and the liturgy, but first and foremost promises a calming musical composition:

[Your letter] urged me to add a sweet melody of verse to the horrible din of battle and the raucous blast of trumpets, since the music of sweet melodies softens the fierce emotions of the mind... You wished that the savagery of your boys be mitigated by the sweetness of some song or other.[21]

One can well imagine that both the king and his 'boys' needed their boiling blood tempered. They were engaged in the summer of 798 in a military campaign of extraordinary brutality. The Saxons, chafing under harsh edicts issued by Charlemagne a decade and a half before, and smarting from strings of disastrous defeats, had seized and murdered royal legates in early 798. Outraged, the king gathered a great army, which came together at Minden on the Weser river in July and mounted a terrible campaign of destruction, moving from the Weser to the Elbe, laying waste to everything in their path by fire and sword. The Saxon army opposing them allowed itself to be trapped, hemmed in on a field bordered by the Schwentine river, where four thousand of them were slaughtered. Those who fled in panic were pursued and killed by the Franks.

Under these circumstances one can appreciate Charlemagne's need for some palliative and tempering force: the savagery of battle rage only half-controlled could break out anew in the camp, and the return from killing frenzy to civil behavior required strong medicine. But Alcuin's letter aims also at pacifying the king himself, not only tempering the 'savagery of [his] boys'. The mind rasped with anger cannot think straight, Alcuin says, and wise counsel is lost on it – a consideration that must weigh more heavily with the king and general than with his troops in the field, though the tactful courtier rushes to assure his lord that the royal mind stabilized by unshakeable fortitude requires a lesser dose of the medicine of music – or none at all. But the antithesis of counsel and music suggests that words have their limit and beyond that music must take over. It is no coincidence that the paragraph following that on rage-calming music is a reflection on friendship:

...a friend is so called as the custodian of the soul. He strives with all his loyalty to keep the soul of his friend harmoniously integrated so that no point of the sacred law of friendship may be violated... And if it is incumbent on a friend and coequal to preserve the integrity of his friend's mind inviolate, how much more so on a lord and on one who loves to raise up and govern his subjects in all honor.[22]

The context of the passage encourages us to connect the civilizing force of music with friendship,[23] though Alcuin does not make the point directly. He is promising to help restore peace and the rule of love among his soldiers through music.

What is important for the topic of peace-making is that Alcuin uses the occasion of the musical composition to admonish the king himself to restraint. The 'royal path' between the extremes of savagery and lassitude is good for men in the battlefield; this golden mean will 'compose all things according to the way of peace'. Temperance, like music, calms the raging mind and becomes, in Alcuin's prose sermon, the highest virtue of a ruler waging war:

> We read in the ancient books of history that this is the sort of virtue most essential for those waging war, that a wise temperance should rule and govern all things that must be done.[24]

Alcuin's 'seed-sowing' intent is perfectly clear. Asked by the king to calm the rage of his soldiers through music, he attempts to calm that of the general through reminders of friendship, temperance and moderation as high military prudence and humane virtues. Interestingly, mercy is not among them, and so the passage seems to lack any appeal to spare helpless Saxons, though there is certainly an implicit plea to make friends of enemies and exercise temperance in warfare. Violence done (by Charlemagne and his boys) in what Alcuin sees as a just cause may be less in need of restraint than arbitrary violence (by Aethelred and his boys). In any case, Alcuin is ready and willing to help, 'if the flute of Flaccus can avail to mollify ungentle minds'.[25]

'Softening harsh minds' is a duty of the counselors of kings, closely connected with music, to which there is abundant evidence from the early Middle Ages well into the twelfth century.[26] It is likely that the study of poetry and music, which became an indispensable part of education, aimed at just this function: taming the anger of raging seculars, and particularly that of kings. Alcuin knows this counselor's duty well, and he connected it with his own mission of seed-sowing.

Alcuin's admonitions to the king bring us to the real context and focal point of love and friendship in Charlemagne's kingdom: the royal court and its culture. It may well be that communal friendship was part and parcel of the York traditions in which Alcuin grew up and was educated.[27] But a cult of passionate friendship is documented far more abundantly around the person of the king himself, from whom traditions seem to arise. Whatever traditions flowed into the Carolingian cult of friendship, the king himself nurtured and made good use of them.

Love and friendship are well known as virtues of a ruler in antiquity. Aristotle devoted two books of his *Nicomachean Ethics* to the subject. He connects love with the themes of justice and governance, because love is a higher form of regulating the state and human affairs than law. Loving friendship in rule characterizes the most civilized states; lack of it, tyrannical ones.[28] This commonsense precept was also known in the Middle Ages, though not necessarily attached to the name of Aristotle. The 'Laws of Henry I' (early twelfth century) restate it: 'Agreement is better than the law, and love is better than a judge's edict.'[29]

The friendship of good men, based on the love of their inner worth, *areté* or *virtus*, became a social ideal of the aristocracy, Greek and Roman, and received its classical formulation in Cicero's *De amicitia*, one of the most widely circulated books from antiquity in the Middle Ages. To take only one example of this inheritance in the political realm, let us examine the poems of Venantius Fortunatus, an Italian who visited the courts of various Merovingian potentates in the middle of the sixth century.[30] His poems speak a fervent language of friendship. He writes to King Sigibert that his own, Fortunatus's, talents do not prompt him to write, but rather it is 'love of you which spurs me on'.[31] Sigibert has chosen his counselor and favorite, Gogo (perhaps *major domo*) because, 'being wise [Sigibert] has chosen a wise man, and being a lover has chosen one who loves (*elegit sapiens sapientem et amator amantem*)'; 'You [Gogo] love [the king] so much that you've won good fortune for him.'[32] He praises Conda, another court official of Sigibert, for having won 'the singular love of such great kings'; when Conda held power at the 'great court' of Chlotharius, the household was 'ruled with the same love'; Conda enjoys 'the great love of the king' and therefore from love receives lavish gifts.[33] The 'sweet name' of Duke Lupus of Champagne is 'always inscribed on the page of my heart', which possesses a 'wealth of love, a rich affection forging pure gold by its own feelings!'[34] These are a few passages (there are many more) characterizing the love language in which Fortunatus regularly addresses members of royal courts. In his rich body of poetry he hails his friends as the other half of his soul; he dwells on the beauty of their faces in their absence and finds refreshment, even salvation, in the cultivation of friendship. The erotic component of his language is strong. The 'beautiful shape' of the courtier Gogo 'ignites him with love' (7.12). Kisses and embraces were among the *signa amoris* (along with gifts, letters, poems). It is not clear to me that such expressions were widespread in Merovingian courts. Gregory of Tours does not paint a picture of courts of love.

As suggested earlier, of the many courts which developed cults of friendship in the Middle Ages, the best documented is the court of Charlemagne.[35] We should be clear on one point: the royal court is the originator and focal point of friendship in the Carolingian age; the monasteries and cathedrals receive the social practice from the court,[36] as they receive the educational program from the court. Smaragd of St Mihiel says in his *Via regia*, written around 810 for Charlemagne, 'This truly...is the royal virtue...to give sweet kisses to all and to embrace all lovingly with open arms.'[37]

The richness of the Carolingian sources allows us to observe the uses of the 'royal virtue' at the court in some detail. First, the language of passionate friendship provided a ceremonial form of address, probably also a ceremonial form of behavior. Carolingian court life had a 'staged' and 'composed' character. The close friends and advisers of the king took on classical and Old Testament epithets: the king was 'David', Alcuin was 'Flaccus Albinus', Angilbert was 'Homer'. The language of love is part of a scenario of court life and a style of courtly representation based on a mixed neoclassical and Old Testament idiom. Emplotted in this scenario are three of the main themes of Carolingian court verse: learning, poetry and friendship.

The much quoted poem of Angilbert (Homer) sending greetings to the court in his absence is a good example.[38] The poem is written in the mannered style of court poetry with strong reminiscences of Vergil's pastoral poems and fainter ones of the Psalms. It has a ceremonial aspect to its plot: Angilbert sends his flute to the court as his messenger; he bids it to sing as though, self-activated, it could deliver his messages by its own breath. The idea that structures the song is the flute's progress through the court. It moves from one member to the next, greeting with its song all the poet's friends. There are flattering descriptions of each, the verbal counterpart of a court ceremony of receiving and being received, bowing, paying compliments.

The song's ritual progress through the court is musical both within the metaphorical frame (the flute plays a song to the court) and in the character of the song. The dance-like nature of its progression is underscored by the refrain, repeated in some variant eighteen times in 108 lines:

> David loves poetry; rise up, my pipe, and make poetry!
> David loves poets, David is the poet's glory... (ll. 2–3)

In its choreographed progression the flute's song assumes the role of a love messenger. It calls to the other poets to respond to the king's love ('David loves poets') by joining in the chorus:

> and so, all you poets, join together in one,
> and sing sweet songs for my David! (ll. 3–5)

The singers are to draw their inspiration from their love for the king:

> May David's sweet love inspire the hearts of singers,
> and love for him make poetry in our hearts!
> Homer the poet loves David; make poetry, my pipe!
> David loves poets...
> May David's name resound on your lips in poetry,
> and love for him fill your heart! (ll. 7–13)

The song posits and makes audible a love flowing from Charlemagne and circulating through the court. The song is to run along 'through the holy palaces of David' and bring greetings 'to all his dear ones' (*cunctis caris*), 'embracing' them with its sweet tune (ll. 72–8). He bids it to throw itself down before the king and 'sweetly kiss the hallowed toes on his feet!' (l. 77). He varies the refrain to repeat the love theme:

> David is our love, David is dear above all.
> David loves poets, David is the poets' glory.
> David loves Christ, Christ is David's glory. (ll. 90–2)

This love language has in Angilbert's poem a particular honeyed sentimentality and preciosity, but the tone is common in poetry from the court circle. Paulus Diaconus expresses his love for the king in the conceit of a compulsion:

> What need of cells or chains to restrain me. The love of my lord king conquers me... Just as Saint Peter burned in the immense love of Christ...so also the strong love of you inflames my heart.[39]

Like Angilbert, Alcuin sent a 'love song' (*carmen amoris*) to the king as a love messenger: 'May my flute make songs for my beloved David.' And again in the same poem: 'As my spirit pursues you, so also does my song of love... O beloved David.'[40] The poet of the 'epic' on Charlemagne's meeting with Pope Leo, possibly Einhard, speaks of the radiantly happy figure of Charlemagne illumining the nobles of the court 'in the glow of his great love'.[41] The poet called 'the Irish exile (Hibernicus Exul)' addresses Charlemagne: 'With these unkempt verses but with the highest love of spirit, I contrive these things for you, O Caesar.'[42] And Theodulf protests to young Charles, the king's son: 'My head's dual lamps [eyes] thirst for the sight of you with unquenchable longing, and the lofty love in my breast desires you.'[43]

If the language of love were restricted to poetry, we might think it was determined somehow by the lyrical genre. But it registers in other forms. Here are some excerpts from the dedication of the *Via regia* of Smaragd of St Mihiel:[44]

> We dwell in our memory incessantly on the thought of all your good qualities and of your manifold gifts; those embraces which your royal arm has sweetly bestowed on us are painted on the secret surfaces of our mind, your honey-dripping kisses carved on the tablets of our heart, your words – kingly, honey-flowing, sweet and gentle – we treasure in the innermost recess of the mind...[45] Your mild and beautiful presence brings happiness to all, exalts and glorifies all, distributes to all gifts, affection and love. Stirred to action by this royal and sweet love, we, little as we are, have composed this little booklet...[46]

Smaragd was plain in connecting his love for Charlemagne with the gift he had received from him. The conflict between *honestum* and *utile*, which for Cicero was acute in the relations of friends, seems solved for this writer. The connection of emotion and political ends in the king's love is an important element of the style of Carolingian rule. Far from being decoration and overlay, the language and gestures of love made up the code in which favor relationships were publicized.

The documents from the Carolingian court give us a consistent picture of a court of love. Love beams from the king like light, engulfs the court, bathes its members in its warmth, compels them with its chains, charms them with its songs. It circulates back and forth between the king and the poets; the king's love inspires their writings. They live, act and speak in metaphors: they are players in a pastoral idyll, they are ancient sages and Old Testament patriarchs reborn. But the overarching metaphor is love: they are wounded by the king's love, they pine for him and feel immense desire welling through the chambers of memory at the thought of his beautiful face.

It may be that friendship was so fervently celebrated at the Carolingian court because it was rooted in the king's character. Einhard commented in the *Vita Caroli*:

> Charles was, by nature, a good friend, for he easily made friends and firmly held on to them. Indeed he treated with the greatest respect those he had bound closely to himself in a relationship of this sort.[47]

Friendship, Einhard claims, was one of the means by which Charlemagne increased the kingdom. Kings of Spain and Ireland declared him their lord merely by the friendship he showed them. Harun-al-Raschid declared Charlemagne's friendship more valuable to him than that of all the kings of the earth put together, so says Einhard.[48] And this was not only wise politics, but also an expression of the character of the king. Einhard's comments suggest that the love language of the court poetry originates in Charlemagne's personality. The passage sheds some light on the 'utility' of the king's friendship. He says that he 'did everything he possibly could' for intimate friends. That is presumably a lot. We have seen the close company that love and benefits keep in the case of Smaragd.

We find some confirmation for the real belief in love as a code of behavior at the Carolingian court in the Manual (*Liber manualis*) of Dhuoda, practical advice by a woman of high nobility to her son, written in the middle of the ninth century. In advising him on his debut, education, and service at court, she writes:

> If you attain to a position where, along with your companions, you serve within the royal or imperial court...then fear, love [*ama*], venerate and cherish [*dilige*] the famous and distinguished parents and retainers of your lord who are close to royal power... Recall how David was his life long a pure, loyal and true servant to Jonathan, son of King Saul, and to the father no less than the son... Upon their passing away, pressed by the sweetness of a boundless love, he sang this grave lamentation, in a flood of tears of mourning: '...I mourn for you, o my brother Jonathan, my love for you surpassed love [of women]...' You also, my son William..., be loyal to your lord Charlemagne,[49] whoever he may be... There is dignity in such service... For God has selected and elected them, we believe, for the kingdom.[50]

This is an ethic of court service, based on a relationship of loyalty and love like that of David and Jonathan, an important model of ennobling friendship in the Middle Ages. It shows that the power and charisma of high court dignitaries legitimize and dignify servitude, partly because of the divinity of kingship and rule that so clearly plays a part in Dhuoda's conception of royal power.

This passage gives us a prescriptive text enjoining personal, charismatic love as a communal ethic. To some extent it must corroborate the testimony of court poetry indicating that love provided a scenario of court behavior and structured the relations of court to king. The Carolingian cult of friendship is a major factor in court style. It would be quite appropriate to wonder whether the model of David and Jonathan, common though it is in the writings on friendship, were not particularly commended in this case because of the tradition that made Charlemagne into a second King David.

We began with a look at Alcuin as peace-maker with unruly or intemperate kings. Now we will regard him in his role as friend and 'lover'. In this role he appears as the most important and prolific figure in the Carolingian cult of friendship. His love poems and letters show us love at work not only in royal politics, but in the relationship of individuals; in the latter, however, the distinction between public and private relationship is ordinarily not clear. Alcuin's love letters and poems speak a language fashioned from the Song of Songs, the Psalms and the New Testament, with little echo of the classical Roman language of friendship.

He brings a startling innovation to the representation of love. In Cicero, Ambrose, Augustine, Paulinus of Nola, loving friendship was represented as chaste, heroic, idealistic, a love of the virtue in another man, held in tight check in the strictures of temperance, decorum, and self-control.[51] In Alcuin love is passionate and sensuous. With minor violence to the temporal bounds of concepts, one could call it romantic. A reading of some of his poems and letters justifies the provocation.

In one of his most remarkable poems Alcuin addresses an unnamed friend, who is traveling to take up service at a distant court, where he is honored and is vulnerable to the dangers and allurements of court life.[52] In his absence the beloved friend 'shines brighter than all treasures', and the poet desires and seeks with his whole will and his whole mind to restore his presence, 'to have, to hold, to love and to worship' ('*Omnibus et gazis clarior iste nitet,/Quem cupit et quaerit mentis sibi tota voluntas/Ut habeat, teneat, diligat atque colat'*, stanza 1, ll. 6–8; henceforth cited in the form 1.6–8). The poem is a love lament, and states as much in the first lines: 'Sweet love laments with tears an absent friend...' ('*Dulcis amor lacrimis absentem plangit amicum...*'). The poet's mind and heart are troubled, and he breaks into tears as his poem ends:

> We shall end this song with the tears welling up while I write,
> But the love in our breast is never-ending.
> I've written this song weeping, dearest one,
> And I believe that merciful Christ will wipe away the streams
> Of tears from my eyes...
> (*Carminis hic finem lacrimis faciemus obortis,*
> *Pectore sed numquam finem faciemus amoris.*
> *Flentibus hoc oculis carmen, karissime, scripsi,*
> *Flumina, credo, pius lacrimarum Christus ocellis*
> *Abstergat...*) (4.1–5)

There is turbulence; 'many thousands of things' (1.4) press in on him from without, while anxiety and longing for his friend upset him inwardly. He seeks peace and calm in the thought of his friend:

> ...joined to me in great love,
> You are peace to my mind, sweet love to me.
> (*...Iste eris ecce mihi magno coniunctus amore,*
> *Tu requies mentis, tu mihi dulcis amor.*) (ll. 9–10)

And he knows he will never find rest until he sees his friend again (4.5–6). As lovers do, he closes the chasm between longing and fulfilment with the vision of reunion:

> Oh would that the moment of wished-for love might come.
> When will that day be when I may see you,
> O beloved of God...
> (*O quando optandi veniat mihi tempus amoris,*
> *Quando erit illa dies, qua...te cernere possim,*
> *O dilecte deo...*) (2.1–3)

And it is also a lover's vision that imagines love, which otherwise fades, as in this one case eternal:

> The love in our breast is never-ending
> (*Pectore sed numquam finem faciemus amoris.*) (4.2)

The poet is timidly anxious for his friend's well-being: his trip is not without danger, and he equips him for the journey with his poem and his prayers.

This remarkable poem is filled with the tensions of absent love: the turbulence of mind, the longing, the hopes and fears of the lover. That is the *honestum* of the letter; its *utile* is also present, if only indirectly stated. It is a love poem, certainly, but it very probably doubles as both safe conduct and a letter of recommendation. The recipient is clearly headed for a court where he will have a high position, probably exercising his learning, certainly dependent on the favor of the locals. He will also face the dangers endemic to court life and high office. But he comes to his new position with a letter-poem from Alcuin, a powerful and favored member of Charlemagne's court. The writer is careful to invoke the safety of the bearer and to seal the letter with the authority of the writer's name:

> May God keep you safe for all eternity
>   And may you prosper always and everywhere,
>   mindful of Albinus [Alcuin].
> (*Te deus aeterno conservet tempore semper,*
> *Tu memor Albini semper ubique vale.*) (11.11–12)

The language of love must be unmistakable to anyone tuned to the court idiom. It was the language of the royal court, authenticating the letter/poem like a royal seal; it shows the high worth of the man to whom it is directed and enjoins honor and safety, repeatedly invoked in the letter, upon those receiving him.

That is not to deny that Alcuin 'loves' this man as vehemently as he claims to do. The expressions of admiration and respect in modern letters of recommendation are not undermined by the practical purpose of the letter. What is remarkable here is the style, the sentiment and the personal cast of the letter-poem.

Reading Alcuin's poems after the court poetry of Angilbert, Modoin or Theodulf is like moving from the Anacreontic verse of the early eighteenth century, witty but tinny, to Goethe's love poems. Alcuin's poetic language goes well beyond the honeyed and jeweled imagery and the rococo sentimentality of court poems. In fact, I don't think it is an exaggeration to declare Alcuin one of the finest love poets of the Middle Ages. He can represent love as vehement, deeply felt, personal and genuine. He uses the trite images of the 'flames of love' and the 'wounds of love' in many skilful variations. He writes to an unnamed friend:

> O that the spirit of prophecy might be in you...so you might perceive with how sweet a savor the love of you fills my breast... I send you these small jottings as signs of great love, so that what surpasses understanding can at least receive partial expression in words. For just as one can see a flame but not touch it, so also one can make love sensibly perceptible in letters, though in the mind of the writer it is not visible. Just as the fire sprays sparks, so love sparks out from letters.[53]

He particularly likes the image of the wounds of love. To his friend Peter of Aquileia he suggests that he has received 'wounds sweeter than any honeycomb from the sweet lance of love in his heart'.[54] Alcuin's heart also burns with the flame of love for Archbishop Ricbod of Trier; its heat is so intense that 'my heart could say to me, "I am wounded by love"'.[55] He suffers, he burns, he is sick or wounded, he pines, he dreams of his beloved. His love and longing far exceed the body's ability to fulfil; they leave him no rest, they drive him and pursue him. He dreams of a friendship that finds peace in heaven, though hindered on earth – a deeply romantic idea.[56] He would have sympathized with the figure of the driven wanderer in Goethe's love poetry. Both live in turmoil, longing for rest and the peace that comes through the beloved, and both feel magnified by love, since the soul without love – so says Alcuin – is, not just tinkling and empty, but dead.[57] Alcuin was clearly a man who was capable of loving other men deeply and passionately, and it is worthwhile stressing the personal aspects of his poetry, or rather, the aspects that at least present themselves to the modern reader as personal.

It is curious that the theme of friendship in Carolingian sources has attracted so little attention from modern scholars. There is no treatment of it. Those who have observed it do so in passing, though J Fleckenstein recognizes its importance as an element of court style.[58] Brian McGuire devotes a section to it in the context of Christian monastic ideals of community.[59] The reasons for this silence, I suspect, are themselves a chapter in modern cultural history. Wolfram von den Steinen, one of the shrewdest readers of Carolingian court poetry, shows the kind of consideration that has sheltered the subject from study. He commented that a complete inventory of the love declarations between Alcuin and Charlemagne would show Alcuin as 'virtually an intoxicated devotee or even an idolatrous worshipper' of the emperor, and asks, 'What modern scholar would not prefer to avert his eyes?'[60] Some of the hieratic gay heroism of the circle of intellectuals around Stefan George (von den Steinen was on its fringe) may shine through his reading: 'in Alcuin's words here there pulses the masculine devotedness of the loving older man to the younger [disciple], of Flaccus to his David'. Or 'lived experience brought home to him Charlemagne's role as master of a love that was masculine, active/aggressive and severe'.

John Boswell can claim Carolingian expressions of friendship as witness to a widespread tolerance of homosexuality in Antiquity and the earlier Middle Ages.[61] Certainly the earlier Middle Ages fashioned its public discourse of ennobling love from the passionate love of men for each other, and that fact should be of interest to gay history. But I find the issues very muddied by the term 'homosexuality'. The relationship of ennobling love to sexuality is an intriguing problem of historical analysis, but it requires the refashioning of our concepts of love, friendship and sexuality, not the uncritical use of them.

Adele Fisk's coopting of Alcuin for mystical notions of friendship is as misleading as Boswell's coopting him for homosexual ones. The ideals of friendship and love are tightly woven into the social and political fabric of life around Charlemagne, and I believe the least misleading approach to this difficult topic is through its uses. The 'otherness' of Carolingian friendship is evident in its contrast to the role of love and sex in twentieth-century political life. Perhaps it is not inappropriate to stress the usefulness, in fact the pragmatism, of a social value which molds the affective and the erotic into a ruler's virtue parallel to wisdom and strength of character, and an instrument for the exercise of power.

Chapter 6

Scaldic Poetry and Early Christianity

Ásdís Egilsdóttir

In the thirteenth-century *Njáls saga*, the longest and most widely acclaimed Icelandic saga, several passages are devoted to the missionary period and the conversion of Iceland. In them we meet the rather belligerent missionary þangbrandr from Saxony, who had been sent to Iceland by King Ólafr Tryggvason of Norway to preach the faith. The saga describes his successes and failures where heathen poets are among his most ardent adversaries:

> Veturliði the Poet and his son Ari spoke most against them and for this reason they [i.e. þangbrandr and his men] killed Veturliði.[1]

A stanza is composed about this incident. After this, þangbrandr is successful at Njáll's farm, Bergþórshváll, where Njáll and all his household accept the faith. The missionary and his men then proceed to Grímsnes where a band of men is mobilized against them and word is sent to the poet Úlfr Uggason to kill þangbrandr. This message is delivered to Úlfr in verse. Úlfr replies immediately with another verse where he expresses his fear. He concludes his stanza thus:

> bad things are brewing
> I'd better watch out.[2]

His words in plain prose are also quoted in the saga where he says:

> I don't intend to be his puppet and he'd better take care that his tongue doesn't twist itself around his neck.[3]

Words bound in poetry are powerful. One of the stanzas in *Hrafns saga Sveinbjarnarsonar*, dated to 1230, describes the power of poetry in the following way:

> Many a man who now gets away unharmed would long ago have been deprived of life, if a man's big talk bit him in the same way as blades do – the poet lets his beard fall back behind his shield.[4]

Úlfr knows that a poet can certainly harm others with his sharp tongue, but he also knows that it can place the poet himself in danger.

There are more perils ahead for þangbrandr. His ship is wrecked before he completes his journey round the west of the country. There, a heathen poet named Steinunn Refsdóttir comes to meet him:

> She preached heathenism at great length to Thangbrand. Thangbrand was silent while she spoke, but then spoke at length and turned all her arguments upside down.
>
> Have you heard, she said, that Thor challenged Christ to a duel and that Christ didn't dare to fight with him?
>
> What I have heard, said Thangbrand, is that Thor would be mere dust and ashes if God didn't want him to live.
>
> Do you know, she said, who wrecked your ship?
>
> What can you say about it? he said.
>
> I'll tell you, she said.[5]

In two mocking stanzas she tells him that þór had wrecked *Bison*, his ship:

> The shaping gods drove ashore
> the ship of the keeper of bells;
> the slayer of the son of the giantess
> smashed *Bison* on the sea-gull's rest
> no help came from Christ
> when the sea's horse was crushed;
> I don't think God was guarding
> Gylfi's reindeer at all.

Thor drove Thangbrand's beast
of Thvinnil far from its place;
he shook and shattered
the ship and slammed it ashore;
never will that oak of Atal's field
be up to seafaring again;
the storm, sent by him,
smashed it so hard into bits.[6]

The conversion in Iceland is believed to have taken place in 999 or 1000 in the reign of Ólafr Tryggvason and fully confirmed in the reign of his successor Ólafr Haraldsson, whose sainthood was acknowledged soon after his death in battle in 1030.

Several sources contain information about the process of Christianity in Iceland, the oldest being the *Book of the Icelanders (Íslendingabók)* by Ari þorgilsson, from 1125–30. The sources and transmission of Ari's account can be traced to the time of the conversion. Ari says in his book that his account of the acceptance of Christianity was how his informant, Teitr Ísleifsson, had told it. Teitr was the son of Ísleifr, the first bishop of Iceland. Ísleifr was the son of Gizurr Ísleifsson, a Christian leader who was present at that dramatic Alþingi meeting in 999/1000 when the new religion was accepted.[7]

Christianity brought books and the art of reading and writing to Iceland and the oldest manuscripts preserved in Iceland are religious books. The *Book of the Icelanders* tells of Irish monks who dwelt in Iceland before the Norwegian settlement. They left Iceland 'because they did not wish to live here together with heathen men, and they left behind Irish books, bells, and crooks'.[8] The *Book of Settlements (Landnáma)* says that Bishop Patrick of the Hebrides sent an Icelander with 'church timber, an iron bell, *plenarium* and consecrated earth'[9] to Iceland. These sources indicate that books were looked upon as a part of Christian culture. Although writing was begun in Iceland in the eleventh century the earliest signs of Christian thought are to be found in poetry composed by poets who were probably illiterate. This poetry was not put on parchment until later. Most of it is preserved as quotations in prose texts from the twelfth to the fourteenth century. The poets composed their poetry in the same tradition as the aforementioned Úlfr Uggason and Steinunn Refsdóttir.

This traditional poetry, scaldic poetry, also called *dróttkvætt* or court poetry, is strophic, stress-counting and syllable-counting with regulated alliteration and internal rhyme. Each stanza consists of eight lines. Apart from the extremely elaborate meter with complicated word order, other characteristics are the so-called *kennings* and *heiti*. *Kenning* is derived from the verb *kenna*, 'designate'. A *kenning* is probably best described as a periphrasis of a noun. A simple kenning consists of two nouns, or of a name (the base word, *stofnorð*) combined with a noun in the genitive case (the determinant, *kenniorð*), or forming a compound with it. A *kenning* for ship could be a horse of the waves and a battle designated as the storm of weapons. A *heiti*, derived from the verb *heita*, 'call by name', is a noun or name which appears frequently in poetry, but rarely in prose.[10]

The first known poet, or skald, of *dróttkvætt*, also believed to be its originator, was Bragi Boddason, nicknamed the Old, probably of the second half of the ninth century. Whether this is true or not, there is an interesting relationship between the poet Bragi, and Bragi the god of poetry, who is mentioned in several sources. Nothing is known of a cult of Bragi, but it is very likely that this apparently highly esteemed poet came to be regarded by later generations as a god.[11] Snorri Sturluson's *Edda*, a thirteenth-century treatise on scaldic poetry, tells the story of the mythical origin of poetry, in which Óðinn brought the mead of poetry from the world of giants to the gods and men. The poets do not have a priestly or prophetic role, but they sometimes refer to this myth in their poetry.[12] The period of *dróttkvætt* lasted for about four hundred years. The poets came from different strata of society; kings, outlaws, even ghosts could compose a stanza of *dróttkvætt*. Although Steinunn Refsdóttir plays an important role with her poetry in *Njáls saga*, there are not many women among the poets.[13] The first known poets were Norwegians but soon Icelanders took over as court poets of Norway. Their relationship with the royal patron is difficult to define but it can be said that the royal patron needed the poet as much as the poet needed – and gained from – his patron. Court poets were loyal to their patrons and sometimes fought and died alongside them. The poet had a position at court, at least a temporary one. Poets were given seats of honor and occasionally acted as royal retainers. However, as Bjarne Fidjestøl has pointed out, the poets of the Norwegian kings during the missionary period were slow to exploit the religion for political ends in any open and obvious way.[14] In most cases the name of the poet is known. The sources do not give evidence about the schooling of poets or how they acquired their skills, but in many cases poetic talent and knowledge seem to have run in certain families.

Frequently, those families also excelled in other important fields, such as law and the priesthood.[15] Two of the best-known poets, Sighvatr Þórðarson and Arnór earls' poet, were sons of poets, and the poet Steinunn, who used her skills against the Christian missionary, was the mother of a poet.

In the poetry of Steinunn heathen poetic language is used as a weapon against the missonary. Poetry and poetic diction had divine origin since it was believed to be derived from Óðinn, and a considerable amount of the poetic language included names of gods and goddesses and alluded to myth. It may therefore be assumed that the magical power of poetic language was due to this, at a time when belief in the heathen gods and myths was very much alive. In her poetic diction Steinunn Refsdóttir refers to Þór in his protective and defending role as the slayer of giants. Besides, she makes a rather undignified new *kenning* to designate the missionary, where she calls him 'the keeper of bells', a humiliating *kenning* when compared to the elegant, warrior-like *kennings* that usually designate men in scaldic poetry. She never alludes to Óðinn, probably because her stanzas describe a struggle between Christ and Þór. In her opinion Þór was the winner in this battle because he had succeeded in smashing the missionary's ship. Þór had power over weather; Steinunn uses various *kennings* to designate him, and numerous *heiti* for the sea, or the mythical king of the sea. She mentions God and Christ, but without the use of *kennings*. Clearly Steinunn uses the poetic diction to name what she believes in and to give her poetry added power.

After the conversion to Christianity poets continued to compose according to the old tradition. They were reluctant to use heathen *kennings*, instead creating new *kennings* similar to the traditional ones. *Kennings* were now created to designate the king of heaven and creator of the world. The power of the word is in that respect transferred to the Christian poetry and the old heathen magic avoided. The poet who probably best represents the conversion – or what it was like to be a poet during that period – is Hallfreðr Óttarsson, nicknamed 'the troublesome poet' (*vandræðaskáld*) because of his rebellious personality.[16] Hallfreðr began his career as the court poet of the heathen earl Hákon (d. 995) and then joined the missionary king Ólafr Tryggvason. Proud, even arrogant, as court poets usually appear, Hallfreðr agreed to be baptized on the condition that the king himself would stand as his godfather. Hallfreðr admitted in his poetry that he had deep roots in the old religion and that his poetic gifts depended on inspiration from pagan mythology. Hallfreðr composed a poem after his king's death in

1000. There are not many Christian ideas in this poem but considerably fewer heathen *kennings* than in his former works. However, in his poem on the dead king he remembers him as his godfather and the concluding lines of this poem form a prayer where the pure Christ is asked to guard the king's soul in heaven. Hallfreðr seems therefore to have had Christian ideas of afterlife: the missionary king Ólafr Tryggvason deserves a place in heaven. In a verse Hallfreðr is supposed to have composed shortly before his death he confesses that he could easily accept death, were it not for his fear of hell. The problem with this verse is that it is preserved in only one version of the saga and could easily have been made by the saga-writer himself to emphasize the poet's good faith.[17]

Scaldic poetry with Christian themes or ideas can be divided into three periods: conversion period (1000–1050), formative period (1050–1150) and finally the flourishing period (1150–1200).[18] In the poetry of the first period there is a strong emphasis in the *kennings* on Christ and God as kings. The baseword of the *kennings* is a noun meaning king or chieftain; the determinant shows the place he reigns over, heaven or the whole world. The adjectives used in the poetry of this period allude to power. God is strong, powerful and pure. He is the creator of the world and rules over the fate and lives of all human beings. This powerful image is evident in a stanza of the lawspeaker and poet Skapti þóroddsson (d. 1030) who tells his audience about the strong and mighty Christ who created the world and laid the foundations of Rome.[19] Poets compare God with wordly rulers, as can be seen from a poem by Hallvarðr Háreksblesi on King Canute of Denmark. The poet claims that King Canute guards his country as God guards the beautiful dwelling of mountains,[20] a *kenning* for heaven.

The same strong images of God and Christ dominate the poetry of the second period, 1050–1150. According to the lawspeaker and poet Markús Skeggjason, the king of heaven created heaven, earth and mankind. This poet sees people (probably exclusively male) as God's army. In his poem Christ, the king, is the sole ruler.[21]

Although the image of God and Christ is similar in the first and second periods, there is more variation in the use of adjectives in the second period. We find fewer adjectives for power; instead, there is more emphasis on purity, wisdom and glory. God is shown as a judge punishing people for their sins but also giving rewards for righteousness. The poets ask God to give grace to the rulers they are praising or mourning in their poetry. Christian ideas of afterlife are best seen when the poets conclude their poems by praying for their kings' souls. An impressive scene of the last judgement appears in a fragment by Arnór earls' poet, where 'the king of heaven sits on his throne and the archangel Michael weighs the deeds of mankind, good and evil.'[22]

The twelfth century produced several poems on religious themes and some of the known poets are not court poets of kings, but monks and abbots. In additions to *kennings* and occasionally instead of them we find symbolic religious imagery. In this period there is an explosion in the use of adjectives and there is a notable change in emphasis from the use of adjectives designating strength and power towards those of love and kindness.

The scaldic poems from the conversion until the twelfth century are valuable sources for the evaluation of Christian thought and ideas during this period. The poetry which survives does not, however, tell the whole story and it is impossible to judge the poets as Christians only from the existing poetry. The poetry from this period still existing today has probably been preserved because it has been embedded in the kings' sagas and is therefore thematically related to them. The sources mention several poems that are now lost. The previously mentioned Hallfreðr Óttarsson is believed to have composed a poem on the story of the creation, as a penalty for his lack of faith.[23] Among other lost poems of other poets are a poem on St Thomas the Apostle and a poem on the Rood. One stanza from the last mentioned poem has been preserved. This stanza describes a battle of kings but the part on the Rood is completely lost.

We may ask how or if Christian community is reflected in this poetry or how the poets perceived themselves as belonging to a group of Christians. Again, we have to bear in mind what has been said before about the preservation of writings. The relationship between God and mankind is frequently depicted as the relationship between a king and a court or subjects. Angels are also the army or court of God, the king of heaven.

The poetry of the prolific, witty and elegant Sighvatr þórðarson best reflects the relationship between poet and patron although his position and esteem may have been exceptional.[24] Sighvatr þórðarson was born near the turn of the eleventh century and became one of Ólafr Haraldsson's court poets. Although loyal to his patron, Sighvatr could also be politically independent, as is evident in his composition of a poem in honour of Erlingur Skjálgsson, the king's long-time enemy. Sighvatr went on diplomatic missions for his king, described in his versified travelogues *Austrfararvísur* and *Vestrfararvísur* (*Verses on a*

Journey to the East/West). Later he gave outspoken advice to King Ólafr's son Magnús in his *Bersöglisvísur* (*Plain-speaking Verses*). In the beginning of *Austrfararvísur*, Sighvatr addresses the king's court. The court is the community he belongs to, where he is among other Christian men. Then he proceeds to describe the journey, which was not always easy; the route was difficult and he met inhospitable people on his way. The hostile people he mentions are heathens. He arrives at a farm where he finds the doors closed. He manages to open them enough to be able to stick his nose in but the people inside do not ask him in, telling him that he has arrived on a sacred day. The heathens send him away and he curses them when he leaves. At the next farm, the housewife prevents him from entering her home because a heathen feast is being celebrated in her home and she fears Óðinn's wrath. Sighvatr describes the heathen woman as *ópekk*, unsympathetic. In this poem the poet distinguishes himself from the heathens he meets on the journey. He belongs to another community as does his audience.

Sighvatr composed an *Erfidrápa*, a memorial ode for his king after he was killed in the battle of Stiklarstaðir in 1030. Sighvatr reminds his audience that not all of the king's army was Christian. The army was divided into two parts and the king asked his Christian soldiers to stay on his right side, which can be seen as an allusion to the Last Judgement.

A significant part of Sighvatr's Christianity is his relationship with his king and patron Ólafr Haraldsson. He sternly expresses his feelings about those who are about to betray or have betrayed their king. 'You will have a place for you in black hell if you sell your king for gold,'[25] he warns his audience in a poem. He is convinced that the traitors will end in hell, a deserved punishment for their crime.

Sighvatr went on a pilgrimage to Rome and was unfortunate enough to do this Christian deed at the same time as the king was fighting his final battle. According to the saga of St Ólafr the other court poets scorned him because of his absence. In one of the stanzas Sighvatr composed on his pilgrimage he states that Christ can send him to hell if it had ever been his intention to betray the king. A similar idea is expressed in a stanza by Sighvatr's contemporary, þorgeir Flekkr, when reproaching young King Magnús: 'You loved those miserable men, the traitors that pleased the devil.'[26]

In the poetry from the conversion period we find Christian ideas emerging and the eleventh century reflects their growing acceptance. The great age of Christian scaldic poetry was the twelfth century. This period consolidated with the establishment of monasteries in Iceland.

Two of the most interesting poems of this period are *Geisli* (*Sunbeam*)[27] by Einar Skúlason and *Harmsól* (*Sun of Sorrow*)[28] by Gamli the Canon. Both poets were learned men in the new, Christian sense. Einar Skúlason was a priest and and Gamli an Augustinian canon.

Einar Skúlason was probably born in the last decade of the eleventh century and a kinsman of well-known poets and writers including Egill Skallagrímsson and Snorri Sturluson. Einar was a prolific poet and court poet of more than one king. *Geisli* is his masterpiece, a long encomium on St Ólafr Haraldsson, delivered in Trondheim in 1152 or 1153. The poem compares St Ólafr to Christ using typological parallels. Einar composed his poem in the old scaldic meter but, understandably, he avoids mythological *kennings*. Instead, he creates metaphors and symbolic imagery based on his knowledge of theology, liturgy and the Latin poetry of his time. The image of God and Christ in Einar's poem is a royal image, supported by numerous inventive *kennings*. The mightiest of kings invites men to dwell with him in heaven and to join his court. God is depicted as the king of angels sitting on a throne above them. The angels form his court and bow respectfully to their king. The dead king, St Ólafr, is invited to stay at Christ's royal palace. *Geisli* is delivered in the presence of the reigning kings and the poem is addressed and dedicated to them as well as the saint and the heavenly king. Einar stands before the kings, almost as arrogantly as any court poet before him, expecting his rewards. He says that God's blessing will be his rewards, if his poem is well liked, but can't resist implying that a poem like that should be rewarded with valuable rings.

Much less is known of Gamli, the poet of *Harmsól*, a canon in the Augustinian cloister (*Þykkvibær*), founded in 1168. Besides *Harmsól* he composed a poem on St John the Apostle. Harmsól is also composed in the old *dróttkvætt* meter, a complicated poem with a striking number of *kennings*. In the opening words of *Harmsól* the poet calls upon the 'high ruler of the storm canopy (God)' – to open his 'gate of the poetry fortress (lips)'. The first stanzas are a prayer in which Christ is apostrophized. According to scaldic tradition Christ is praised as a king in more than eighty *kennings*, depicting him as a king in his heavenly kingdom. In addition there is a new emphasis on the sorrowful, suffering Christ, who is closer to the individual than the more remote *rex triumphans* of the older poets. The poet then turns to his fellow men, whom he addresses in homiletic style as his dear brothers and sisters (*góð systkin*). The main theme of the poem is the basic tenet of Christianity, concentrating on sin and Christ's work on salvation. He concludes by asking his audience to pray for him and then prays for all Christians. As one of the last court poets, Einar Skúlason is a man of two worlds. He is a learned Christian but also a court poet. He is self-conscious in the style of the older court poets, which makes him conscious of himself as a performer in front of an audience. The humble, penitent Gamli is a master of the poetic diction of *dróttkvætt* but he neither needs nor has a worldly king or a court to address. He asks God to open his lips so that his humble words can be a prayer of mercy for sinful mankind. After having confessed his own sins he compares himself to other sinners who have been forgiven and by doing so he gains hope. In that way he also identifies himself with the brothers and sisters he addresses.

Gamli is one of the poets who marks a turning point. He is one of those who belong to the Christian community of the monastery, but also identifies with the broader Christian world.

Chapter 7

Heloise and the Abbey of the Paraclete

Chrysogonus Waddell

During the past several decades no twelfth-century theologian has been the object of so much scholarly attention as Master Peter Abælard. Editions of his various works, major and minor, have abounded, as have articles, monographs and book-length studies concerning seemingly every aspect of his life and writings.[1] Thanks, too, to the perennial fascination attaching to Abælard's autobiographical *Historia Calamitatum* and his correspondence with Heloise, scholars and novelists and even movie producers have kept the memory of Heloise alive – alive, yes, but almost always only with reference to and in subordination to her husband and father in Christ, Abælard.[2] For most readers, the final letter in their correspondence spells not only the end of their exchange of letters, but also the end of Heloise. She simply disappears – even though she outlived her husband by at least 22 years.[3]

All this is very likely soon to change. The distinguished New Zealand medievalist Dr Constant Mews, who currently teaches at Monash University, Australia, has recently produced a major work. This important contribution is bound to focus attention on Heloise in quite a new light. In *The Lost Love Letters of Heloise and Abelard: Perceptions of Dialogue in Twelfth-Century France*,[4] Mews argues that the collection of 65 letters from a famous teacher and of 48 from his female student known as the *Epistolae duorum amantium* does indeed represent an authentic exchange of letters between the young Heloise and her mentor, the famous dialectician Peter Abælard.

First edited by Ewald Könsgen in 1974,[5] this collection of letters exists in a single manuscript from Clairvaux (Troyes, Bibliothèque municipale, ms 1452, fos 159–67ᵛ). Copied only in the late fifteenth century by the scribe Jean De Vepria, and included in a miscellany of letters and tracts on letter-writing and related topics, these letters, on the basis of internal evidence, can safely be dated to the first half of the twelfth century.

In an unpublished lecture entitled 'Philosophical Themes in the *Epistolae duorum amantium*: The First Letters of Heloise and Abelard?',[6] Mews suggested that the lack of critical attention given this letter-collection 'may be related to renewal in the 1970s and early 1980s of sometimes vitriolic debate about the authenticity of the letters of Heloise [and Abælard] ... [F]ew scholars risked sticking their neck out for some anonymous letters which might have even less claim to authenticity than the more well known letters of Heloise [and Abælard]'.[7] Prominent among such scholars was Peter Dronke. In a few remarkable paragraphs devoted to the *Epistolae duorum amantium* in his Ker Lecture of 1976,[8] Dronke rehearsed the evidence in favor of the authenticity of this correspondence; but just at the moment when the reader might well expect the author, on the basis of the evidence he so tellingly adduces, to conclude that the two correspondents are therefore necessarily the young Heloise and her teacher and lover, Dronke draws back, cautions us that 'these letters take their place within a specific tradition', and offers three examples of similar exchanges between 'a young girl hesitantly in love with, and still somewhat over-awed by, her older *magister*' ...[9] Heloise, however, is not just hesitantly in love. She is passionately in love. Nor is she particularly overawed by her older *magister*. She is her own woman, and easily stands her own in these often subtle dialectical exchanges with her mentor. However, whether or not the jury will still be out after Mews' *The Lost Love Letters of Heloise and Abelard* has had a chance to circulate, scholarly attention will have been brought to bear on Heloise in the light of an idea central to the author's understanding of his subject: that is to say, Heloise's remarkable independence of spirit. In a personal communica-tion, Mews refers to his 'discussion [in his book] of the similarities between the ideas of Heloise and' – of all people! – 'Bernard [of Clairvaux]'. He goes on to write: 'I am confident that Heloise was cer-tainly closer to Bernard than to Abelard in many things ...'[10]

The Heloise on whom Mews focuses is, of course, the Heloise of the years 1114–16. But it is much to be hoped that, in the light of renewed interest in the relationship between Abælard and the *très sage* Heloise, attention will be extended beyond the *Epistolae duorum amantium* and the more famous collection of frequently edited and translated letters, to the still little known and therefore little appreciated Heloise of the period 1142 to 1164, that is to say, the period from the death of Abælard in 1142 (some say 1143) to the death of Heloise in 1164. Indeed, it might almost be suggested that Heloise came fully into her own only upon the death of her rather exigent spiritual father and husband, Abælard. It can be asserted with a fair amount of confidence, however, that the discovery of this latter-day Heloise will also be the discovery of the community which she governed, first as prioress (1129–c. 1132), then as abbess, for a total period of some thirty-five years – the community of the Paraclete, a community so dynamic and alive that, during Heloise's abbacy, it gave birth to a half-dozen other houses, all of which together formed the Congregation of the Paraclete.

Indeed, Abælard's love for Heloise had reached out at an early date to embrace also the community which had formed in 1129 around Abælard's abandoned Oratory of the Paraclete (originally dedicated to the Holy Trinity) in the woods near Quincy, diocese of Troyes. In 1129, as the result of litigation initiated by Suger, abbot of St Denis, the nuns of the Carolingian abbey of Argenteuil, including their prioress Heloise, had been expelled from their monastery.[11]

Abælard, in taking up his duties as abbot of St-Gildas-de-Ruy in Brittany, had left his woodland oratory vacant. He now invited Heloise and a group of her companions to settle there and form a new religious community. Anything but successful as abbot of St-Gildas, Abælard had returned to Paris by 1132 or 1133, where he became attached to the school of Ste-Geneviève. If we are to take Heloise's first letter to Abælard at face value, his rapport with the Paraclete community during the first years was somewhat ambiguous. True, Heloise can state: 'You after God are the sole founder of the place, the sole builder of this oratory, the sole creator of this community'[12] – and this is certainly correct: it was Abælard who had first acquired the Paraclete property, Abælard who had built the original oratory, and Abælard who, by making possible the transfer of Heloise and her companions from Argenteuil to the Paraclete, had brought this new religious community into being. Yet it emerges from what follows that, during those first critical and formative years, Father Founder had left the fledgling community to fend pretty much for itself.[13] This distancing of Abælard from Heloise and her community was not to last for long. As the correspondence continues, it becomes painfully clear that Abælard now aspires to play Jerome to Heloise's Paula, and with a vengeance. In no time at all Heloise, writing in the name of herself and her companions, is asking two things from Abælard, the first being a history of women religious, the second, a Rule. 'All of us handmaids of Christ,' she writes, who are also your daughters in Christ, are now humbly asking two things from your paternity, two things which we foresee as being quite necessary for us. The first is that you be willing to teach us how the order of nuns first began, and what authority there is for our profession. But the other, that you will draw up some kind of rule for us, and write it down and send it – a rule which is proper to women, and which describes fully the manner and habit of our way of life.[14]

Abælard was eager to oblige. His response was the monumental Letter VII, a detailed and prolix history of women religious and, introduced by Letter VIII, a still more monumental and more detailed and more prolix Rule. Indeed, if we take the history and the Rule together, these, as Sir Richard Southern notes with no little dismay, are 'much longer than all the rest [of the correspondence] put together'.[15] Southern is quite candid in his estimation of this history and this Rule:

They are by no means readable, and they are seldom read. They have no personal interest. They must have cost him much dreary toil... Having started as a brilliant expression of early twelfth-century learning, rhetoric and personal vanity, the correspondence ends as a series of monastic documents.[16]

'Monastic documents' ... What, indeed, could be more lethally, more devastatingly anticlimatic than 'a series of *monastic documents*'? Indeed, the translator of what may currently be considered the standard English version of the correspondence, Betty Radice,[17] also finds Letter VII, the history of nuns, 'prolix and not very logical in [its] arrangement', and mercifully spares the reader by providing, not a translation, but a mere summary of its main points. (We might ask ourselves by what miracle the equally undeserving Rule escaped the same fate at the hands of the bored translator.) Pascale Bourgain is even more eloquent. This Rule, she writes, is 'a monument of incoherence and disorder'.[18]

But if I may now interject a personal note into this exposition, let me confess that I myself find Abælard's history of nuns almost Euclidian in its logical arrangement, and endlessly fascinating to boot. Worse still, I would venture the same enthusiastic response as regards the Rule. Far from costing Abælard much dreary toil, these two documents, I should like to suggest, represent the enthusiastic climax, the culminating point

of the entire correspondence. Elsewhere I have outlined my own working hypothesis as regards the nature of this correspondence,[19] which
may here be summarized in a few words.

Medieval monastic customaries are frequently introduced by prefatory material offering information about the nature and origin of the
customary in question. At times this prefatory material consists of no
more than a *monitum* or relatively brief letter, as in the case of Lanfranc's
Decreta.[20] However, at other times the prefatory material takes the form
of a lengthy historical narrative. The *Prooemium* to the *Regularis
concordia* linked with the names of both Dunstan and Ethelwold is a
good example: in the Symons edition[21] it accounts for nine of the sixty-
nine pages, and includes both historical narrative and synodal deci-
sions. Even more ample are the introductions to the various recensions
of the Cistercian customary, where we find a historical narrative, the
fundamental constitution of the Order and a lengthy series of select
instituta or statutes of the General Chapter.[22] This introductory
material provides the monastic with an understanding of the origins
and spirit of his or her observance. Accordingly, I suggest that the
Paraclete dossier is a particularly novel variation of the sort of arrangement we find in the *Regularis concordia* and the Cistercian customary.
Here the form of the material leading up to Abælard's history of nuns
and his Rule is not that of historical narrative interspersed with letters
and official documents, as in the case of the Cistercian customary, but
narrative in the form of letters. As I have written elsewhere,[23]

> The literary genre adopted offers the author a unique advantage:
> he can describe the pre-history and early history of the Paraclete
> not as recorded by a chronicler, but as experienced 'from within'
> by the chief protagonists of the drama, the founder Abælard and
> the first abbess Heloise. Future generations of Paraclete nuns
> would be introduced to the way of life set forth in their unique
> Rule, not by a run-of-the-mill introductory letter or historical
> narrative, but by a series of 'letters' that not only detail the his-
> torical facts, but also bare the souls of founder and foundress,
> and describe their spiritual evolution [or conversion].

And let it be noted, too, that this Rule of Abælard's is rather more than
a monastic rule. It is also a spiritual directory that spells out the spiritual values and inner motivations which should animate the outward
observances. Scholars familiar with Abælard's ethical writings will here

recognize his characteristic emphasis on the role of intention and of inner dispositions in determining the morality of human acts.

It might also be noted that the monastic cachet of the correspondence seems to have been recognized by the compiler of the only complete manuscript of the correspondence,[24] Troyes Bibliothèque Municipale ms 806, since the manuscript includes not only the eight letters plus Abælard's Rule, but a further set of Paraclete institutes known by its incipit, *Institutiones nostrae*; lengthy excerpts concerning nuns and abbesses from Ivo of Chartres' *Panormia*;[25] canons concerning monastics from the Council of Rouen of 1231;[26] eleven Premonstratensian statutes concerning nuns;[27] and canons 7–28 from the statutes on monastic life decreed in 816 at the Synod of Aix-la-Chapelle, and here presented as a *Regula sanctimonialium*.[28]

But Abælard's contributions to life at the Paraclete went far beyond his history of women religious and his Rule. He was prodigal in his efforts to provide Heloise and her daughters with all that was needed to live their monastic commitment enthusiastically. There is, for instance, his *Expositio in Hexameron*[29] (1133–7) addressed to Heloise, and his replies to various theological problems raised by her – the *Problemata Heloissae*[30] (c. 1137–9?). He wrote a bulky hymnal for the Paraclete, compiled a biblical Night Office lectionary, pieced together a series of Office canticles, authored a collection of sermons and composed an entire Holy Week Office, to say nothing of sequences, collects, responsories and antiphons of various kinds.[31] A substantial amount of this material is not only recoverable but has actually been recovered.[32]

But anyone who would conclude from the preceding remarks that Heloise and company submissively and uncritically received the Rule from Father Founder and put it into practice, or allowed his liturgical contributions to determine the shape of their liturgy, is taking far too much for granted – as we shall now see.

First, to touch briefly upon the Paraclete liturgy. The sources for our knowledge of this unique liturgy are relatively late. For Abælard's hymns, the principal source is fairly early, a manuscript now at the Brussels Bibliothèque Royale, dating from the late twelfth or early thirteenth century.[33] A few individual hymns are to be found in various reasonably early manuscripts.[34] But, after the Brussels manuscript, the next most important witness to Abælard's hymns is a late fifteenth-century Paraclete breviary now at the Bibliothèque Municipale in Chaumont.[35] Though basically a breviary for only the Day Hours, this manuscript does include a certain amount of material for the Night

Offices. Thanks to this manuscript, we can recover an abundance of Abælard's contributions to the Paraclete liturgy (though only for the texts, since the manuscript is without music). There are, furthermore, two absolutely priceless liturgical directories: an Old French Ordinary, with a Latin *Ordo* for processions.[36] This manuscript dates from the late thirteenth century. An analysis of these sources, however, leads inexorably to the conclusion that the decades and centuries which followed the springtime of Heloise's abbacy were anything but creative. The problem seems not to have been, on the part of Heloise's successors, their excessive conservatism, but rather their lack of imagination and learning. For instance, by the time we reach the early fourteenth century, the recently promulgated Corpus Christi Office celebrated at the Paraclete was, on the basis of the Chaumont breviary, simply the Roman rite Office as regards both content and structure.[37] No attempt was made to adapt the Roman rite structure of the Office to the monastic form of the Office. Again, with few exceptions, such as the Corpus Christi Office, the liturgical calendar appears virtually frozen in the form it had in the late twelfth century. Even universal favorites such as the early thirteenth-century St Francis and St Elizabeth of Hungary are conspicuous by their absence.

Perhaps the most astonishing thing to be noted about the Paraclete Office as transmitted by these sources is that this Office is fundamentally Cistercian in structure and content. For a monastery founded by Peter Abælard this is, to say the least, somewhat surprising given what we know about the somewhat less than cordial relations between the Abbot of St-Gildas, Peter, and the Abbot of Clairvaux, Bernard. Further, Abælard's only extant letter to Bernard, his Letter X,[38] is one long litany cataloguing the stupidities and contradictions of Cistercian liturgical practice. Yet, it is difficult to avoid the evidence that the Cistercian liturgy was known at the Paraclete from a very early date indeed. Take, for instance, the case of the Paraclete hymn repertory.

The Paraclete hymn repertory, compared with the hymn repertory of most other monasteries, was mammoth. It drew on a number of sources. First of all, there were Abælard's hymnic contributions represented by the hymnal of the Brussels manuscript (ninety-six hymns – but the manuscript is lacunose at the end), by a Holy Week Office composed by Abælard (known from the Chaumont breviary), and by an additional nine hymns for various saints (also known from the Chaumont breviary). There were another twenty-nine hymns standard in Gallican territory, and borrowed for the Paraclete from an unidentified source or sources. Finally, and this astonishes, there were all thirty-four hymns from the primitive Cistercian hymnary.

As regards the ninety-six hymns known from the Brussels manuscript, all but four of the Sunday and weekday hymns were eliminated, and the hymns from the temporal and sanctoral cycles were pruned; those which survived were placed often enough in a position subordinate to the hymns from Gallican and Cistercian sources. The case of the primitive Cistercian hymnal is especially noteworthy, since it was retained in its entirety. Here the word 'primitive' is important, since it distinguishes this hymnal from its later counterpart redacted during the 1140s, but before 1147, under St Bernard's supervision.[39] The Paraclete hymn sources include absolutely nothing from this Bernardine revision of 1140/1147, whereas the texts of the pre-Bernardine version are retained *in toto*. This clearly suggests that, at least for the hymns, the primitive Cistercian hymnal was already part of the Paraclete liturgy during the period prior to 1140/1147. Since it was supplemented by hymns from Gallican sources and from the pen of Master Abælard, there would have been no need to introduce material from the later Bernardine recension, since all that was proper to this recension was already included in the repertory of Gallican hymns.

The case of the antiphonary material was somewhat different – the antiphonary material including antiphons, responsories of various kinds and versicles. About ninety per cent of this material is pure Cistercian, but belongs to the Cistercian antiphonary reformed under Bernard's aegis, once again during the 1140s, but before 1147.[40] The nature of the antiphonary current at the Paraclete prior to the 1140s is a matter of pure conjecture. Perhaps it was the primitive Cistercian antiphonary; and this problematic antiphonary would have been replaced by the later Cistercian version at the same time this later version was promulgated for Cistercian use. Then again, the early Paraclete antiphonary may have had a quite different origin. What we do know on the basis of manuscript evidence is that, as of the 1140s, Abælard's considerable liturgical contributions had been inserted into an Office that was Cistercian through and through in form and content. All this would have taken place, of course, during the period of Heloise's abbacy, which extended from (probably) 1132 to her death in 1164.

The Paraclete liturgical calendar goes parallel with the hymnal and antiphonary. The substratum of the calendar is distinctively Cistercian.[41] Though fundamentally based on the calendar of the period after 1147, elements from the primitive Cistercian calendar may still be discerned.

The influence of Abælard, however, is considerable. Inserted into the Cistercian calendar are the deacon saints of Acts and other deacons and their companions, all of whom were illustrative of Abælard's emphasis on the role of the deacon vis-à-vis the holy women-disciples of Christ.[42] Saints particularly associated with the Master also are represented – St Gildas, St Ayoul, St Hippolytus. Also present are the patron saints of the houses dependent on the Paraclete, all of which were founded between 1142 at the latest and 1163, the year before Heloise's death, and all together of which formed the Congregation of the Paraclete.[43]

The sources reveal that, contrary to Cistercian practice, which until around 1147 admitted of only two liturgical processions within the liturgy (Candlemas and Palm Sunday), processions were held in high honor at the Paraclete.[44] There is, however, a good chance that the Sunday processions date from a period later than the twelfth century.

For the Mass rite and the Mass chants, we have only the pertinent references of the Old French Ordinary. These suffice to indicate, however, that the Paraclete Mass rite and Mass books were definitely non-Cistercian.

While obviously allowing for an evolution of the Paraclete liturgy after the death of Heloise, most of the evidence points to a liturgy which had attained its characteristic shape during the abbacy of Heloise. She draws heavily on Abælard; she draws even more massively on the Cistercians; she also draws eclectically on still other sources. She is a free woman who exercises her liberty creatively in such a way as to leave her stamp on the Paraclete liturgy up to the time of the seventeenth-century catastrophes, when the abbesses and their subjects energetically disassociated themselves from all that remained from their heritage of former times.[45]

Let us now return to the important matter of Abælard's Rule at the Paraclete. Was Abælard's Rule ever implemented at the Paraclete? There is no clear evidence that such was ever the case; and there is, indeed, a negative *a priori* argument against the likelihood of any such Rule ever being implemented. Eager as Abælard may have been to assume the reforming role of a new Benedict, a new monastic legislator, the odds were stacked against him. Canon 26 of the Second Lateran Council (1139), was eloquently to the point:

> We decree...that there be abolished the pernicious and detestable custom of certain women who, though they live neither according

to the Rule of the blessed Benedict, nor of Basil, nor of Augustine, nevertheless want to be reckoned in common repute as nuns...[46]

The reference to these three Rules is in keeping with twelfth-century curial jurisprudence, which Fr Jacques Dubois describes in this way:

The Gregorian reform had re-invigorated the two forms of religious life which had found their definitive shape in the heyday of the Carolingian Empire, the canons and the monks. On the latter the Rule of St Benedict was imposed with such vigor as to admit of no discussion; and it was only by way of concession to the usages of an earlier time that mention of the Rule of St Basil was introduced [in papal privileges] for a few monasteries in southern Italy.[47]

Now, it is quite certain that Heloise and her companions from Argenteuil had already made monastic profession according to the Rule of St Benedict. Further, in asking Abælard to write a Rule more suitable for nuns, Heloise, in Letter VI of the correspondence, indicates that the Rule she considers less suitable is indeed the Rule of St Benedict, of universal obligation:

Nowadays women of the Latin west make profession of the one single Rule of the blessed Benedict, even as men do; although, just as it is clear that this Rule was written for men only, so also is it clear that it can be fulfilled by men only...[48]

Had our latter-day Benedict, Master Peter, been content to supplement the Rule of Benedict on particular points, or to treat of matters not specifically covered by the Rule, while retaining the Rule of Benedict as the central point of reference, there would have been no problem. However, with characteristic but nonetheless egregious *chutzpah*, Abælard chucks out the Rule of St Benedict and replaces it with the Rule of...Master Abælard. This willingness of Abælard to take his place alongside Basil and Benedict as author of a monastic rule is disarmingly naive. One wonders, for instance, how willing the Bishop of Troyes would have been to have within his jurisdiction a community of women who took vows according to the Rule of the Blessed Peter Abælard, twice condemned for heterodoxy, first at the Council of Soissons (1121), then at the Council of Sens (1140). Again, it is difficult to envisage a papal privilege conferred upon the Paraclete, and beginning with the necessary adaptation of the formula consecrated by curial practice: *secundum Deum et beati Petri Abælardi Regulam*. No, at the Paraclete as elsewhere, the Rule of Benedict necessarily retained its centrality as the norm of monastic observance, no matter how this norm may have been interpreted or misinterpreted in concrete practice. As for the need of supplementary monastic customary material, this was clearly recognized in chancery practice. This is why references to the Holy Rule are combined, in papal privileges, with references to observances of a more particular sort: *secundum Deum et Benedicti Regulam et normam Cluniacensis monasterii...*; or *secundum Deum et beati Benedicti Regulam et institutionem Cisterciensium fratrum...*[49] As Fr Dubois writes,

> no community of religious was able to invoke the protection of the Holy See unless it proved faithful to its ideal. In order to keep this ideal from being imaginary or confused, the papal bulls themselves defined that ideal by naming the Rule and the *institutio* which were supposed to be normative for the life of these religious. This distinction soon became standard, for it was in keeping with the legislation of the new Orders founded in the twelfth century, such as the Cistercians and Premonstratensians, who claimed to observe the traditional Rules strictly, but would have been unable to do so without completing them and making them more explicit with the help of carefully prepared juridical texts...[50]

It is precisely such a juridical text that we find in the brief text, *Institutiones nostrae*, which follows immediately upon Abælard's Rule in the Troyes ms 807. This brief directory, made up of less than two folios, is astonishingly rich, as I have suggested elsewhere by providing a detailed commentary on the text.[51] Let me here draw attention only to a few features of this remarkable document. It derives in part from Abælard, in part from the Cistercians, and in lesser part from the Rule of St Benedict.

The opening paragraph is pure Abælard. It states, in summary, that 'Our observance is based on the teaching of CHRIST, who preached and practiced POVERTY and HUMILITY. We also imitate the APOSTLES, who provide the pattern for our COMMON LIFE, with its corollaries of RENUNCIATION OF THE WORLD and COMMITMENT TO A LIFE OF PERFECTION.' To each of these practices preached and practised by Christ and the Apostles – poverty and humility, the common life, renunciation of the world, and commitment to a life of perfection – corresponds a chapter or paragraph of the directory. The poverty and humility of Christ provide the theological *locus* for chapter III (on clothing), chapter IV (on bedding), chapter V (on food and drink); and Christ's humility underlies chapter VI (on obedience). The common life of the apostles gives rise to chapter VII (on material resources and the distribution of goods). Renunciation of the world has its pendant in chapter VIII (on enclosure and separation from the world); and to commitment to a life of perfection corresponds chapter IX (on newcomer nuns), chapter X (on the stability of lay sisters), and chapter XI (on the monastic vocation). The directory concludes with a fairly detailed summary of the daily exercises of the community, from dawn to dusk.[52]

As for chapter II, this chapter is by way of providing the historical background, and of laying down the principle of uniformity of observance so dear to the Cistercians.[53] Since this paragraph presupposes the existence of more than a single house founded by the Paraclete, this would date our text to around 1147 at the earliest, since it was in this year or soon after that La Pommeraye (Yonne), the second foundation of the Paraclete, was established.[54] It would also date our text to a period within the abbacy of Heloise, since all the Paraclete foundations were made between 1142 and her death in 1164.

As for the sources of Chs. III–XI, the principal source is a set of abridged and thematically arranged *statuta* belonging to the Cistercian customary in the recension current probably between c. 1136/7–c. 1147.[55] This dependence on Cistercian legislation emerges from a line-by-line comparison of the texts. Even when the Paraclete text states the opposite of the Cistercian text, it is clear that our author – who can be only Heloise – had before her eyes the Cistercian text which she is contravening. Thus, in Ch. VII, 'Where necessary provisions come from', Heloise states realistically: 'It would be truly monastic for us to live off farming and our own work – if only we could do so.' She then candidly goes on to state that, in point of fact, they cannot do so, and uses this consideration to justify the admission of lay brothers and lay sisters and the acceptance of donations and revenues. The parallel Cistercian text states without qualification: that 'Provisioning for monks of our Order ought to come from manual labor, farming, and the raising of livestock.'[56] This Heloise accepts as an ideal, but an ideal unrealizable at the Paraclete.

The presence of Abælard, however, is frequently to be glimpsed behind a turn of phrase or a snippet borrowed from his Rule. It is to be seen, too, in some of the major orientations evident in this directory for Paraclete religious. The Paraclete work schedule, for instance, fits wonderfully well with the spiritual and intellectual pursuits described by Abælard in the concluding sections of his Rule. Conversely, it is hopelessly at odds with the 'work-mystique' of the White Monks.[57]

Important as it is to track down the sources which lie behind the texts of *Institutiones nostrae*, this is secondary to a reading of the text as a whole. It would be pleasant indeed to pass in review each of the details of life at the Paraclete as described by this extremely rich monastic directory. But this is the work of a detailed commentary.

One further remark about Heloise's authorship of the *Institutiones*. In a personal letter dated 21 October 1998 Dr Constant Mews, who has studied in careful detail the prose style of Heloise, reassures me: 'I can confirm that from a stylistic point of view [Heloise] did write those *Institutiones nostrae* too.'

In the meantime, the portrait of Heloise as it emerges from the *liturgica* and *monastica* of the Paraclete is impressive. With a sovereign liberty of spirit she was able to draw upon sources as disparate as Abælard and the Cistercians, and adapt them to her purpose within a harmonious unified whole.

While it would be unjust to separate Heloise from her husband and father in Christ, Abælard, it would also be unjust to consider her solely in her relationship with Abælard. What is more, there is another relationship which deserves further exploration, and that is the relationship between Heloise and her Paraclete community.

The twelfth century was a century rich in new forms of religious life. Some of these prospered and endured; some prospered for a while, then died. As for the Paraclete, its golden age lasted all too briefly. From the late thirteenth century onwards its story could be told under the general title of *Historia calamitatum*, with chapter after chapter filled with disaster after disaster. It is a story of fires, of the horrors of war, of the plague; the story of devastation during the long century of war with England, and of further devastation during the Wars of Religion; the sad story of the abandoning, around 1609, of all that had once made the Paraclete unique; and, worst of all, the story of the gradual descent of a once vibrant community into the morass of respectable mediocrity, until, at last, with the coming of the Revolution, the history of the abbey came to an end with scarcely a whimper.

Nevertheless, once there was a Camelot. With the beginning of a new millennium we look back to a Heloise, and find her ever meaningful for the life of the spirit and for our perception of the human experience; and surely, as one author has expressed it, 'we shall not be the last to do so'.[58]

Chapter 8

Communities of Reform in the Province of Reims: The Benedictine 'Chapter General' of 1131

E Rozanne Elder

In 1131 William of St Thierry, who four years later entered the Cistercian abbey of Signy and has become known as one of the 'four evangelists of Cîteaux', celebrated the feast of St Luke at Reims as a Benedictine abbot in the company of the pope, the king of France, 13 archbishops, 263 bishops[1] and a great throng of other abbots, monks and secular clerks of the province, which included Champagne, Hainault and Flanders. During the provincial synod, which continued at the royal city over the next fortnight, William would have seen Pope Innocent II marshal support in his contest against Anacletus II and perhaps glimpsed the king, Louis VI, and his queen. William may have had mixed feelings about the prohibition passed there forbidding monks and canons regular from studying canon law or medicine[2] – later one of his own interests. He may even have witnessed the coronation of the heir apparent to the throne of France, the future Louis VII.[3] These great events, however, do not here concern us. It was what William did before or, more likely, immediately after this provincial synod that interests us. At least 18 – perhaps 21 – of the Benedictine abbots in attendance at the feast met in a 'General Chapter'. Yet Benedictines did not at the time have general chapter meetings, which were a Cistercian innovation. After their discussions, the superiors of these autonomous abbeys agreed together to limit liturgical memorials, to slow the pace of the office and if necessary to shorten it, and to simplify the use of vestments; they also pledged to follow the Rule literally in certain matters liturgical and ascetic, to allow the temporary transfer of monks between houses and finally to meet at annual intervals in an abbatial chapter of review.[4]

The documents relative to this unprecedented Benedictine chapter are few but now, through the efforts of scholars, well known:

- The agreement of the abbots, dated 1131 at Reims, and signed by 18 abbots, with two erasures allowing the probable identification of an additional three abbots.[5]
- A letter chiding the abbots, written by Cardinal Matthew of Albano, papal legate and former Grand Prior of Cluny, a much longer document than the agreement.[6]
- The reply of the abbots to Cardinal Matthew, almost equal in length to his letter.[7]
- Bernard's letter 91 to a group of abbots who had invited him to another such chapter at Soissons, either in 1130 or 1132.[8]
- A later letter of Innocent II approving and authorizing annual general chapters,[9] and thoughtfully providing the initials of 10 of the abbots while lumping an indeterminate number of others together; probably datable to 1136/7.[10]

Background

Several of the 21 Benedictine abbeys had been reformed more than once in their long history.[11] Three had been founded in the reforming zeal of the eleventh century.[12] Monastic memories are long, and the abbots at Reims surely recognized the cyclical nature of monastic zeal. In 1131 moreover they, like many abbots, were struggling in the 'complex and tightly interrelated reforming world'[13] of their generation to reinstitutionalize the ancient monastic ideal in contemporary form. As one way of reinvigorating monastic observance, all the abbeys represented at the Reims 'Chapter' had adopted the customary of Cluny.[14]

General chapters were one of the novelties for which the White Monks of Cîteaux were criticized, along with their smugness, by the Benedictines in the years before the Reims synod.[15] Yet the fact that these same abbots at some point invited the Cistercian abbot of Clairvaux to meet with them – an invitation he declined with some vexation but with no lack of advice[16] – indicates that some of the organizers knew Bernard either personally or by reputation.

With the clarity of hindsight, it has generally been assumed by Dom Jean Mabillon and all those who have relied on him over the intervening centuries that, whoever the Benedictine movers and shakers may have been, the *éminence grise* behind the Black Monks' chapters was certainly the energetic, charismatic and manipulative Bernard of Clairvaux, and have concluded therefore that the Black Abbots most closely connected to him must have provided the impetus for the chapter.[17] These were

William, known to be Bernard's personal friend, and Geoffrey, who, at Bernard's recommendation, was consecrated in August 1131[18] to the bishopric of Châlons-sur-Marne, which the abbot of Cîteaux himself had refused.

But in October 1131 the abbot of Clairvaux was not yet a superstar; his public career was just beginning. Even so, few people who attended the Synod of Reims could have failed to know of him. They saw him at the side of Innocent II during the synod,[19] and heard his sermon – if indeed he preached it[20] – on the failings and probable fate of bishops who tolerated laxity.[21] His satirical *Apologia* and his public letter to his nephew Robert had been in contentious circulation for six years or more – since 1125 if Leclercq is right,[22] or even earlier if we accept Holdsworth's dating[23] – long enough to make the rounds in the relatively small area of Hainault and Champagne, where major trade roads led from Bar-sur-Aube to Lagny, Reims and Laon; particularly if the very abbot who had urged that the *Apologia* be written,[24] William of St Thierry, had seized the opportunity of sharing it with his confrères now assembled in chapter, as in fact Bernard had expected him to do.[25]

In the same region, Bernard had also attracted attention by his foundation of three daughter houses between 1118 and 1129,[26] and by his reforming activities after he had, in his words, been 'dragged'[27] to a synod at Arras in 1128. At least some of the Benedictine abbots of the province then in office may have met him there.[28] Bernard's eloquent endorsement of Innocent II against the claims of Anacletus had brought him further attention at the Council of Étampes in 1130, and his presence in the papal party as it wound its ceremonious way towards Reims in late September 1131 had brought him into contact with still more of the abbots.[29]

Bernard was also the abbot of the Cistercian proto-abbey closest to the province of Reims and had had 16 years' experience in the workings of general chapters. The autonomous Benedictine world realized, as did the inexorably centralizing papal and episcopal world and the courts of Champagne, that the White Monks had found their annual chapters very effective in maintaining discipline and fervor.

To ascribe responsibility glibly to Bernard, however, overlooks a medieval attribution by the *Gesta abbatum Lobbiensium*[30] of credit, or blame, for the chapters to Pope Innocent II and Archbishop Reginald of Reims. It ignores the zeal of such non-monastic reformers as Bartholomew de Vir, bishop of Laon, or Thibaud II, count of Champagne; and neglects other possible connections, such as the bibliophilia

displayed by a number of early twelfth-century abbots bent on amass-
ing libraries of the works of the Fathers of the Church and cloister.
Finally, it disregards the possibility that the Benedictine abbots had
planned their chapter well in advance of the Synod of Reims in 1131
after discussing among themselves possible avenues of renewal.

In addition to the documents directly relating to the 'Chapter of
Reims', other sources of information have gone largely as yet untapped.
By scouring the published classics of the medieval French church – the
Gallia Christiana, the *Annales OSB* and the *Histoire littéraire de la
France* – by ferreting out local historians' accounts in (usually nine-
teenth-century) journals, by combing the letters and narratives of con-
temporaries and by tracking down all surviving medieval charters from
or relating to these 21 abbeys, the picture can be expanded.

The all too often random survival of documentation on these reforming abbots may not allow us to answer all our questions, nor will
it provide an entirely accurate indication of the various abbots' relative
importance in the twelfth-century scheme of things. But the documents
do allow us to uncover some of the activities of these reforming abbots
in the years prior to 1131 and some of their connections with one another, with William of St Thierry, and with the Cistercian abbeys being
founded within the province of Reims.

Present Questions

What, or who, moved these heads of traditional, autonomous abbeys
to take the untraditional step of meeting together in chapter and of
proposing to continue to meet annually?[31] Was William of St Thierry
the driving force behind this untraditional General Chapter – as the
late Stanley Ceglar has recently and repeatedly argued?[32] Did William
collaborate with his former prior at St Nicaise, Reims, and his predecessor as abbot of St Thierry, Geoffrey Hartneck – as Dom Ursmer
Berlière hypothesized more than a century ago?[33] Or does credit belong
to Geoffrey alone – as Dom Jean Mabillon conjectured in the seven-
teenth century?

Is Adriaan Bredero right when he alleges that William of St Thierry
was less a Cistercian-inspired 'mole' in the Benedictine network than
an opportunistic would-be leader of 'an opposition in search of
renewal',[34] a disillusioned abbot who had persuaded Bernard to his
public and combative defense of monastic reform after Cluniac traditionalism had reasserted itself in the wake of a failed attempt at reform

in 1124 by the ill-fated former abbot Pons of Melgueil? Was the irregular chapter part of a 'struggle between the age-old tradition and the renewal under way', as Bredero maintains?[35]

Is the chapter attributable chiefly to the influence of Bernard and the Cistercians? What previous associations had the abbots had with Cistercians, particularly with the rising star of Clairvaux? Has Bernard by his Letter to Robert and the *Apologia* forever muddied the waters of Benedictine historiography by contrasting reform and tradition in terms of Cistercian and Cluniac, whereas everyone else, not least the abbots at Reims, saw it purely as an internal Benedictine matter?[36]

Does the documentary evidence support Father Ceglar's contention that William played the 'leading role' at the chapters of the Benedictine abbots in the fourth decade of the twelfth century? Who, besides William, attended the chapter at Reims? Which of them might have collaborated with William in planning it? Why did they, and not dozens of other abbots in the province,[37] band together? What previous connections had their houses had with one another and what similarities existed among them in the early twelfth century?

The Abbots

The aggregate overview of these abbots which emerges from these limited documents affords us some clues as to the motivation of these capitular pioneers who incurred the displeasure of the papal legate, that devoted son of Cluny who, when he became a prince of the church, 'relaxed nothing of the Offices, nothing of the chant, nothing of the protracted Cluniac psalmody'.[38]

In his 'Letter to the Chapter Abbots', Matthew of Albano refers to them as beacons of holiness in the bleak northern monastic landscape,[39] reformers who had 'repaired Christ's glorious sheepfolds'.[40] Early in his letter, he reminds them that their cloisters had only recently been notorious as 'shrines of pleasure [where] the hedgehog dwelt, screech owls lurked, sirens sang, [and] furry creatures abounded',[41] and that credit for the recovery of their good name was due entirely to the adoption of the ancient and venerable customs of Cluny,[42] the very customs which these same abbots are now 'refuting and abandoning'.[43]

Stung but unrepentant, the abbots sent off a sharp but politic reply, from Soissons in 1132 if Ceglar is correct, in which they tell us something more about themselves. Time spent in conversation 'is never useful',[44] but as abbots they are obliged by extreme necessity to treat with their employees and overseers 'frequently, morning and evening',[45] a need probably heightened by the preceding decade of harsh weather, famine and resultant epidemic illness in the area.[46] Compared with the likes of Cluny, their abbeys are small,[47] which is both a disadvantage and an advantage in that their small numbers do not permit the full Cluniac liturgical cycle, but does let them 'know the souls of our flocks'.[48] From this they realize that following the customs of Cluny, as they have done and continue to do,[49] has not produced the monastic reality which is more to be sought after than renown.[50] Which abbeys were these?

The Abbeys

If we supplement the eighteen signatures with Ceglar's addenda, we arrive at the following list of twenty-one abbeys:

In the diocese of Reims:
  St Thierry
In the diocese of Soissons:
  Chezy-sur-Marne; Orbais; and probably St Médard Soissons[51]
In the diocese of Laon:
  St John Laon; St Vincent Laon; St Nicolas-aux-Bois; St Michel-en-Thiérache
In the diocese of Noyon-Tournai, linked canonically until 1142 and episcopally until 1148:
  St Eloi Noyon; Homblières; Mount St Quentin; St Amand;
In the diocese of Cambrai:
  St Sépulcre Cambrai; Hautmont; Liessies; and perhaps Lobbes[52]
In the diocese of Arras, recently formed:[53]
  Hasnon; and perhaps Anchin[54]
In the diocese of Beauvais:
  St Lucien Beauvais
And outside the province of Reims, two *abbayes comitales* of Count Thibaud of Champagne:[55]
  Lagny (in the diocese of Paris) and Rebais (in the diocese of Meaux)

Abbots by Rank

The abbots who attended (or, in three cases, may have attended) the chapter at Reims can with two exceptions[56] – those of Homblières and

Orbais – be precisely identified. In addition to organizing abbots by diocese, one can also order them by rank, that is, by the number of years each had held abbatial office. Following this system, we arrive at the following 'classes:'

The Veteran Abbots – those who had been in office longer than ten years.

The Middlers – those who had taken office some time in 1123 or 1124.

The Freshman – those who became abbots after c. 1128.

The Latecomers – those who had only recently taken office by the time the synod was held.

The Alumni – abbots who had moved on to episcopal office or to glory.

The Veteran Abbots

The doyen among the abbots was Henry of Mount St Quentin, who had been in office at least by 1098 and would die two years after the synod, in 1133.

The other two veterans were roughly coeval, both in assuming and in laying down abbatial office. They are: William of St Thierry (c. 1120–35); and his schoolmate, perhaps brother, Simon of St Nicolas-aux-Bois (1120–34).

The Middlers

These six abbots seem all to have taken office in about 1124 and, with one exception, to have continued into the 1140s. They are: Gilbert of St Michel-en-Thierache (c. 1124–33);[57] Ralph II of Lagny-sur-Marne[58] (c. 1124–48); Wedric of Liessies (1124–47); Valbert of Hautmont (1124–37); Absalon of St Amand-en-Pevele (1124–45/6); and Thierry of St Eloi Noyon (1123–44).

The Freshmen

Some seven abbots[59] who had been in office two to four years by October 1131. They are, in order of office: Warin of Rebais (1127–33) – although there is some confusion about his tenure in office in 1131; Simon of Chezy-sur-Marne (1128–56); Drogo of St John Laon (1128–37); Serlo I of St Lucien Beauvais (1129–47); Parvin of St Sépulcre Cambrai (c. 1129–c. 1161); Anselm of St Vincent Laon (1129–45/6); and Hugh I of Hasnon (1129–40).

The Latecomers

These three abbots were new when the pope convoked the 1131 synod. The names of their abbeys do not appear on the list and have been supplied by scholars.[60] Granting the uncertainty of their participation and, even if they did attend, their effectiveness in swaying senior peers, they are: Goswin of Anchin (1130/1–65); Leonius of Lobbes (1131–7); and Odo of St Médard Soissons (1131–c. 1138).

The Alumni

Finally, we include three former abbots whose very recently elected successors attended (or likely attended) the Reims Synod. Of them, one had quite recently died; two had been promoted to bishoprics. Seifrid of Vincent Laon, died probably in the winter of 1128–9, and had been succeeded by Anselm. The other two attended the Synod of Reims in their new position as bishops: Alvisius, formerly abbot of Anchin, now bishop of Arras; and Geoffrey Hartneck, formerly abbot of St Médard Soissons and now bishop of Châlons-sur-Marne.

Space prevents a detailed consideration of every abbot; let us instead summarize those occasions on which two or more of them were together in the decade leading up to 1131.

1120 Simon and probably William left St Nicaise Reims to become abbots.

1121 At Soissons, in the presence of the papal legate,[61] Abbots Geoffrey of St Médard Soissons, William of St Thierry and Fulbert of St Sépulcre signed an accord settling a dispute between the abbeys of Mount St Quentin and St Nicolas-aux-Bois.[62]

Simon of St Nicolas-aux-Bois had several dealings, through Bishop Bartholomew of Laon, with Norbert of Xanten at the foundation of Prémontré, as did Seifrid of St Vincent Laon.[63]

At roughly the same time, if the dating of the Letters of St Bernard can be trusted,[64] Bernard of Clairvaux advised Simon to act prudently in introducing a stricter way of life to his resistant community 'in the order of Cluny'.[65]

1122 Simon and Seifrid at Laon witnessed a charter together.[66]

1123 Seems to have been uneventful, perhaps because harsh winter weather had produced economic hardship in the area.[67]

1124 Bishop Bartholomew of Laon put the declining abbey of St Martin

Laon into the care of Norbert of Prémontré, a transaction witnessed by Abbots Seifrid of St Vincent, Simon of St Nicolas-aux-Bois and Bernard of Clairvaux.[68]

At Reims that year, a donation was witnessed by Abbots Thierry of St Eloi, William of St Thierry and Geoffrey of St Médard, together with Gilbert, the prior of St Nicolas-aux-Bois who would soon be the abbot of St Michel-en-Thiérache.[69]

1125 Sometime between August and October, William of St Thierry and Geoffrey of St Médard were among those who witnessed the gift of several altars to the their home abbey, St Nicaise.[70]

1126 While the activities of several of the abbots can be documented, none of them appears together.

1127 William of St Thierry witnessed the foundation charter of the Cistercian abbey of Igny;[71] none of the other abbots in this study was present.

1128 A busy year for the abbots.

William convalesced at Clairvaux in January and February.[72]

On the Ides of May that year,[73] the reforming Bishop Bartholomew of Laon was at a synod at Arras attended by King Louis VI, *ceterisque illius diocesis episcopis et abbatibus*, among whom was Bernard of Clairvaux and, if Bernard's secretary Geoffrey of Auxerre can be believed, William of St Thierry.[74] During the synod, Bartholomew turned the ancient royal nunnery of St Mary and St John, close by the cathedral, into a house of monks and appointed as its first abbot Drogo, a monk of William's former abbey of St Nicaise.[75] Bernard later referred to the nunnery as 'a brothel of Venus',[76] and Matthew of Albano, who was also there, probably had it in mind when he referred to the reforming abbots generally as heads of notorious shrines of pleasure, now corrected by adherence to the venerable customs of Cluny.[77] Although most scholars take it for granted, we cannot be sure whether this newly appointed abbot was the same 'very dear' 'very holy and most observant'[78] Drogo who had stirred up a hornet's nest four years earlier by leaving St Nicaise for Pontigny, and caused Bernard to write four letters: one to advise abbot Jorannus of St Nicaise 'to control [his] outbursts of indignation',[79] one to advise Hugh of Pontigny to ride out the storm but to hang on to the monk,[80] one to praise Drogo for his action[81] and one to Cardinal Haimeric halfheartedly to disavow any responsibility in the matter.[82] Leclercq and Mabillon both thought Bernard deserved full credit or blame.[83] That Drogo could leave his own abbey without permission in 1124 and then be given the post of prior on his return, however, raises certain questions.

Among the witnesses of a confirmation issued by Bishop Simon of Noyon-Tournai were Geoffrey of St Médard, Thierry of St Eloi, along with his prior and his cellarer, Simon of St Nicolas-aux-Bois, Henry of Mount St Quentin, Alvisius of Anchin, William of St Thierry, and the papal legate and former Grand Prior of Cluny, Matthew of Albano.[84]

In July of 1128, Abbot Drogo, probably with Simon of St Nicolas-aux-Bois and possibly with Seifrid of St Vincent[85] witnessed another charter for Bartholomew of Laon.[86]

At Reims at the beginning of August, Henry of Mount St Quentin, Simon of St Nicolas-aux-Bois, Thierry of St Eloi, Alvisius, still abbot of Anchin, and Geoffrey, still abbot of St Médard, along with Matthew of Albano, witnessed the donation of an altar for the support of the monks of St Thierry, although William's name does not appear on it.[87]

According to Orderic Vitalis, writing in Normandy, Abbots Natalis of Rebais and Warin of St Evroul visited Bernard at Clairvaux in this year and were favorably impressed.[88] Orderic seems to have confused his abbots, however, for Natalis first appears in the documentary evidence c. 1133, whereas abbot Warin of Rebais is found in 1127 and again in 1133.

1129 There is no evidence of contact among the abbots. Simon of St Nicolas, having outraged his adopted community by handing over altars and therefore income to Bishop Alvisius of Arras, retired, only to be recalled by the monks, 'who preferred to do without the altars rather than their abbot'.[89]

1130 By the end of the Council of Étampes, held 'probably at the end of August or early in September',[90] the eloquence of the abbot of Clairvaux in defending the moral superiority of Innocent II over Anacletus and so his claim to the papal throne, had begun to make its mark on the Church of France.[91]

1131 Innocent II spent most of the year in France and Flanders,[92] where he had dealings with several of the abbeys, although evidence that the abbots were together at the same place at the same time is slight.

Between March 16 and 22, Innocent visited Lobbes, accompanied by Bernard of Clairvaux and eleven cardinals,[93] and a month later, April 26, while at Paris, issued to it a bull of protection. This was no doubt welcomed by the new abbot, Leonius, who had had to be escorted to his contentious new abbey by Alvisius, bishop of Arras and former abbot of Anchin. Leonius had begun his abbatial reign by re-moving the organ installed by a tenth-century predecessor and donat-ing it to the cathedral at Arras, and by suppressing the abbey school.[94]

Also in March Innocent visited Cambrai, where the abbots of St Sepulcre, Hautmont and Liessies could be expected to have turned out.[95] We know that the pope communicated with Abbot Gilbert of Hautmont[96] and on March 28 (5 kal April 1131) confirmed the pos-sessions of Liessies.[97]

Shortly after Easter, Innocent was at Beauvais,[98] where it is only reasonable to expect that Abbot Serlo of St Lucien would have turned out to greet him. On 16 April, Bartholomew of Laon let it be known that Abbot Anselm of St Vincent had lodged a complaint with the pope against Milisent, the widow of the infamous Thomas de Marle, and her son Enguerraud, who had, under threat of excommunica-tion, by then restored usurped lands to the abbey.[99]

On August 10,[100] Geoffrey of St Médard became bishop of Châlons-sur-Marne, and on September 30 the pope, then at Orléans, consecrated Odo as the new abbot of St Médard.[101]

And, not least, following an episcopal judgement at Laon, con-firmed by Innocent II who was then in the city, William and the monks of St Thierry were promised reparation by Hugh, Count of Roucy and his viscount, Levoldus, for damage caused at the village of Trigny belonging to St Thierry.[102]

Conclusions

1128 and 1131 were the two years which best provided opportunities for Benedictine abbots with ideas of reform to talk with one another, to talk with the abbot of Clairvaux and to begin thinking about ways in which they could, at their next plenary opportunity, assemble in a mini-General Chapter and take action.

Who were the abbots most conspicuously together in the decade be-fore the chapter at Reims?

William of St Thierry, Simon of St Nicolas-aux-Bois, Seifroid of St Vincent (who died before 1131), Geoffrey of St Médard, Gilbert of St Michel-en-Thiérache (Simon's former prior) and, after 1128, Drogo of St John Laon.

Were they the senior abbots?

Three were senior abbots and two, Drogo and Gilbert, had been priors before becoming abbots.

Were they abbots of monasteries of the same diocese?

No, but with the exception of William (Reims) and Geoffrey (Soissons), they all lived in Laon under Bartholomew de Vir, who had appointed four of them: Simon of St Nicolas-aux-Bois, Drogo of St John, Gilbert of St Michel and Anselm of St Vincent; and recommended two others (Thierry of St Eloi and Absalon of St Amand) to his kinsman by marriage, Simon of Noyon.[103]

Did they have Cistercian – specifically Bernardine – contacts?

Yes, most of them:

- William had known Bernard perhaps since 1119.
- Simon carried on an extensive correspondence with him.
- Geoffrey of St Médard had been asked by Bernard to placate the abbot of Anchin after one of his monks went to Clairvaux[104] and in 1131 Bernard recommended him for the see of Châlons-sur-Marne.[105]
- In July 1121 Gilbert of Saint Michel exchanged land to allow the foundation of the Cistercian abbey of Foigny[106] and can be expected to have attended the dedication of the Church by its Father Abbot, Bernard, on November 11, 1124.[107]
- Drogo of St Jean was very likely the same monk who had left St Nicaise for Pontigny[108] although the letter he received from Bernard suggests that the latter knew him only by reputation.[109]

What else, in addition to this, did these abbots have in common? William, Simon, Geoffrey and Drogo are all known to have entered monastic life at the abbey of St Nicaise Reims – as almost certainly had Gilbert, Simon's reforming prior at an abbey which vigorously resisted reform.[110] Of the abbots at the Chapter of Reims, three others had also been monks of St Nicolas-aux-Bois: Thierry of St Eloi, Absalon of St Amand and Ralph of Lagny.[111] From the fact that they were chosen to introduce reform elsewhere from within a community which was resisting its own abbot's reforms, we may suspect that they too may have been trained at St Nicaise.[112]

We are drawn therefore to ask why the abbot of St Nicaise himself was conspicuously absent from the Reims Chapter. That Abbot Jorannus had sympathies with the 'new monasticism' is attested to by his decision in 1138 to enter the Charterhouse of Mont Dieu. That he knew the Cistercians is clearly indicated by Bernard, who referred to him as *'familiarissimus nobis abbas'*[113] and St Nicaise as *'notissimum monasterium'*.[114]

The answer provides what I think is the most important clue to the motivation of the abbots who did attend. The abbots at the Reims chapter all came from houses which followed the Customary of Cluny. St Nicaise followed the Customary of La Chaise Dieu in the Auvergue.[115]

The abbots who seem to have been most often together and therefore able to plan the unprecedented chapters of Black Monks had probably all been formed in the Casadean tradition and had subsequently become abbots of houses which followed the more demanding liturgical customary of Cluny. Cistercian liturgical simplicity quite aside, they had been obliged to adjust to a more elaborate and time-consuming ritual than they had originally known as novices and young monks and, in trying to balance the demands of life in a small community with the hardships wrought by hard times and the demands of charity, it would have been only natural for them to think of trimming what seemed to them overelaborate liturgy. This may lie behind Bernard's explicit reference in his letter to Simon to the difficulties of having taken responsibility for a monastery 'in the Order of Cluny'.[116]

In sum, the documentary evidence seems to me to support Ceglar's hypothesis that the chapter at Reims was the first, not the second, such meeting, and further to suggest that several of the abbots, all of them from the tradition of St Nicaise, had at various times in the preceding decade – principally in 1128 – discussed how best to achieve a strict but traditionally Benedictine monastic routine. It would appear that they seized the opportunity the papal synod provided to enlarge their circle and hold a first meeting and that, having heard of the Cistercian confederation and seen the abbot of Clairvaux over the years and probably after having talked with him at Reims, they then invited Bernard, the closest Cistercian abbot with experience of the Cistercian system of General Chapters, to join them at a second General Chapter in 1132.

Chapter 9

When Jesus Did the Dishes: The Transformation of Late Medieval Spirituality

Brian Patrick McGuire

Any understanding of the meaning of Western civilization relies to a great extent, even in these postmodern times, on interpretations of the Middle Ages. Here, most historians propose a model built on three different periods: the primitive age, the age of growth and the age of decline.[1] The primitive age lasts from the fall of the Western Roman Empire until the eleventh century. Then comes the age of growth, from about 1050 to 1250 or 1300, when anything seemed possible and medieval institutions from monarchy to monasticism took on new and more durable forms. Finally follows the age of decline, the fourteenth and fifteenth centuries, leading to the Reformation and its rejection of the central factor binding together medieval civilization, the universal Christian Church.

A continuing debate about the place of the Italian Renaissance in this scheme makes it less satisfactory when we deal with Southern rather than Northern Europe. Was the Renaissance a part of the Middle Ages, or was it a new period in Western history?[2] However the historian replies, he or she usually concludes that at some point in the last medieval centuries, something went wrong with the unified Latin culture that the Christian Church once offered.[3]

The twentieth century's most influential interpretation of the breakup of the medieval synthesis appeared in 1919, with Johan Huizinga's *The Waning of the Middle Ages*.[4] Huizinga's book, which has recently been retranslated into English,[5] continues to fascinate because of its magisterial overview and magnificent prose. But Huizinga's treatment, like so many others of this period, tends to emphasize the breakup of culture and its inability to renew the content of institutions and beliefs.

In what follows here I will be looking at the cult of the saints, in particular the cult of St Joseph as a member of the Holy Family, in order to respond to Huizinga's view of decadence and decline in the later Middle Ages. This approach might seem to be narrow and specialized, but my contention is that by understanding how saints were visualized, it is possible to reach a fuller understanding of how medieval people expressed their own needs and desires.[6] The projection of feelings on a saint provides an indication of what men and women sought in their own lives. My thesis will be that a new cult of St Joseph contributed to a renewal of medieval spirituality in terms of a greater awareness of what can be called affective Christian masculinity.[7]

I will concentrate on one central theological figure, the chancellor of the University of Paris, Jean Gerson (1363–1429). Gerson's own views and experience might seem to be too individual to represent the development of an entire culture, but Gerson deserves attention not only because he was centrally placed in the Church but also because in his life and writings he proposed new forms of spiritual expression. In Gerson's efforts to commemorate St Joseph, a new spiritual orientation began which continued and grew after the chancellor's death. In the early 1480s the papacy responded to a growing interest in Joseph and included him in its calendar of saints.[8]

Huizinga did not like what was happening in this respect. He was aware of Gerson's attention to St Joseph and took Gerson to task for what he thought was excessive interest in the details of Joseph's life:

> ... he [Gerson] himself becomes guilty of a curiosity which to us seems out of place and deplorable. Gerson was the great promoter of the adoration of St Joseph. His veneration for this saint makes him desirous of learning all that concerns him. He routs out all particulars of the married life of Joseph: his continence, his age, the way in which he learned of the Virgin's pregnancy.[9]

Huizinga could not understand why Gerson wanted to know about Joseph's inner emotional life, and he found it a waste of time to speculate in this manner. There was something of the Calvinist iconoclast in Huizinga, who had difficulty in accepting the use of symbols and images in medieval religion. For him these symbols had multiplied far beyond necessity and had become overdeveloped. His moralizing response to religious phenomena makes Huizinga a rather narrow, even if brilliant, participant in a debate about the worth of medieval spirituality. This debate started with the Reformation itself and still continues in our postmodern world.

Instead of judging the validity or acceptability of late medieval

perceptions of sainthood and spirituality, I want to understand them
better. Here I find myself in good company with the group of scholars
who a few years ago looked at the late medieval cult of St Anne, the
mother of the Virgin.[10] They concluded that Anne became available and
important for many different groups in society and that her life and
story were interpreted in new ways. In speaking of the symbolic meaning of sainthood, one must be aware, as these scholars have been, of the
polyvalence of symbols: saints functioned in church and society not as
eternal figures but as human beings whose importance or relevance to
individual persons or social groups could change and grow.

In looking at new cults or attachments to saints such as Anne or
Joseph, I find a way of understanding the meaning of late medieval
spirituality. This is an easy and therefore dangerous word, one that
our medieval ancestors themselves only used in a very narrow context
and which has only recently appeared in European languages.[11] Spirituality is not a phenomenon that exists in itself. It needs to be seen in the
context of living individuals and institutions and is the sum of their
religious practices and imaginations. Spirituality is rarely systematic or
predictable: it is a whole that is greater than the sum of its parts, the
fashioning of behavior and the expression of beliefs which are not always articulated but are still present in a person or a social group.

St Joseph and his Family

Before I take a look at Gerson and his reformulation of the meaning of
St Joseph and his family, it is necessary to start with the view of Joseph
that predominated in the medieval world right into the fifteenth century. If we turn to the obvious place for the stories of the saints that
were preached to the people in the Latin West, the late thirteenth-
century *Legenda Aurea* by Jacob of Voragine, there is no day of the
year dedicated to the sainthood of Joseph.[12] In spite of the fact that a
few churches and even dioceses did have commemorations for him, the
Roman breviary did not include a feast day for St Joseph before the
1480s.[13] Joseph is visible in the *Legenda Aurea* only in terms of his
secondary role in the early life of Christ. Here the stories found in the
first two chapters of Matthew and Luke are repeated, with a few apocryphal additions, but Joseph does not take on any prominence.[14]

Elsewhere in medieval art and literature Joseph does not receive any
flattering attention. Among medieval mystery plays there is one dedicated to Joseph.[15] Here he is the fool who does not understand the

workings of the Incarnation and has to be convinced by miracles that Mary really is the virgin she is said to be. Before he is convinced, Joseph turns to the audience and complains that people will think he is a cuckold: 'Alas, alas! My name is shent [disgraced]/ All men may me now dyspyse/ And seyn "Old cokwold" ...'[16] Joseph is depicted as an aged fool who does not understand that God can do anything and that Mary would never have allowed herself to break her vow of virginity. She has to be patient with Joseph and wait until he finally can see the light.

Long before fifteenth-century miracle plays, Romanesque art presented a picture of Joseph as a tired old man, whose role at the Nativity consisted in being off by himself and putting his hand up to his chin, to support his head while he started to fall asleep.[17] Joseph is depicted in terms of his fatigue after a long journey. He does not seem able to rejoice in the birth of Christ, and so it is implied that he does not grasp the significance of what has happened. In Gothic wall paintings in fifteenth-century Denmark this theme is repeated but is sometimes varied with the depiction of a more useful Joseph. He is seen off to the side in the Nativity scene, making soup for Mary.[18] But he is still a tired old man, resigned to the long journey ahead that cannot be avoided.

In such scenes, Joseph plays only a bit part in the history of the Redemption. If he is not a cuckold, he is at best a rather secondary participant in the greatest story ever told. The viewer was perhaps expected to smile at this man, so close to the main event of history and yet so distant.

Behind the representation of Joseph in medieval art and literature there was a debate going back to Late Antiquity not so much about the person of Joseph as concerning his status as Mary's spouse. The church father Augustine had posed the question whether the relationship between Joseph and Mary was a genuine marriage.[19] Since Mary had to remain a virgin, the relationship could not be consummated. At one point in his writings, Augustine insisted that a permanent bond between the two sexes based on consent and love is a marriage. Elsewhere, however, he replied to heretics such as the Manichaeans, who looked upon sexual intercourse as impure, by insisting on the necessary and rightful place of sex in marriage.

Augustine's concern with the relationship between Joseph and Mary is paralleled in the writings of his contemporary, Jerome, who in attacking an opponent on the worth of marriage emphasized the greater value of virginity.[20] Thus for Jerome, Joseph and Mary had a marriage that was better than a marriage precisely because there was no sexual intercourse.

The question of the relationship between Joseph and Mary appeared again in the twelfth century, when canon lawyers generally insisted on the necessity of intercourse to seal the bond of marriage, while theologians placed emphasis on mutual consent. For Peter Lombard the marriage of Joseph and Mary was genuine and did not require intercourse.[21] Joseph's care and concern for Jesus as his own child made Joseph not only the husband of Mary but also the father of Jesus, at least in earthly terms, for he was the one who together with Mary brought up the child.

These debates about the marriage of Joseph and Mary may seem rather theoretical, the stuff of good theological discussion but not very important for the lives of ordinary people. But theological ambiguity about the status of Joseph as the husband of Mary and the father of Jesus is directly reflected in the lack of a popular or widespread cult of St Joseph. He remained a shadowy figure, hardly noticed except when the status of the Virgin Mary was being discussed. As late as the thirteenth century, when the scholastics were making their syntheses and female visionaries were speaking to Christ and Mary, Joseph seems almost absent from the life of the Christian Church.[22] In Byzantium he apparently had a different status, and there his cult had been continuous from the early centuries.[23] But in the warrior society of the West, with its celibate clerics who tended to identify with the Virgin Mary and all that she could give them, the figure of Joseph did not normally invite great admiration in the popular or learned imaginations. No warrior or martyr, Joseph remained a silent witness to the Incarnation. His resigned manner and his great age made him too subdued for a society that sought dramatic supernatural intervention to resolve its ills and traumas.

Jean Gerson and the Renewal of Theological Discourse

For the fourteen-year-old Jean, oldest son of a wheelwright in a hamlet of the Ardennes, the University of Paris in the year 1377 was hardly the place to come for a greater appreciation of the saints, not to mention the obscure Joseph.[24] Gerson obtained a scholarship at the prestigious College of Navarre, worked hard, isolated himself and soon made a name by preaching at the royal court. He was well connected: his friend Pierre d'Ailly became in the 1380s a reform-oriented chancellor of the university and saw to it that when he left the post in 1395 Gerson succeeded him. The brilliant young theologian suffered from a lack of funds in an office that no longer could allow the personal payments for services that had supported earlier chancellors. Surrounded by rich aristocratic students and courtiers, Gerson found himself so much in need of money that he had to take on boarders in his lodgings. At the same time he found his political obligations in the chancellorship so pressing that he felt he was losing contact with his own spiritual life. By the end of the 1390s he was questioning his own motives and the very meaning of his brilliant career.

We know about Gerson's doubts from letters he wrote to his colleagues in Paris. In 1399–1400 Gerson went into a self-imposed exile and tried to concentrate on his duties at the collegiate church of St Donatian at Bruges. Here he would have preferred to remain for good, but his fellow canons were not interested in Gerson's reforming plans and made him realize that Paris, with all its drawbacks, was perhaps not the worst place in the world for a priest and intellectual in the service of the Christian Church. When Gerson returned to Paris in the autumn of 1400, he was able to resume his teaching and administrative duties with new energy, as we can see from a flood of writings in both French and Latin that poured from his pen.[25] The year of exile had contributed to his own sense of who he was: a theologian. In an almost old-fashioned manner going back to the early thirteenth century, Gerson believed that the duty of the professor was to prepare his students not only to discuss texts but also to contribute to the pastoral life of the Church.

Theological discourse in the schools was a point of departure for Gerson's own involvement in what he called the reformation of the Church (reformatio ecclesiae). If he is at all known today, it is usually in connection with his tireless work to end the papal schism.[26] Because he ended up siding with those who would have limited papal power, Gerson's orthodoxy has been questioned.[27] Certainly he envisioned a church less dominated by the papacy. But Gerson's central concern was not the limitation of papal power. He sought a much more far-reaching renewal of Christian life, as can be seen from the sermons he preached to the people in a local Paris church and from his lectures in the winter of 1401 on mystical theology in its practical and speculative aspects.

During these busy years Gerson showed no sign of any special devotion to St Joseph. The first manifestations of his attention to the saint came after Gerson emerged from one of the most traumatic episodes of his life, the so-called 'revolt of the Cabochiens', the butchers of Paris. These important tradesmen allied with the Duke of Burgundy against the supporters of the mad King Charles VI's brother, the Duke of

Orléans, who had been murdered in 1407. In 1413 important university figures who had 'sided with the royal party were hunted down. Gerson's rooms in the cloister of Notre Dame cathedral were plundered, and he had to hide in the vaults of the great church for several weeks.[28] When he emerged and the revolt was suppressed, Gerson apparently found the explanation for his salvation in the protection provided not only by the Virgin Mary to whom the cathedral was dedicated, but also by her husband, St Joseph. As far as Gerson was concerned, Mary and Joseph had saved him from the mob, and now it was time to do something in order better to celebrate the bond between the couple.

An early indication of Gerson's attitude is to be found in a letter dated November 23, 1413 and addressed to the Duc de Berry, the king's uncle and one of the most influential people in the kingdom. Here Gerson argued for a yearly commemoration of the 'holy and sacred marriage' of Mary and Joseph, to be held on the Saturday of Ember Week before Christmas. Gerson emphasized the favors that Mary had done for the needs of the Duke and the miracles she had performed for many who had gone to her in need. He did not mention his own situation, but he went on to emphasize the special status of Joseph, 'who was the governor of the infant Jesus, often carried him, often kissed him…in a manner more familiar than for any other man'.[29]

At the end of the letter Gerson named some of the immediate sources for his devotion to St Joseph: his teacher Pierre d'Ailly and the Celestine monk Pierre Bourgignon. St Joseph had been a special patron for these men, who 'often experienced his aid in their own needs and those of others, by way of miracle'.[30] Finally Gerson mentioned Master Henry Chiquot, former master in theology of Paris, who was now at the church of Chartres, where he already had begun this annual commemoration for St Joseph.[31]

Gerson's letter has long been known and is part of his efforts beginning in mid-1413 to arrange a yearly commemorative feast for the Marriage of the Virgin and Joseph.[32] What has not been sufficiently noticed, however, is the kind of language Gerson used, emphasizing the tenderness of the bonds between Joseph and Jesus. In a Latin letter, already written on 17 August and addressed to all churches in the world, Gerson had dealt with the old question about the definition of the marriage of Mary and Joseph.[33] Now writing in French and addressing a lay audience, Gerson ignored any theological questions and assumed the bond to have been a genuine marriage. At the same time he did not feel called upon to explain in what way Joseph was the father of Jesus. It was sufficient for him to point out that Jesus was 'born of the sacred marriage of Our Lady and St Joseph and nourished' by them.[34]

The mentions of Pierre d'Ailly and other significant theological figures indicates that Gerson was by no means alone in his attention to St Joseph as the husband of Mary and the father of Jesus. Outside Paris, other contemporary figures such as St Bernardino of Siena (d. 1444) were also pushing for greater devotion to St Joseph and for a feast day for him.[35] But, once convinced of the importance of St Joseph in the history of salvation and the life of the Church, Gerson began a veritable campaign that used all his talents and influence. The 'humble chaplain and orator Jean Gerson, unworthy chancellor of Paris', as he signed his letter to the Duc de Berry, began to expand his vision of St Joseph and to use his influence to spread devotion to the saint.

A few months before he wrote this letter, Gerson had already expressed his interest in the cult of St Joseph in his treatise, *Considérations sur Saint Joseph*.[36] Here Gerson reviewed the evidence for the assertions that he was able to make in November in his letter to the Duc de Berry. Joseph was to be seen as a virgin and as the husband of Mary and thus as the father of her son Jesus. Joseph did everything that a father could be expected to do for a son: 'Joseph fed him, carried him, brought him into Egypt...taught him and disciplined him according to parental authority. Briefly he carried out all the care that a good and loyal and wise father can and should show to his true son.'[37] Such descriptions of paternal care are, however, rare in this list of theological considerations. Gerson's main concern was to show that Joseph and Mary engaged in a real marriage. The theological discussions of Late Antiquity and the twelfth century still concerned him, and he wanted once and for all to answer them.

At the same time, however, Gerson felt obliged to deal with contemporary and popular views of Joseph. Painters, he surmised, had shown Joseph as an old man in order to make the chastity of his bond with Mary more believable.[38] They did not want to support those heretics who formerly had doubted the fact of virginity. But Joseph was not an old man when he married Mary, Gerson insisted: old age does not begin until fifty, and Joseph was under that age.[39]

Again and again Gerson had to return to the meaning of true marriage and to point out that it is based not on intercourse but on consent. There should be no question of the marriage arrangement as being difficult or dangerous for Joseph. Mary pleased Joseph, 'without any base thought or evil concupiscence' on his part. This bond was expressed 'in all honesty' and not because their rooms were 'separate and secret' from each other![40]

It is not necessary to go into great detail with the contents of Gerson's *Considérations*, but his various arguments recalling a thousand years of discussion concerning the status of the marriage of Mary and Joseph are a landmark in the history of theology. Here, just as in his work on mysticism written for his sisters, *La Montaigne de contemplation*, Gerson took a debate that had formerly been reserved for Latin-trained scholastics and made it available for those who only read the vernacular. Gerson was determined to make theological questions accessible for ordinary people and to provide answers that such people could apply to their own spiritual lives. He concentrated on questions of virginity, chastity and marriage, but in so doing prepared his conclusion: that the time for theological debate was over and now it was right to provide a special feast to commemorate this marriage. As part of this commemoration, the bond between Joseph and his son Jesus could be remembered in a more intimate and vivid manner. The man who had touched and fondled Jesus was a man to be celebrated.

Gerson's *Josephina*: A New Spiritual Hero

Gerson's next step in his new devotion to St Joseph was to write a poem in hexameter of 3,000 lines to celebrate the story of the Holy Family as seen through the eyes of St Joseph. The *Josephina* is one of the least known of Gerson's works, for its Latin is difficult and at times obscure.[41] There is some distance from the clear French text of the *Considérations* to the abstruse theological meandering of the *Josephina*. Such a procedure was standard for Gerson, however: he wrote both for learned and for lay audiences. He tried to convince both of them that it was necessary to rethink the meaning of God's revelation and presence in human life.

The *Josephina* may have been begun in 1414 while Gerson was still resident in Paris, but most of it was probably written while he was attending the Council of Constance, where he arrived on February 21, 1415. It is perhaps difficult to imagine how he would have time, amid all the deliberations and uncertainties of the Council, to dedicate himself to a poem whose precise language and form would have required some of the best hours of his day. But Gerson had always been a tireless worker and someone who needed to convey his thoughts in writing. Thus it is not surprising that he could have created such a poem at this time, and its learned content reflects the erudite atmosphere in which Gerson lived at Constance. Here he did not divide up his worlds between Latin and vernacular: now he thought and wrote and spoke in the language of the universal Church.

Gerson had in youth been well trained in classical texts, and his early writings reflect this erudition.[42] Later in life he never forgot his authors, and in writing his poem to St Joseph in epic form, like a new *Aeneid*, Gerson bore witness to the new French humanism of which he was so important a part. Instead of starting at the beginning of the Gospel narrative about the Annunciation, Gerson used his imagination to provide a point of departure that would take hold of his listeners or readers: the dramatic action of the Flight into Egypt. Gerson then advanced according to what he called *distinctiones*, scholastic divisions of argument that each in themselves provided a separate picture of the life and work of Joseph in the context of the drama of the Incarnation and Redemption. Each distinction can be taken on its own as an independent portrayal of the life of Joseph, but each one also contributes to the whole epic story of the man whom Gerson called his hero.

We see Joseph in this role from the opening of the first distinction, where Gerson describes his and Mary's reaction to Joseph's dream where an angel tells him to take his family and flee into Egypt. Here Mary's initial reaction is one of near-despair. She asks how they can cope and questions the promises given her by the angel Gabriel. But Joseph is strong and tells her not to weep: '*Flendi, carissima, non est/Hora modo.*'[43] He knows that God's command is to be obeyed. The reaction of the infant, which wakes and chuckles with laughter, seems to confirm Joseph's confidence.

Gerson's description of this scene is precise and powerful: God has become a fugitive, he says; the all-powerful God lets himself be pursued by a man: '*Deus est fugitivus et advena.*'[44] In considering this example, we can recognize that we are pilgrims in his care.[45] Gerson varies narrative with commentary, sometimes just reflecting on the scene he has described, sometimes asking theological questions. The strength of the poem lies in this combination of everyday scenes from the life of a family and theological considerations. On the first evening of the flight, Joseph finds a fitting house in a village where they can stay. He takes the infant lovingly into his arms. A fire is made to warm them. They eat and retire to bed, until the infant 'sleeps whose heart always keeps watch'.[46] This scene is contrasted with the habitats of those who seek pomp and splendor. This modest little house was enough for the Son of God and so should put the ambitious to shame.

Gerson compared his name with the Hebrew word for pilgrim and envisioned himself in the role of pilgrim for God.[47] Already at the Council of Constance he may have known that he would not be able to return to Paris and would remain a pilgrim for the rest of his life. Thus Gerson in the *Josephina* was to a certain extent describing his own situation: he too had embarked on his flight from his home and was seeking an Egypt where he could dwell for the time being before he would be able to return to his own country. This life was one of hardship, and so he could think of what Mary and Joseph experienced: hunger, thirst, heat and cold ('*quotiens sitis, algor et ardor/ Atque fames potuit inopes vexare viantes*'[48]).

At the same time, however, Gerson visualized Mary and Joseph as having had time and energy to discuss the meaning of their actions. The first distinction includes a long section in which the two travelers are supposed to have considered the meaning of fortune in human life as compared to the fact of faith, hope and charity. They complain that most people only consider what they see around them: 'they do not wish to perceive heavenly things through the light of faith'. It is necessary to take into account the role of grace in human life and its victory over nature.[49]

Gerson might seem to have forgotten his protagonists in the midst of such considerations. But he ends the discussion by making the point that such 'learned speech makes the road easier and removes fatigue' ('*Doctus sermo viae relevat fallitque laborem*').[50] Again Gerson may have been thinking of his own situation and recalling how good conversation about theological questions could relieve the tedium of the road from Paris to Constance. He projected his own experience back on that of Mary and Joseph: 'Many things on these subjects were reviewed on other days,' he suggested ('*Plurima sunt super his aliis repetenda diebus*').[51] In the given situation, Mary is seen in the role of Joseph's teacher: '*Qualia Virgo virum potuit docuisse viando.*' Mary and Joseph talk together like two university professors, but two professors who are devoted to each other and aware of the meaning of their exile.

The second distinction returns to the narrative. Arriving in an Egypt whose inhabitants are known for their sexual license, Joseph is afraid that Mary will not be safe from attack. He asks Mary to tell everyone that she is his daughter. The Egyptians find her to be exceedingly beautiful and attractive.[52] Joseph explains in a kind of speech to the people of Memphis that he and his daughter had to flee with her son after a catastrophe in their home country. The Egyptian king hears of the family and invites them to his palace. Here Joseph tells their story without ever lying about their identity: they are of royal stock but came on hard times. They had to flee the ferocious Herod, and the child's father ordered Joseph to protect him. They ask for asylum and assure the king that they have every intention of working for their bread and of not being a burden to anyone: 'Nulli nos erimus oneri.'[53]

The king is won over and orders that the family be given a house. Both king and people treat them well and show them hospitality. Now that the worst dangers are over, Gerson describes the Holy Family in all its domesticity: Mary nurses the infant and bathes it; it then falls asleep. She and Joseph thank God for protecting them. Gerson completes this section by writing of how we are all pilgrims and should remember the example of Jesus, Mary and Joseph:

> Quisquis es ad cives patriae coelesis anhelans
> Sic age, sic retinens meditare quod advena tu sis.
> Exemplum tibi sint Christus, Joseph atque Maria.[54]

Now Gerson was ready to describe the everyday life of Mary and Joseph in Egypt. Just as with his narrative concerning their scholastic discussion on the road, Gerson used his imagination in order to provide material for pious meditation. I have not found specific literary models on which he could draw. In using his own inner resources, Gerson revealed what mattered to him: hard work, tenderness, cooperation, and hope for a better future:

> Jesus grew and passed the age of two
> His mother made for him a garment
> Now he could stand shakily and speak
> He stammered with imperfect speech
> Which seemed so sweet to both parents.
> He rushes into their embrace when called
> Lifting his little arms he wants to hang on the necks of his parents.
> With tender embrace to give chaste kisses,
> He places his hand in yours, Mary and Joseph.
> And with his uneven step, he follows you all over the house.
> Whatever he sees he marvels at, asking questions so he can know all.
> Perhaps sometimes he interrupts your work.

> Containers, strainer, baskets, threshing instruments and small
>   hatchets
> He handles and tries to carry about.[55]

This remarkable passage is Gerson's visualization of Jesus the two-year-old at home with his parents.[56] Such a description of the child Jesus provides ample warning that the facile conclusions of Philippe Ariès about medieval views on childhood are based on lack of knowledge. Medieval people like Gerson, even if they did not themselves have children, visualized childhood as a special, unique age. Children were not little adults but were adorable creatures when they were in a loving environment.

It is not my purpose here, however, to discuss perceptions of childhood. What matters for our concern is that Gerson was willing to spend intellectual energy on imagining the content of daily life for the Holy Family. The parents worked at their respective jobs, Joseph the carpenter and Mary the weaver. Gerson was perhaps remembering from his own childhood. He knew that such attention might invite a smile from his learned audience, and he dealt directly with its possible objection that such childhood concerns were unimportant: 'Someone might say here that to talk about childish things is laughable. We admit that our concern is childhood, but God as a child.'[57] There is no better way to soften hard hearts than to let faith see God acting as a child. He wants us to act in the same way, to return to the innocence of childhood.

This portrait of Mary and Joseph hard at work with the infant at their feet is not purely idyllic. Gerson imagined how the child, perhaps a few years later, might have been taunted by one of his playmates for his dubious background. Out of 'a malignant heart', this child called Jesus a 'bloody foreigner' ('*miser advena quod sis*') whose father and fatherland were not known.[58] The child hit Jesus and he came weeping to his mother. She kissed him, dried his tears, and listened to his story. 'Is Joseph not my father? Is this not our own country?' the child could have asked: '*Ergo Josephne pater mihi? Nonne haec patria nobis?*'

Mary's response here is long and detailed. She told Jesus of the prophecies about his coming and the sufferings he had to endure. She explained how humankind was made in God's image but had fallen. Death had come into the world, and Herod's killing of the innocents is described as a manifestation of this evil.[59] Now redemption from sin would come, but: 'Alas, your death will be the price, most sacred son,' Mary wept and sobbed.

Gerson did not allow into his story the type of apocryphal tales about the childhood of Christ that imagined how the boy performed miracles and impressed his playmates. His vision of Jesus is that of a real human child who had to find out who he was, both the hard way through the assaults of playmates, and the gentle way through the teaching of his parents. Gerson's description of how the Christ child learned shows how a medieval theologian perceived the history of the Incarnation in terms of the growth and development of a human being. When Jesus learns of his fate, his reactions are varied: 'he hopes, fears, rejoices, is sorrowful'.[60] Gerson, ever aware of the simultaneous divinity and humanity of Christ, made a Jesus who really was a child and who had to come to terms with an identity involving both joy and sorrow. Gerson describes eloquently the child's tears and those of his mother when they face what is to come. But Gerson also adds Joseph's reaction, imagining that he just then returned from work and 'sensed when he entered the tears of both of them' ('*Sensit in ingressu primo lacrimas utriusque*').[61] Realizing that his son now knows what will happen to him, Joseph too 'weeps with those who weep'. This is a Pauline phrase, linking Gerson's narrative to the language of salvation and reminding his audience how it is necessary to 'weep with those who weep' in order to 'rejoice with those who rejoice'.[62]

Gerson uses such linguistic devices to discipline his mode of expression and never descends into sentimentality. At this point Gerson has Joseph continue Mary's narrative in order to place Jesus's story in the context of the history of Israel's people. Joseph tells the story of his namesake, the patriarch, and how he also had once come to Egypt.[63] The first Joseph gained great influence by being able to interpret the dreams of Pharaoh. Now the time was coming when the Egyptians no longer would worship their idols but the true God.[64]

But it was time for the Holy Family to leave their exile and return to Israel. Gerson describes the tenderness of the departure scene, with tears, embraces and words of parting. Jesus was now seven years old. Gerson describes his own desire to see the Holy Family on the road and to be able to speak with them.[65] Gerson reflects that children at this age are very quick to speak about everything they experience which is new to them. The child Jesus would have been caught up in the sights and beauty of nature around him: the birds, beasts and reptiles, the fields full of flowers. He would have asked his parents many questions about what they were seeing.[66] Once again Gerson reminds his audience that Christ had been a real human child and had grown and developed as children do.

At this point Gerson described Christ's extended family, known today as 'The Holy Kinship (*Die Heilige Sippe*)' and based on the apocryphal story that Mary's mother Anna married twice again after the death of her first husband Joachim and had daughters who in turn had children.[67] This crowd of relatives of Christ is known from late medieval art and explained the biblical phrase 'the brothers of Christ'.[68] For Gerson it was a convenient way of guaranteeing the virginity of Joseph, who in Late Antiquity was thought to have produced brothers for Jesus by previous relationships before he came to know Mary. For Gerson, following the tradition of Jerome, it was unthinkable that Joseph had ever been sexually active. Therefore Christ's extended family had to emerge from Mary's mother and not from Joseph.

These are some of the people whom Gerson imagines would have welcomed Jesus and his parents on their arrival at Nazareth. Gerson describes how they must have spent the whole day in telling about their seven years in exile.[69] From this time onwards, Jesus did many things from that time which are not written down, Gerson explains, but it is still legitimate to imagine how he lived:

> Thus our meditation does not rashly assert anything about what is not known but only uses in a modest way the logic of conjectures. From what is written the mind by pious effort can infer what is not written. Thus a certain faith reveals what is uncertain, what has been done or could be done.[70]

This remark is a rare and valuable summary of the manner in which Gerson proceeded. He based his 'logic' about Jesus on conjecturing what seems likely on the basis of what is generally known about children and families. On this basis it is possible to draw many conclusions about the life of the young Jesus. Gerson's 'contemplative mind' can make a number of plausible deductions, especially about the love that bound the family together.

Following this method of logical deduction, Gerson takes the familiar Biblical sentence about how Jesus 'was obedient' to his parents[71] and asks what this would have meant:

> Thus Christ was subject, as he was to you, Mary and Joseph,
> What kind of subjection did he wish for himself?
> Was he not showing obedience in your midst, as one who rightly
>   serves?
> Carefully and often he lights the fire and prepares the food;

He does the dishes and fetches water from a nearby fountain.
Now he sweeps the house, gives straw and water to the donkey.
He brings the neighbors his mother's weaving,
Or gives himself over to learning his father's carpentry,
With different kinds of woods: therefore, he was called carpenter.[72]

At this point Gerson added a detailed description of the types of wooden objects Jesus learned to make, including the carriages of a type Gerson's father himself may have produced. The description is so technically precise that it looks as though he is betraying his own childhood training by his wheelwright father.[73] Whatever Gerson's own background, it was important for him to present a Christ child who really helped out his parents, not by performing miracles, but by doing chores for them.

Gerson soon made it clear why he wanted so much to emphasize how the Christ child did the dishes and other tasks for his parents. Earlier in his *Considerations*, Gerson attacked the lazy and idle. Such proud people wanted to live by the sweat of others.[74] But we should all sweat for our bread.[75]

Having established the content of the early life of Jesus, Gerson now returned to his favorite theme of how Jesus found out his identity. Jesus turns to his father and asks him to explain his lineage. Once again Gerson visualized the Christ child in terms of a process of gradual learning. Joseph welcomes the query and takes Jesus into his lap: '*Mox puerum rapit in ulnas gremioque reponit*' (Gl. 4.52). The answers come both from Joseph and from Mary, who tells him how she had chosen Joseph as part of her decision to remain a virgin. Here Gerson is dependent on the Gospel narrative, and from this point onwards, the *Josephina* becomes more conventional, following the language of Matthew and Luke. The fourth distinction starts with the story of the Annunciation, while the fifth provides a long explanation concerning the meaning of Joseph and Mary's marriage, thus returning to the main theme of the *Considérations*. The sixth distinction tells of the Visitation, the seventh of the Nativity, the eighth of the shepherds, the ninth of the Magi, the tenth of the presentation of Christ in the temple, the eleventh of the finding of Jesus in the temple when he was twelve years old. Only when we come to the twelfth and final distinction, the death of Joseph, do we leave the Gospel narrative and return to material that calls for Gerson's own meditative imagination.

Since Gerson was more closely bound here to the biblical text and at times felt obliged merely to rephrase it, these middle distinctions do not show the imaginative power of the first three. But he continued to interpret the drama of Christ's life on the basis of Joseph's participation in it. He regularly returned to his theme that Joseph was the real father of Jesus, at least in legal terms, because he was the one who brought up or nurtured him. Joseph can rejoice because he could say of the Lord, 'Behold, this is my son.' The image of father and son together were for Gerson a *pietatis imago*, what we today would call an icon of piety.[76] Gerson returned again to the assertion he had made earlier, in his *Considérations*: Joseph was not an old man. Age had not yet broken him, and he was able to work hard for his family: '*Aetas quem nondum frangit vel reddit ineptum.*'[77] At the same time he was free from any sexual temptation and could enjoy the presence of his wife in unremitting virginity.

Every image and every word to be found in the Bible is taken by Gerson and examined for all possible levels of meaning. This is a practice of which Huizinga disapproved, for it seemed to be a kind of insatiable need to know of indifferent matters. But Gerson's interest was based not on idle curiosity but on a desire to emphasize the importance of the heroic role that Joseph had played. By meditating at length on the content of Jesus's early life, Gerson could find a new understanding of the meaning of parenthood, chastity and marriage. These themes are summed up in the twelfth and final distinction where Joseph's death is described. Gerson assumes that Jesus was present, describing how Mary embraced him and gave 'chaste kisses to his lips'. 'My man,' she is supposed to have cried, 'are you going away and deserting me, leaving me a widow?'[78] Mary weeps at her loss, while Jesus is shown consoling his mother. He asks her to look inward 'with the eye of faith': '*Cara mihi in primis mater, nolito doloris. Accumulare tibi causas.*'[79] Also, she will not be alone, for Jesus and his disciples and the holy women will look after her.

Jesus is described here as preparing himself to go out into the desert and be tempted. But Joseph is not forgotten. Mary ends the distinction with the assurance to Joseph that she will see him again. Gerson concludes with a prayer to Joseph as 'guardian of Mary, witness, nurturer and minister of the faith of Christ, aware of the mystery which former ages did not know'.[80] Joseph is described as a man (*vir*) and as a lord (*dominus*) who was privileged to have dominion over the Lord himself. Gerson asks him to support pilgrims, to comfort the weary and to remove hindrances from our paths in life. Joseph is seen as the strong, virile man, who will guard us as he guarded Christ.

Some of this language is traditional, but Gerson's leisurely pace and constant reformulation of familiar themes provide many surprises. At the end of the eleventh distinction, for example, when the now grown-up Jesus tells his father that he is going out into the world, Joseph weeps and tells him that without Jesus's presence, he will have no life: 'You have been a consolation to us. What then will be life worth? (*Tu solamen eras nobis. Quid vita deinceps/Profuerit)*'.[81] Joseph asserts that he will hardly be able to love if he is not allowed to live together with his son. Such an outburst, so far as I know, has no literary source on which Gerson could draw. He may have been expressing what he himself had felt some years earlier when two of his younger brothers to whom he was closest left him in order to become Celestine monks.[82] Gerson allowed himself in his poem to Joseph to reflect on the pain of human separation. He did not try to pretend that because of the love of God, it is easy to forget the love of other human beings. The reaction of Joseph was the natural reaction of a father to the departure of a beloved son, what Gerson called '*naturalis amor*'.[83]

The Meaning of Gerson's Devotion to St Joseph

Gerson's devotion to St Joseph can be understood in the context of the late medieval attempt to concentrate on the meaning of Christ's life by meditating on the exact content of its events. Certainly the procedure Gerson here recommended was the same that would make devotion to the rosary a universal phenomenon by the end of the Middle Ages.[84] Gerson provided fruitful 'images of piety' that renewed and expanded the repertoire of faith. One can see a parallel development in Gothic art, where we in the fifteenth century begin to see depictions of Joseph as a mature but not old man, holding his little son Jesus by the hand.[85] Here Gerson's point of view is triumphant. Joseph is a virile male, not a decrepit old man, and his son Jesus looks up to him.

Devotion to the infant Christ preceded this new devotion to Joseph. We find in St Francis with his Greccio crib scene a point of departure for the later medieval fascination with the child. This can also be seen in the fourteenth-century *Meditations on the Life of Christ*, which asks the viewer to 'kiss the beautiful little feet of the infant Jesus who lies in the manger and beg his mother to let you hold him a while'.[86] Here it is the infant and his mother, an infant who really is a child and whom the

viewer can kiss and fondle until he is handed back. But Joseph is absent
– or left discreetly in the background.

What does it mean, this entrance of a virile, hardworking and loving
man into the drama of salvation? The easy answer, in a superficial
sociological manner, would be that the coming of Joseph asserts the
new vitality of town culture, where physical labor, guilds and produc-
tion had become an integral part of everyday life. St Joseph the carpenter was a model for the kind of hardworking people to whom Gerson
preached on Sundays in his parish church on the right bank of the Seine
in Paris. But as studies on the growing late medieval cult of St Anne
have already shown, new attention to a saint does not have to reflect a
one-dimensional use of symbols. Gerson was just as eager to present
Joseph as a royal person who could be a model for members of the
French royal family, such as the Duc de Berry. Finally, Joseph was in
Gerson's eyes a learned man who discussed grace and free will with his
wife and who could be a model for theologians and other clerics: they
were obliged to learn and express the vocabulary of salvation. At the
same time, learning was not enough: they had to live in chastity and
devotion to Mary, just as their model St Joseph had done.

The appearance of St Joseph as a model for different groups in
medieval society could not have been so convincing, however, if the life of
the saint had not been personally important for Gerson. Here one moves
from sociological explanations to psychological ones, questionable as
they are, but there are some obvious factors worth mentioning. First of
all, as I showed earlier, Gerson made a great deal of Joseph as an exile
and pilgrim. The chancellor of the university felt for much of his life that
he was an outsider whose real home was in heaven, and when he was at
the Council of Constance, his sense of exile may have become all the
more immediate. He could identify with the Joseph who had to leave his
homeland and venture out into the unknown, following God's will.

A second possible personal element in Gerson's fascination with
St Joseph is found in the chancellor's unusual attention to the education of children. He wrote at length on this subject and at the same time
felt he had to defend his concern for children and their upbringing.[87] He
says in one place that he was criticized for bothering with such a puerile
subject: theologians were supposed to have better things to do.[88] But
Gerson insisted on paying attention to the boys he saw at the Notre
Dame school and was concerned about how they were taught and
lived. In describing in detail the education of Jesus – and the approach
to education of Mary and Joseph in slowly revealing to their son the

coming joys and sorrows of his life – Gerson was formulating a view of education as a slow, careful process. The parent and other educators had to respond to the awareness of the child in whom God's plan was revealed.[89]

A final personal aspect in Gerson's attention to Joseph lies in his search for a means to express human attachments and affectivity in celibate terms. Here we are up against twentieth-century prejudices which insist that the voluntary renunciation of overt sexual activity is usually a form of self-deception. I would not deny that for many medieval clerics, especially parish priests, celibacy was more an ideal than a reality. But for Gerson in his personal life and his reforming program for the Church, celibacy was a very important matter and a necessary way of life. At the same time Gerson was aware of the gap between what priests said and what they did. He himself sought to express his feelings without falling in love and seeking sexual union.[90]

I have shown elsewhere how Gerson tried to resolve this dilemma by concentrating his affective impulses on his immediate family members.[91] His brothers apparently found Gerson's affections too demanding and distanced themselves from him. His sisters Gerson cultivated through letters and treatises of advice. Gerson ended up expressing his affective impulses not to the living but to the saints. Here he could turn first to Mary, whose great church dominated his everyday life, and to Mary's husband, the ideal of a chaste man who had expressed warmth and affection to wife and son without being sexually involved. Joseph in this sense was the perfect man for Gerson: active, virile, masculine and not plagued in any way by sexual concerns.

If we look at the scenes from saints' lives inscribed on the portals of the great French Gothic cathedrals, such as Chartres, there is a great emphasis on the sufferings of the martyrs. Certainly these witnesses to the faith of Christ were to be celebrated for their courage and stamina, but there is an element of sadomasochistic sexuality in the depiction of their tribulations. Whether it is a question of the breast of a female saint being cut off or an attractive male form being filled with arrows, it is impossible for anyone in our time to look at these scenes without wondering about repressed sexuality. An easy conclusion would be that the clerical culture of the Middle Ages created a hothouse culture that turned 'natural' impulses into something perverted. A more sophisticated response would be to see clerical culture as using the cult of the martyrs in order to reflect and comment on the violence and pain in the lives of ordinary people. Not that they experienced martyrdom, but they lived in a society where physical and psychological violence were part of everyday life.

Gerson did not criticize clerical or popular martyrs' cults, but he added to the larger cult of the saints by emphasizing the importance of St Joseph. Here was a saint who was not a martyr, a strong and capable man who chose to live celibately within marriage. This decision did not lead to some kind of excruciating martyrdom of the flesh. For Gerson Joseph's life was peaceful and harmonious. What mattered for Joseph was to be with his wife and son and to make a family. Gerson, the cleric who chose not to have a family, idealized the Holy Family and provided a model of masculine affective spirituality where masochism and martyrdom were absent.

It has been suggested that this projection of male Christian affectivity on Joseph was the beginning of a reaction to the prominence of women visionaries and their spiritual challenge to a masculine church.[92] The cult of Joseph can be seen as the first step towards the Protestant Reformation, 'when fathers ruled' and women were made to leave their religious houses and to get married and have children.[93] The Lutheran ideal of 'Kinder, Küche und Kirche' can be interpreted as a desire to recapture power in religion from women visionaries such as Birgitta of Vadstena and Catherine of Siena, women who openly criticized popes and kings and threatened them with God's wrath. In the new Lutheran churches of Northern Europe, the king was the head of the church and thus God's representative in both spiritual and temporal matters. It would be dangerous for any woman to challenge such power.

Was Gerson one of the earliest contributors to this development that ended by replacing female religious authority with male? It is still thought today by some medieval historians that Gerson was 'notoriously' skeptical about women visionaries and did his best to 'put them in their place'.[94] But this view does not take into account Gerson's continuing interest in women who claimed to share in God's revelation and his willingness, for example, to accept the revelations of Birgitta of Vadstena (Bridget of Sweden) as genuine. For Gerson it was important to find out whether revelations were genuine or not, and he dedicated three treatises to this question.[95] But here there was no preference for men over women: both sexes had to submit their visions to the judgement of the Church in the person of qualified and careful clerics.

Gerson was not concerned with replacing female spiritual authority with male. What was important for him was to use the world of saints, both male and female, in order to influence his own world. At the end of his life he was even willing to believe in the revelations of a peasant girl in order to save the French monarchy and nation. In the cult of St Joseph, Gerson wanted to focus attention on a man who was physically close to God, but a God who made himself loveable as a child and who could be held, touched and fondled without any worries about chastity or celibacy.

The Protestant Reformation rejected this attempt to reconcile family affection with a celibate way of life. Gerson's stories about Joseph, in so far as they went beyond the contents of the New Testament, were ignored or forgotten. A man like Martin Luther found that he could not handle the demands of the celibate life and threw himself into the joys of sexuality within marriage as not only his personal solution but every man's preferred way of behavior. In Northern Europe, the celibate Joseph lost the prominence in the history of salvation that Gerson tried to give him.

The varieties of religious expression and experience that characterized the last medieval centuries eventually settled into one of two great patterns: the Northern European search for simplicity and authority within state churches; the Southern European reconstruction of medieval religion in a new church that also emphasized authority and criticized the proliferation of cults and religious imaginations. Both the Protestant and the reformed Catholic churches were dependent on absolute male authority. Joseph could be tolerated in the Catholic version, but now he was a magisterial Joseph and not Gerson's loving, affectionate father.[96]

In order to understand this development it is important to be aware of the creativity of late medieval spirituality. The historian Giles Constable has long made his colleagues aware of how late medieval religious expression was dependent on the writings of twelfth-century theologians.[97] It is true that much in the later Middle Ages was borrowed from the earlier period, but the renewal and expansion of the cult of St Joseph and the images used to describe him should make it clear that something new also was taking place. While the popular imagination continued to dismiss the saint as a tired old man, a new vision of Joseph was beginning to make an impact in medieval art and theology. Here Gerson made use of his own life, its hopes and dreams, in order to imagine a man who was father, guardian, nurturer, friend and celibate lover. Gerson was thereby describing the kind of man he himself wanted to be. The fertility of Gerson's imagination cannot fairly be dismissed in Huizinga's way as a misuse of the cult of the saints. The spirituality of the later Middle Ages did more than to multiply religious images. It related them to human needs and experience.

Notes

Preface

1. Glen W Bowersock, 1982, 'The Imperial Cult: Perceptions and Persistence', repr. in his *Selected Papers on Late Antiquity*, Bari, 2000, p. 56.
2. Matthew, 19.29; cf. Mark, 10.29 (cited here and below from the Douai version).
3. Luke, 14.26.
4. Acts, 4.32.
5. See Giles Constable, *The Reformation of the Twelfth Century* (Cambridge, 1996), pp. 8, 155, 159.
6. Brian Stock, *The Implications of Literacy* (Princeton, 1983).

Introduction

1. cf. Cicero *de Amiticia*, 27.101.
2. Aelred, *de Spir. Am.* i, 25–30.
3. C Stewart, 1998, *Cassian the Monk* (Oxford, 1998), p. 39.
4. Ep. 22.28.
5. J Lienhard, *Paulinus of Nola and Early Western Monasticism* (Cologne, 1977), p. 118.
6. R Bartlett, *The Making Of Europe* (Princeton, 1993), pp. 5 ff.
7. R Fletcher, *The Barbarian Conversion* (Berkeley, 1997), pp. 451 ff.
8. cf. Sunnia and Frethela debating scripture interpretation with Jerome.

Chapter 1. The Disruptive Impact of Christianity in Late Roman Cappadocia

1. A Harnack, *The Mission and Expansion of Christianity in the First Three Centuries*, trans. J Moffatt, 2 vols. (New York, 2nd edition, 1908), 1:312.
2. Basil, *Homiliae in Hexaemeron*, 1.4, ed. S Giet, *Basile de Césarée: Homélies sur l'Hexaéméron*, Sources chrétiennes, 26 (Paris, 1950), p. 104; E Amand de Mendieta and S Y Rudberg, *Basilius von Caesarea, Homilien zum Hexaemeron*, Die griechischen christlichen Schriftsteller der ersten Jahrhunderte, Neue Folge, Band 2 (Berlin, 1997), p. 8.

3. This chapter is a condensed version of a more extensive discussion of the impact of Christianity in Cappadocia, with full references and bibliography, in my *Becoming Christian: The Conversion of Roman Cappadocia* (University of Pennsylvania Press, forthcoming in 2003). The original lecture was the basis for the chapters in the book; for comments and reactions, I am most grateful to the audience and the other participants at the conference, and in particular Mark Williams.

4. Basil, *Epistula* 188, Canones 1–16; *Epistula* 199, Canones 17–50; *Epistula* 217, Canones 51–84, ed. R J Deferrari, *Saint Basil: The Letters*, 4 vols., Loeb Classical Library (Cambridge, Mass., 1926–34), 3:4–46, 102–34, 240–66.

5. Basil, *Epistula* 217, Canon 51, in Deferrari, *Saint Basil*, 3:244.

6. Basil, *Epistula* 217, Canon 55, in Deferrari, *Saint Basil*, 3:246.

7. Basil, *Epistula* 199, Canon 27, in Deferrari, *Saint Basil*, 3:116–18.

8. Basil, *Epistula* 217, Canon 70, in Deferrari, *Saint Basil*, 3:254.

9. R Cagnat et al., ed., *Inscriptiones graecae ad res romanas pertinentes*, vols. 1, 3–4 (1906–27, repr. Chicago, 1975), 3:43–4, no. 115.

10. Basil, *Epistula* 199, Canon 23; *Epistula* 217, Canones 68, 78, in Deferrari, *Saint Basil*, 3:114, 252, 258.

11. Basil, *Epistula* 160, in Deferrari, *Saint Basil*, 2:398–410.

12. Basil, *Epistula* 217, Canon 79, in Deferrari, *Saint Basil*, 3:258–60.

13. Basil, *Epistula* 199, Canon 22, in Deferrari, *Saint Basil*, 3:112–14.

14. Basil, *Epistula* 199, Canon 25, in Deferrari, *Saint Basil*, 3:116.

15. Basil, *Epistula* 199, Canon 38, in Deferrari, *Saint Basil*, 3:126.

16. Basil, *Epistula* 217, Canon 53, in Deferrari, *Saint Basil*, 3:244–6.

17. Gregory of Nyssa, *Vita Macrinae* 2, ed. P Maraval, Grégoire de Nysse: Vie de Sainte Macrine, Sources chrétiennes, 178 (Paris, 1971), p. 144.

18. Basil, *Epistula* 199, Canon 30, in Deferrari, *Saint Basil*, 3:122.

19. Basil, *Epistula* 270, in Deferrari, *Saint Basil*, 4:140–2.

20. *Mosaicarum et Romanarum legum collatio*, 6.4, ed. J Baviera, *Fontes iuris romani antejustiniani, Pars altera: Auctores* (Florence, 1968, pp.558–60). This law was issued in 295AD.

21. *Codex Theodosianus* 9.24.1, ed. Th. Mommsen, *Codex Theodosianus 1.2: Theodosiani libri XVI cum Constitutionibus Sirmondi[a]nis* (1905; repr. Hildesheim, 1990), pp. 476–7. This law was issued in 326 AD.

22. Gregory of Nyssa, *Vita Gregorii Thaumaturgi*, in *Patrologia Graeca* 46.909B, 953D.

23. Gregory of Nyssa, *Epistula* 17.14–15, ed. P Maraval, *Grégoire de Nysse, Lettres*, Sources chrétiennes, 363 (Paris, 1990), pp. 224–6.

24. Basil, *Homiliae in Hexaemeron* 8.4–8, in Giet, *Basile de Césarée*, 446–76, and Amand de Mendieta and Rudberg, *Basilius von Caesarea*, pp. 133–45.

25. Gregory of Nyssa, *Vita Gregorii Thaumaturgi*, in *Patrologia Graeca* 46.921B-C.

26. Gregory of Nyssa, *Vita Gregorii Thaumaturgi*, in *Patrologia Graeca* 46.909A.

27. Gregory of Nazianzus, *Epigrammata* 30.1–2, in *Patrologia Graeca* 38.99A.

28. Gregory of Nyssa, *Vita Gregorii Thaumaturgi*, in *Patrologia Graeca* 46.924B-C.

29. Strabo, *Geographia* 11.2.10, 12.2.3–7, ed. H L Jones, *The Geography of Strabo*, 8 vols. Loeb Classical Library (Cambridge, Mass., 1917–32), 5:200, pp. 350–62.

30. Strabo, *Geographia* 12.4.6, in Jones, *The Geography*, 5:462.

31. Strabo, *Geographia* 12.3.8, in Jones, *The Geography*, 5:380.

32. Procopius, *Bellum Persicum* 1.17.18, ed. H B Dewing, *Procopius*, vol. 1, Loeb Classical Library (Cambridge, Mass., 1914), pp. 148–50.

33. Gregory of Nazianzus, *Orationes* 43.22, ed. J Bernardi, *Grégoire de Nazianze, Discours 42–43*, Sources chrétiennes, 384 (Paris, 1992), pp. 170–2.

34. Philostorgius, *Historia ecclesiastica* 9.12, ed. J Bidez, rev. F Winkelmann, *Philostorgius Kirchengeschichte: Mit dem Leben des Lucian von Antiochien und den Fragmenten*

eines arianischen Historiographen, Die griechischen christlichen Schriftsteller der ersten Jahrhunderte 21 (Berlin, 3rd edition 1981), p. 120.

35. W Dittenberger, ed., *Orientis graeci inscriptiones selectae: Supplementum sylloges inscriptionum graecarum*, 2 vols. (1903–5; repr. Hildesheim, 1970) 1:571, no. 358.
36. Gregory of Nazianzus, *Orationes* 43.63, in Bernardi, *Grégoire de Nazianze*, 260–2.
37. Gregory of Nazianzus, *Orationes* 43.25, 42, in Bernardi, *Grégoire de Nazianze*, 182, 216.
38. Photius, *Bibliotheca* 40, ed. R Henry, *Photius: Bibliothèque*, 8 vols. Collection des Universités de France publiée sous le patronage de l'Association Guillaume Budé (Paris, 1959–91) 1:23.

Chapter 2. Constantinople: Christian City, Christian Landscape

1. The text of the two recensions of the ancient *Life of Daniel* is published in H Delehaye, *Les Saints stylites*, Subsidia Hagiographica, 14 (Brussels, 1923), pp. 1–94. Annotated French translation by A J Festugière, *Les Moines d'Orient II: Les moines de la région de Constantinople* (Paris, 1960), pp. 93–165. The English translation by E Dawes and N H Baynes, *Three Byzantine Saints* (London, 1948), pp. 1–48, will soon be replaced by Professor Miriam Raub Vivian of California State University at Bakersfield. The historicity of the *Life* is explicated by Robin Lane Fox, 'The *Life of Daniel*' in S Swain and M J Edwards, eds., *Portraits: Biographical Representation in the Greek and Latin Literature of the Roman Empire* (Oxford, 1997), pp. 175–225.
2. *Vita Danielis*, 9 (Delehaye, pp. 9–10). For Daniel's origins, see *Vita Dan.*, 2 (Delehaye, pp. 2–3). He came from a little village in the territory of Samosata, now under a large Turkish lake formed by damming the Euphrates.
3. *Vita Dan.*, 10–11 (Delehaye, pp. 11–13). Adjuration in the name of God had particular force: Epiphanius, Bishop of Salamis, had his deacons gag one unwilling ordinand 'lest in his eagerness to free himself he might adjure me in the name of Christ': Letter of Epiphanius to John Bishop of Jerusalem, translated into Latin by the brother of the ordinand, Jerome, *Ep.* 51, 1 (of 394 AD).
4. *Vita Dan.*, 13–14 (Delehaye, pp. 14–15) tells how he came to a place called Anaplous, where there was an oratory of the Archangel Michael. J Pargoire ('Anaple et Sosthène', *IRAIK (Bulletin of the Russian Archaeological Institute of Constantinople)*, 3 (1898), pp. 60–80), argues that the name Anaplous may be understood in three ways: as the journey up the Bosporus, as the European shore of the Bosporus and as a particular place on that shore.
5. N H Baynes, 'The Supernatural Defenders of Constantinople' in his *Byzantine Studies and other Essays* (London, 1955), pp. 248–60.
6. Macarius Melissenus [Phrantzes], *Chronicum Majus*, III, 8, cf. S Runciman, *The Fall of Constantinople 1453* (Cambridge, 1969), pp. 121–2.
7. For recent consideration of this aspect of conversion, T D Barnes, 'Statistics and the Conversion of the Roman Aristocracy', *Journal of Roman Studies*, 85 (1995), pp. 135–55.
8. The question is asked by R A Markus ('How on Earth Could Places be Holy?', *Journal of Early Christian Studies*, 2 (1994), pp. 257–71), and is a persistent theme of his *The End of Ancient Christianity* (Cambridge, 1990).
9. Eusebius, *Life of Constantine* (hereinafter *Vit. Con.*), III, 48, 1.
10. Columella (in describing winnowing: II, 20, 6) allows for the possibility that grain may be kept for more than one year. Ausonius stored two years' supply at his estate: *Herediolum*, II. 27–8. The army kept a year's supply on hand: G Rickman,

Roman Granaries and Store Buildings (Cambridge, 1971), p. 288. P Horden and N Purcell, *The Corrupting Sea* (Oxford, 2000) emphasize the instability of the Mediterranean environment (chapter VIII) and the complexity of Mediterranean reliance on cereals (pp. 201–9).

11. R A Markus, *End of Ancient Christianity*, p. 141. This is spelled out for one great city by G M Rogers, *The Sacred Identity of Ephesus: Foundation Myths of a Roman City* (London, 1991).

12. Arnobius, *Adversus Gentes*, VII, 10, 1 and VII, 33, 1, G E MacCracken, tr., *Arnobius: the Case Against the Pagans*, Ancient Christian Writers, 8 (Westminster Maryland, 1949), pp. 489, 516. For change in civic calendars in the fourth century, R A Markus, *End of Ancient Christianity* (Cambridge, 1990), pp. 107–24, and Michele Salzman, *On Roman Time: the codex-calendar of 354 and the rhythms of urban life in late antiquity* (Berkeley, California, 1990).

13. Lights in the Holy Wisdom guide the sailor who has left the Black Sea and is following fearfully a course towards the City: Paul the Silentiary, *Descriptio Sanctae Sophiae*, lines 903–14.

14. A detailed description of the geography and monuments of the Bosporus in Roman times is provided by Dionysius of Byzantium, *Anaplus Bospori*, ed. R Güngerich (Berlin, 1927, repr. 1958). An annotated translation of this text is being prepared by the present writer.

15. Dionysius mentions Lasthenes at section 63 (the etymology differs significantly from that of Sosthenion offered by Malalas on whom see below, note 57), Amphiaraus at 34 and 63, a temple of Hecate at 62, temples and altars of Apollo at 26, 38, 46, 74 (with the Mother of the Gods), 86 (set up by Romans) and 111 (with an oracle second to none) and a temple of Poseidon (father of Byzas, 24) at 9; Jason and the Argonauts are mentioned at 24, 46, 49, 75 (Jason sacrificed to the Twelve Gods at Fanum/ Hieron; cf. Polybius IV, 39, 6), 87 and 88 (tower of Medea).

16. Antiphilus of Byzantium, *Anthologia Palatina* X, 17, elegantly explicated by L Robert, 'Un voyage d'Antiphilos de Byzance, *Anthologie palatine*, X, 17, 'Géographie antique et byzantine', *Journal des savants* (1979), pp. 257–94.

17. For the temple and the activities of the demons *Vit. Dan.*, 14–15 (Delehaye, pp. 14–16). The alternative recension (D', Mss P and V) of the *Life of Daniel (Vit. Dan.* (Delehaye, p. 14, line 31, with Delehaye's explanation on p. xxxviii) adds that the temple was at a place called *to Philemporin* – this is the only reference to this name in R Janin, *Constantinople Byzantine* (Paris, 1964), p. 476. The demons' stone-throwing is again mentioned in *Vit. Dan.* 22 (Delehaye, p. 23).

18. *Vit. Dan.*, 23–5 (Delehaye, pp. 25–6) describes how the location of the column was chosen. The *Life* repeatedly emphasizes Daniel's connections with Symeon: *Vit. Dan.* 21 (Delehaye, pp. 21–2) (vision); and 22 (Delehaye pp. 23–4) (Sergius gives Daniel Symeon's garment).

19. *Vit. Dan.*, 36 (Delehaye, p. 34, lines 13–14, 17–18). The poem is found also in *Anthologia Palatina*, I, 99; on it, see H Delehaye, *Revue des études grecques*, 9 (1894), pp. 216–24, lines. On Cyrus, see note 53 below.

20. The location of the column at Sosthenion by the harbor of Stenos is given by the Life of the tenth-century holy man St Luke the Stylite: *Vit. Luc. Styl.*, 3, in H Delehaye, ed., *Les Saints stylites*, p. 197, lines 34–6; cf. R Janin, *Eglises et monastères*, pp. 86–7 and 347.

21. *Vit. Dan.* 17 (Delehaye, p. 17).

22. Hestiai: Sozomen, *Historia ecclesiastica*, II, 3, 8–13. J Pargoire ('Anaple et Sosthène', *IRAIK*, 3 (1898), p. 60), Dagron (*Naissance*, p. 396) and Janin (*Eglises et monastères*, pp. 459–62) distinguish clearly between this and the oratory of St Michael at Sosthenion.

23. For their earlier moves, Callinicos, *Vita Hypatii*, 41, in G J M Bartelink, ed. and tr., *Callinicos: Vie d'Hypatios* (Paris, Sources chrétiennes 177, 1971), pp. 242–7, and *Life*

of Alexander the Sleepless, ed. E de Stoop, Patrologia Orientalis VI/5 (1911). After the death of Alexander the Sleepless at Gomon in Bithynia (*Vita Alexandri*, 52 (de Stoop, p. 60); Janin, *CP Byz*, p. 485) in about 430, his community finally constructed a monastery (*Vita Alexandri*, 53 (de Stoop, pp. 60–1)) at Irenaion on the Asiatic shore of the Bosporus, modern Çubuklu, (Janin, *CP Byz*, pp. 486–7). For the location of their monastery vis-à-vis Daniel, *Vit. Dan.*, 22 (Delehaye, p. 23, line 14).

24. C Mango, 'The Date of the Studius Basilica at Istanbul', *Byzantine and Modern Greek Studies*, 4 (1978), pp. 115–22, reprinted in his *Studies on Constantinople* (Aldershot, 1993), study XII with additional notes pp. 6–7, which places the building before 454.

25. Callinicos, *Vita Hypatii*, 24, 36 (Bartelink, pp. 156–8).

26. Callinicos, *Vita Hypatii*, 43, 16–23 (Bartelink, pp. 260–2).

27. Callinicos, *Vita Hypatii*, 45 (Bartelink, pp. 270–72).

28. Callinicos, *Vita Hypatii*, 1, 6 (Bartelink, p. 74). For further sources on Isaac, see G Dagron, 'Les Moines et la ville: le monachisme à Constantinople jusqu'au concile de Chalcédoine (451)', *Travaux et mémoires*, 4 (1970), pp. 229–76 at 232. Sozomen (II, 14, 38) and Socrates (II, 38) record the foundation of monasteries at Constantinople by the heresiarch Macedonius in the time of Constantius II (337–61), but ecclesiastical disapproval meant that they remained marginal: Dagron, 'Les moines et la ville', pp. 238–9, 244–53.

29. In general on monks and monasteries in Constantinople, see G Dagron, 'Les moines et la ville'. M Kaplan ('L'Hinterland religieux de Constantinople; moines et saints de banlieue d'après l'hagiographie', in C Mango, G Dagron and G Greatrex, eds., *Constantinople and its hinterland: papers from the Twenty-seventh Spring Symposium of Byzantine Studies, Oxford, April 1993* (Society for the Promotion of Byzantine Studies 3, Aldershot, Variorum, 1995), pp. 191–205) points out that for some monks settling in the outskirts rather than in the City itself was 'un pis-aller' (p. 192).

30. J F Baldovin, *The Urban Character of Christian Worship: the Origins, Development and Meaning of Stational Liturgy*, Orientalia Christiana Analecta, 228 (1987), p. 268, elaborates the significance of this sentence from John Chrysostom on Antioch (*Homily 15, On the Statues*; in Patrologia Graeca, XLIX, col. 155). A procession bearing martyr's relics from Constantinople to a suburban shrine made the sea into a church: John Chrysostom, *Homilia in S Phocam martyrem* 1; in Patrologia Graeca, L, col. 699–706 at col. 700. For general discussion of the evidence for religious processions in Constantinople, see Baldovin, pp. 181–7.

31. Socrates, *Historia Ecclesiastica*, VI, 8; Sozomen, *Historia Ecclesiastica* VIII, 8.

32. *Chronicon Paschale*, p. 586 Bonn ad ann. 447 AD, tr. M. and M. Whitby (Liverpool, 1989), p. 76. The *Chronicon Paschale* provides a doublet of its account of the earthquake of 447 in its record for the year 450.

33. Orosius III, 3, 2; Sozomen II, 4, 4.

34. The records of the commemorations of the earthquakes of 438 and 447 are disentangled by Brian Croke, 'Two Early Byzantine Earthquakes and the Liturgical Commemoration', *Byzantion*, 51 (1981), 122–47; see also Brian Croke, *Christian Chronicles and Byzantine History, 5th–6th Centuries* (Aldershot, Variorum, 1992), study IX.

35. John Chrysostom, *Homilia in martyrio...*, 2; in Patrologia Graeca, LXIII, col. 467–70. The emperor arrived with a military detachment the following morning: *Homilia* 3; in Patrologia Graeca, LXIII, col. 473.

36. Jerome, *Chronicle*, 240i Helm, ad ann. 357 AD, *Consularia CPana* ad ann 357; in T Mommsen, *Chronica Minora* I, 239, *Chronicon Paschale*, p. 542 Bonn ad ann. 357 AD; Paulinus of Nola, *Carmen* 19. C Mango, 'Constantine's Mausoleum and the Translation of Relics', *Byzantinische Zeitschrift*, 83 (1990), pp. 51–62, reprinted in his *Studies on Constantinople*, study V (with addendum), pp. 52–3, places the translation in its context.

37. C Mango, 'The Date of the Studius Basilica at Istanbul', *Byzantine and Modern Greek Studies*, 4 (1978), pp. 115–22; his *Studies on Constantinople* (Aldershot, 1993), study XII, 122.

38. Jerome, *Contra Vigilantium*, 5. The other sources are discussed in H Delehaye, *Les Origines du culte des martyrs* (Brussels, Subsidia Hagiographica, 20, 2nd edition, 1933), p. 56. The relics lay initially in the Great Church (*Chronicon Paschale*, p. 569, Bonn, ad ann. 406 AD) but were moved in 411 to a sanctuary at the Hebdomon (*Chronicon Paschale*, pp. 570–1, Bonn ad ann. 411 AD).

39. Stephen: Theodore Lector, II, 64, cf. Theophanes, *Chron.* ad ann mund., 5919–20. Chrysostom: Socrates, *Hist. Eccl.*, VII, 45; Theodoret, *Hist. Eccl.*, V, 36.

40. Socrates, *Hist. Eccl.*, I, 17.

41. Alan Cameron, *Circus Factions* (Oxford, 1976), pp. 157–92. For the particular instance of Julian at Antioch in 363: Maud W Gleason, 'Festival Satire: Julian's *Misopogon* and the New Year at Antioch', *Journal of Roman Studies*, 76 (1986), pp. 106–19 at 110–11.

42. A A Vasiliev, *Justin the First* (Cambridge, Mass., 1950), pp. 68–82, discusses the accession of Justin I in detail.

43. *Canon* 28. The two things are not always the same. C M Kelly points to ways that an efficient bureaucracy could threaten the free play of the emperor's authority: 'bureaucracy's marked preference for order directly challenged the whimsicality and unpredictability of action fundamental to the unfettered exercise of imperial power': 'Later Roman Bureaucracy: Going through the Files', in Alan K Bowman and Greg Woolf, eds, *Literacy and Power in the Ancient World* (Cambridge, 1994), pp. 161–76, at 167.

44. The first miracle of a pagan wonder-worker of the time of Christ was to persuade the potentates of Aspendus in Cilicia to disgorge their hoarded grain: Philostratus, *Life of Apollonius of Tyana*, 2. Lactantius explains the lost plenty of the ancient Golden Age by the fact that in that distant time so unlike his own the barns of the righteous rich stood open to all: *Divine Institutions* V, 5, 8. In the fourth century bishops were concerned about grain-hoarding by the powerful. Ambrose, *De officiis*, III, 6, 39–44 answers the self-justifications of rapacious landowners who claimed they were emulating Joseph in storing grain. In the Cappadocian famine of 369 AD, Basil used influence with the magistrates and most powerful men of the city to open up the storehouses of the rich: for sources and discussion see P Rousseau, *Basil of Caesarea* (Berkeley Ca., 1994), pp. 136–9. For further references P Horden and N Purcell, *The Corrupting Sea*, p. 267. On Julian at Antioch, see note 76 below.

45. Dagron, *Naissance*, p. 119, traces the development of the Senate of Constantinople. 'Le sénat de Constantinople n'est d'abord que l'ensemble des sénateurs qui ont suivi Constantin dans sa nouvelle résidence' (p. 120). Reforms in the latter years of Constantius II opened it 'à des catégories de plus en plus larges de fonctionnaires' (p. 130). On the Senate's local government functions, pp. 141–3.

46. Such are the continuities of life in Whitehall. The prologue to *Dialogus de Scaccario* describes how in 1175/6 the author of the *Dialogus* was inspired to write a description of his own government department (p. 6); the editors discuss its places of business on pp. xliii–iv (*Dialogus de Scaccario: The Course of the Exchequer by Richard, Fitz Nigel* (eds C Johnson, F E L Carter and D E Greenway (Oxford, 1983)).

47. They went back to the reign of Valens (ob. 378): John Lydus, *De Magistratibus* III, 19, cited by C M Kelly (art. cit. n. 43 above), pp. 161, 165.

48. John Matthews, *Laying Down the Law: A Study of the Theodosian Code* (New Haven, Connecticut, 2000).

49. Rochelle Snee, 'Gregory Nazianzen's Anastasis Church: Arianism, the Goths, and Hagiography', *Dumbarton Oaks Papers*, 52 (1998), 157–86.

50. Gervase Mathew, *Byzantine Aesthetics* (London, 1963), p. 70.
51. He was his friend 'from the start': *Vita Dan.*, 23, (Delehaye, p. 25, line 16) and erected his first pillar: *Vita Dan.*, 23–6 (Delehaye, pp. 25–7). Marcus is known only from the *Life of Daniel*; see J R Martindale, *The Prosopography of the Later Roman Empire* II AD 395–527 (Cambridge, 1980), hereinafter *PLRE*, II, p. 720 s.n. Marcus 3.
52. *Vita Dan.*, 25–30 (Delehaye, pp. 26–30). Gelanius is known only from the *Life of Daniel: PLRE*, II, p. 499, s.n. Gelanius.
53. For the career of Cyrus: *PLRE*, II, pp. 336–9, s.n. Cyrus 6; cf. note 19 above.
54. For the career of Zosimus: *PLRE*, II, p. 1206, s.n. Zosimus 6. The text of the history ed. F Paschoud, *Zosime: Histoire nouvelle* (Paris, Budé, 1971–) with comprehensive notes. On his views see Walter Goffart, 'Zosimus: the First Historian of Rome's Fall', *American Historical Review* 76 (1971), 412–41.
55. Callinicus, *Vita Hypatii*, 33 (Bartelink, pp. 214–18). On Leontius, Prefect of the City of Constantinople 434–45, *PLRE*, II, p. 669, s.n. Leontius 9. The anti-Nestorian edict addressed to him is *Cod. Theod.*, XVI, 5, 66 (August 3, 435).
56. Malalas, *Chronicle*, IV, 13 (Bonn, pp. 78–9). The Michaelium at Sosthenion is mentioned again in Malalas, XVI, 16 (Bonn, pp. 403 and 405); Agathias wrote an epigram about an icon of the archangel there, for which see *Anthologia palatina*, I, 35. Further references in Janin, *Eglises et monastères*, pp. 346–50. On the story in Malalas and the possible connection with Attis, see C Mango, 'St Michael and Attis', *Deltion tes Christianikes Arkhaiologikes Hetaireias*, 12 (1984, – publ. 1986), pp. 39–62. On Malalas' reinterpretation of other Greek mythology to maintain continuity with the past: Roger Scott, 'Malalas' View of the Classical Past' in Graeme Clarke et al. (eds), *Reading the Past in Late Antiquity* (Rushcutters Bay, NSW, 1990), pp. 147–64.
57. Fragments in Th. Preger, *Scriptores Originum Constantinopolitanum* (Leipzig, 1901), I, pp. 1–18. Summary of scheme in Dagron, *Constantinople imaginaire*, pp. 23–6. The schemes of historians like Malalas and Hesychius sustain the Early Christian interest in universal chronography first evident in Theophilus of Antioch, *Ad Autolycum*, cf. A Luneau, *L'Histoire du salut chez les Pères de l'Eglise* (Paris, 1964).
58. F Millar, *The Emperor in the Roman World* (London, 1977), pp. 43 ff., provides considerable detail about the 'gradual shift from Rome'. The next generation's estimate of Gallienus' administration was expressed by Lactantius, *De mortibus persecutorum*, 5, 5 (did not rescue his father from captivity in Persia) and a panegyrist in 297–8: *Latin Panegyric* VIII (V), 10, 1–3; further historical references in the notes of C E V Nixon and B S Rodgers, *In Praise of Later Roman Emperors: The Panegyrici Latini* (Berkeley, California, 1994), pp. 122–4. At Rome, Gallienus patronized Plotinus (Porphyry, *Vita Plotini*, 12) and encouraged fine sculpture in the classical manner (Gervase Mathew, 'The Character of the Gallienic Renaissance', *Journal of Roman Studies*, 33 (1943), 65–70). Maxentius faced Constantine in Gaul, Galerius and then Licinius in the Balkans and for a time Domitius Alexander in Africa: T D Barnes, *Constantine and Eusebius* (Cambridge, Mass., 1981), pp. 37–9, 41–3, with references.
59. Text of the Bordeaux Pilgrim ed. P Geyer, *Itineraria et Alia Geographica* (Corpus Scriptorum Ecclesiasticorum Latinorum, 38 (Vienna, 1898), reprinted in Corpus Christianorum Series Latina, 175, Turnhout, 1965). The route of the road across Asia Minor is studied by David H French, *Roman Roads and Milestones of Asia Minor fascicle 1: The Pilgrims' Road* (British Institute of Archaeology at Ankara monograph, 3, British Archaeological Reports International Series, 105 (Oxford, 1981).
60. Constantine: T D Barnes, *The New Empire of Diocletian and Constantine* (Cambridge, Mass., 1982), p. 39. Valentinian I: A H M Jones, J R Martindale and J Morris (eds.), *Prosopography of the Later Roman Empire*, I, 260–395 AD (Cambridge, Cambridge

University Press, 1971), hereafter *PLRE I*, p. 933, s.n. Valentiniaus 7. Maximinus Daia: Lactantius *Mort.*, 49; Constantius II: Ammianus Marcellinus XXI, 15, 2.

61. Lactantius, *Mort.*, 7, 10. Ammianus (XXII, 9, 3) also makes a passing comparison of Nicomedia to Rome.

62. E.g. recently, S Curčič, 'Late-antique palaces: the meaning of urban context', *Ars Orientalis*, 23 (1993), 67–90.

63. To the six mentioned by Lactantius, *Mort*, 29, 2, one may add Domitius Alexander, usurper in Africa.

64. Letter of Constantine to the Shah of Persia in Eusebius, *Vit. Con.*, IV, 9, in *Eusebius: Life of Constantine*, tr. Averil Cameron and Stuart G Hall (Oxford, 1999), p. 157. For a narrative, see T D Barnes, *Constantine and Eusebius* (Cambridge, Mass., 1980), pp. 28–43 and 62–77.

65. For Constantine's movements in 324–5, Barnes, *New Empire*, pp. 75–6 (surrender of Licinius September 19, foundation of Constantinople November 8, 324). For the Troy story, Sozomen, *Hist. Eccl.*, II, 3; Theodore Lector, 17–18; Theophanes, *Chron* ad ann. mund., 5816.

66. Demosthenes, *On the Crown*, p. 87; Eunapius, *Lives of the Philosophers*, 462. For further examples, Peter Garnsey, *Famine and Food Supply in the Greco-Roman World* (Cambridge, 1988), pp. 121–2 (fifth century BC), 135 and 142–3 (fourth century BC).

67. Fergus Millar, *Emperor in the Roman World*, p. 53, points to the frequency of Tetrarchic visits. For the siege of Byzantium in the campaign of 324, *Anonymous Valesianus*, 5, 25 and 27, Zosimus II, 23–5. For the war between Septimius Severus and Pescennius Niger: Dio Cassius (Xiphilinus) LXXXV, 9, 4–14, 6 (with 7, 3 and 8, 3) and Herodian III, 1, 5–7 and 6, 9.

68. C Mango, 'The Water Supply of Constantinople' in C Mango, G Dagron and G Greatrex, *Constantinople and Its Hinterland*, pp. 9–18. Richard Bayliss and James Crow, 'The fortifications and water supply systems of Constantinople', *Antiquity*, 74:283 (March, 2000), pp. 25–6, is the first report of a survey project.

69. Byzantium enjoyed some territory on the Asiatic side of the Sea of Marmara: Polybius, IV, 52, 9 (treaty with Prusias cites lands in Mysia); Strabo XII, 8, 11 (on Dascylium), with L Robert, 'Inscriptions de Yalova', *Hellenica*, VII (1949), pp. 39–41.

70. Polybius, IV, 38, 1–10. It is true that the principal disadvantage perceived by Polybius on the land side was having the 'rich lands' (IV, 45, 7) of the city pillaged by tribes from the Thracian interior, which was not the same problem in the time of Constantine.

71. N Firatli and L Robert, *Les Stèles funéraires de Byzance gréco-romaine* (Paris, 1964), pp. 9–10; C Mango, *Le Développement urbain de Constantinople (IVe–VIIe siècles)* (Travaux et mémoires du Centre de recherche d'histoire et civilisation de Byzance, Collège de France, monographies, 2 (Paris, 1985), p. 15.

72. On the topography of ancient Byzantium, see W Müller-Wiener, *Bildlexikon zur Topographie Istanbuls* (Tübingen, 1977), pp. 16–19, with references.

73. Claudia Barsanti, 'Costantinopoli: Testimonianze archeologiche di età Costantiniana' in G Bonamente and F Fusco, eds, *Costantino il grande dall'antichità all'umanesimo* (Macerata, 1992), I, pp. 115–50 at 116.

74. On the grain supply, Dagron, *Naissance*, pp. 530–41.

75. T D Barnes, *Athanasius and Constantius* (Cambridge Mass., 1993), p. 24 (with note 17) reconstructs the events. Julian, marching east to take power from Constantius II, did not commandeer for his army an African grain fleet destined for Constantinople, and could therefore on his arrival be presented as a benefactor of the City: Mamertinus, *Latin Panegyric*, III (XI), 14, 5–6.

76. For the advice of the notables, Ammianus Marcellinus XXII, 14, 1–2. The dynamics are well presented by Robert Browning, *The Emperor Julian* (London, 1976), pp. 152–5.

77. Zosimus II, 30, 1. His shrewdness was anticipated by Eunapius, *Lives of the Philosophers*, 462.
78. See above at note 12. Amminaus Marcellinus (XXII, 12, 3, cf. 6) reports critics of Julian who considered that the emperor's lack of moderation in sacrifice when things were going well would lead to destruction, his prosperity falling away 'velut luxuriantes ubertate nimia fruges'.
79. M Cook and P Crone, *Hagarism* (Cambridge, 1977), p. 47.
80. Lactantius, *Divine Institutions*, IV, 3, 1–10. See below at note 120.
81. Narrative of the Great Persecution in T D Barnes, *Constantine and Eusebius*, pp. 19–27, 38–43, 148–63 with recent amplification in idem, 'Constantine and Christianity: Ancient Evidence and Modern Interpretations', *Zeitschrift für Antikes Christentum*, 2 (1998), 274–94.
82. Lactantius, *Mort.*, 24, 9.
83. Eusebius, *Vit. Con.*, IV, 23–5 avers that sacrifice was banned everywhere. *Codex Theodosianus* XVI, 10, 2 of 341 AD speaks of sacrifice as 'violation of the law...of our father'. On Constantine's abolition of sacrifice Scott Bradbury, 'Constantine and the Problem of Anti-Pagan Legislation in the Fourth Century', *Classical Philology*, 89 (1994), 120–39.
84. J Gascou, 'Le Rescrit d'Hispellum', *Mélanges d'archéologie et d'histoire de l'école française d'Athènes et de Rome*, 79 (1967), 600–59.
85. Eusebius, *Vit. Con.*, III, 53, 1.
86. *Cod. Theod.*, XVI, 10, 1.
87. Eusebius, *Vit. Con.*, II, 44. For the martyrdom of three Christians who assaulted the governor of Palestine as he was sacrificing, Eusebius *Martyrs of Palestine*, IX, 4–5.
88. The phrase is from the letter to the bishops of Palestine about the pagan cults at Mamre in Eusebius, *Vit. Con.*, III, 52.
89. Eusebius, *Vit. Con.*, III, 48, 2, tr. Hall and Cameron.
90. Themistius, *Oration*, 23, 292–3 (prefers living in Constantinople to living in his native city); 294–6 (students of philosophy at Constantinople). Himerius, *Oration*, 41, may be read as praise of attempts by Julian to alter the Christian character of the City's public life: T D Barnes, 'Himerius and the Fourth Century', *Classical Philology*, 82 (1987); reprinted in his *From Eusebius to Augustine* (Aldershot, 1994), study XVI, 206–25 at pp. 221–2.
91. Mamertinus, *Latin Panegyric*, III, 14, 5–6.
92. *Eusebius: Life of Constantine*, tr. Hall and Cameron, p. 298 in their note on Eusebius, *Vit. Con.* III, 48, 2, claim that 'what Eusebius suggests is impossible', because there would be non-Christian individuals and were non-Christian monuments in the City. On the monuments, see below. What was missing from Constantinople was a calendar of 'feasts of demons' designed to articulate the city's public life.
93. Palinode of Galerius of 311, in Lactantius, *Mort.*, 34, 2.
94. Zosimus II, 36–7, who found an explanation in the words of a Hellenistic oracle concerning King Prusias. The quoted words are from the Palinode of Galerius.
95. Malalas XIII, 8, 322; *Chronicon Paschale*, p. 530, *Parasteis Syntomoi Chronikai*, 5, cf. 56 (Judith Herrin and Averil Cameron, eds, *Constantinople in the Eighth Century: the Parasteis Syntomoi Chronikai* (Leiden, 1984), p. 60, cf. pp. 130–2.
96. Poseidon father of Byzas: Dionysius of Byzantium, *Anaplus Bospori*, 24; his temple was on Seraglio Point (Dionysius 9) and in the sixth century housed the church of St Menas (Hesychius, *Patria* 15). The quotation is from Robert Markus, *End of Ancient Christianity*, p. 33.
97. Robert Markus, *End of Ancient Christianity*, pp. 110–20, contrasts the preaching of Severus of Antioch in the early sixth century with that of Augustine at Carthage in 399.
98. The fullest account of the destruction of the temple of Fortune at Caesarea is by

Sozomen, *Hist. Eccl.*, V, 4, 1–6; V, 11, 8. The earliest allusion to the event is Gregory of Nazianzus, *Oration IV Against Julian*, 92. Basil (*Ep.* 100), connects the temple with Eupsychius, and Libanius, *Oration*, 16, 14 describes Julian's withdrawal of privileges from the city of Caesarea.

99. Sixth century: Malalas XIII, 8, 322; Theodosius the Great: *Parasteis*, 5. The *Chronicon Paschale* does not say if the ceremony continued but refers disparagingly to a similar ceremony as having been performed under the Emperor Phocas in the early seventh century (*Chronicon Paschale*, p. 701).

100. Malalas, XIII, 39, 345, claims that three temples on the Acropolis were destroyed under Theodosius I; that of the Sun was turned into a courtyard, that of Artemis into a gambling den still known in the sixth century as 'The Temple' and that of Aphrodite into a carriage house for the Praetorian Prefect. They are not mentioned by Dionysius of Byzantium.

101. Zosimus, II, 31, 2–3. The interpretation builds on that of Dagron, *Naissance*, pp. 373–4. For references to the pairing of Roma and Constantinopolis (as the City Tyche) on fourth-century coins, S MacCormack, 'Roma, Constantinopolis, the Emperor and his Genius', *Classical Quarterly*, 25 (1975), pp. 131–50 at p. 147.

102. For Julian's sacrifice at the Temple of the Tyche of Constantinople, Sozomen V, 4, 8.

103. 'Si l'on songe que Constantin s'assimile lui-même à l'Hélios byzantin, on ne peut s'empêcher de penser à un transfert de la valeur religieuse de Rhéa-Cybèle sur sa mère': Dagron, *Naissance*, p. 374, note 6.

104. On the Great Statue, see C Mango, *Studies on Constantinople* (Aldershot, 1993), studies II 'Constantinopolitana', pp. 305–13; III 'Constantine's Column' and IV 'Constantine's Porphyry Column and the Chapel of St Constantine', and for this argument my abstract 'The Great Statue at Constantinople', *Bulletin of British Byzantine Studies* 20 (1994), pp. 70–2. *Parasteis* uses the expression 'great statue' in chapters 10, 17, 23, though not, as it happens, in its fullest discussions in chapters 56 and 68a.

105. The passage in quotation marks translates a phrase of Dagron, *Naissance*, p. 373. Lactantius as tutor to Crispus: Jerome, *De viris illustribus*, 80, *Chronicle* 230e Helm. For his account of the earthly rule of the Gods: Lactantius, *Divine Institutes*, I, 8–23, cf. V, 5–7. Saturn lived on earth 322 years before the Trojan War (i.e. around 1,506 years before Christ): *Inst.* I, 23.

106. Jerome, *Chronicle*, 232g Helm.

107. Eusebius, *Vit. Con.*, III, 54, 2.

108. On the common characteristics of Tetrarchic circuses, John Humphrey, *Roman Circuses* (London, 1986), pp. 632–8. For Constantinople, W Müller-Wiener, *Bildlexikon zur Topographie Istanbuls*, pp. 64–71.

109. Zosimus II, 31, 1; Sozomen II, 5, 4; Socrates I, 16. Thomas Madden, 'The Serpent Column of Delphi in Constantinople: Placement, Purposes and Mutilations', *Byzantine and Modern Greek Studies* 16 (1992), 111–45.

110. Zosimus V, 24, 6–7; Sozomen II, 5, 4.; Socrates I, 16, cf. Dagron, *Naissance*, pp. 139–40. Eusebius, *Vit. Con.*, III, 54, 3 places the Muses of Helicon at the palace.

111. Themistius, *Oration*, 31, 355.

112. Socrates I, 16 and II, 16; cf. Dagron, *Naissance*, pp. 392–3.

113. Sozomen IV, 26; Socrates II, 43 and II, 16; *Chronicon Paschale*, pp. 544–5 Bonn; cf. Dagron, *Naissance*, pp. 397–401.

114. Holy Apostles: Eusebius, *Vit. Con.*, IV, 58–60 and 70–1. Altar: Eusebius, *Vit. Con.*, IV, 60, 2; Eusebius uses the phrase 'bloodless sacrifice' of the liturgy at the dedication of the Holy Sepulchre: at *Vit. Con.*, IV, 45. C Mango, 'Constantine's Mausoleum and the Translation of Relics', *Byzantinische Zeitschrift*, 83 (1990), 51–62; reprinted in his *Studies on Constantinople*, study V (with addendum), proposes a sequence of

construction at the Holy Apostles starting with the mausoleum-rotunda and proceeding to the building of the church only under Constantius II.

115. Eusebius, *Vit. Con.*, III, 49. The placing of Christian images at fountains recalls the propaganda value for the German Empire in the years before the Great War of the placing of the Alman Çeşmesi, today rather a lonely-looking monument, near the spot where people gathered to watch the Whirling Dervishes and could get refreshment from its waters.

116. Eusebius, *Vit. Con.*, III, 48, 1.

117. On Sts Mocius and Acacius and their cults, Delehaye, *Origines du culte des martyrs*, pp. 233–6. Socrates, *Historia ecclesiastica*, II, 38; Sozomen, IV, 21, 3–6; Theodore Lector, p. 47; Hansen Theophanes (de Boor, p. 46) tell how the body of Constantine was moved in 359 from the Holy Apostles to the church of St Acacius nearby. Socrates, VI, 23 also mentions an oratory on the site of the saint's execution. David Woods, "The Church of 'St' Acacius at Constantinople," *Vigiliae Christianae* 55 (2001), 201–7 suggests that the association was not originally with the saint.

118. Porphyry, *De abstinentia*, II, 34.

119. Lactantius, *Inst.*, II, 9, 12. The fact is worth emphasizing. Often Helios or Sol are written of as though they were only specific pagan divinities; the Sun is also the Sun, open to appropriation by all Late Roman religions.

120. Lactantius, *Inst.*, IV, 3, 7.

121. Lactantius, *Inst.*, II, 16, 9.

122. The phrase is from C Mango, 'Constantine's Mausoleum and the Translation of Relics', *Byz., Zeitschrift*, 83 (1990), 51–62; reprinted in his *Studies on Constantinople* study V, page 62. Similarly the secularity which R A Markus, *End of Ancient Christianity*, pp. 15–17, sees as characteristic of the fourth century but supplanted by a pervasive sense of the sacred as Late Antiquity proceeds may be seen as an interlude between two eras where the sacred was omnipresent.

123. For Lactantius's selective quotation of an oracle of Apollo at *Inst.*, I, 7, 1–3, D S Potter, *Prophecy and History in the Crisis of the Roman Empire: a Historical Commentary on the Thirteenth Sibylline Oracle* (Oxford, 1990), pp. 351–5, with references, and the basic study of L Robert, 'Une oracle gravée à Oenoande', *Comptes-rendus de l'Académie des Inscriptions et Belles-Lettres* (1971), 597–619. For the demons who manipulate oracles: *Inst.*, II, 15, 1–16, 4, with 'Broadening the Roman Mind: Foreign Prophets in the Apologetic of Lactantius', *Studia Patristica* 36 (2001) 364–74.

124. Above at note 105. For the chronology, 'The Sources of the Dates in Lactantius *Divine Institutes*', *Journal of Theological Studies* 36 n.s. (1985), 291–301.

125. Lactantius, *Inst.*, VII, 24, 11.

126. For the similar appropriation in Lactantius' thought and Constantinian portrait sculpture of pre-Christian notions about the human body, 'Lactantius and a Statue of Constantine the Great', *Studia Patristica* 34 (2001), 177–96.

127. C Mango, *Le Développement urbain de Constantinople (IVᵉ–VIIᵉ siècles)*, pp. 33–4, evokes the way that the old Acropolis became a backwater of Byzantine life until it was used by Mehmet II to build the Topkapi Saray.

128. Lactantius, *Inst.*, IV, 13, 24–7, quoting 26. In *Inst.*, 'ecclesia' denotes the Christian community, though *Mort.*, 12, 3 is the first use of it in Latin to denote a church building.

129. Lactantius, *Inst.*, VI, 25, 3 = Seneca frag. 123. The quotation, like so many of Lactantius' citations from Seneca, is from a lost work.

130. Lactantius, *Mort.*, 15, 7. H. Koch, 'Der Tempel Gottes bei Laktanz', *Philologus*, 85 (1920), 235–8, collects the numerous passages from Lactantius which illustrate this thought. V Loi, *Lattanzio nella storia del linguaggio e del pensiero teologico pre-niceno* (Zurich, 1970), pp. 244–6, compares Lactantius with earlier Christian

authors. R Markus, *End of Ancient Christianity*, pp. 139–42, contrasts pagan holy places with Christian holy people.

131. For the phrase, a favorite of Lactantius, *Inst.*, IV, 10, 1–2; IV, 7, 3; VII, 2, 1 and II, 16, 14; cf. IV, 26, 2.
132. *Inst.*, VII, 25, 6–8; cf. 'Civitas quae adhuc sustentat omnia: Lactantius and the City of Rome' in W Klingshirn and M Vessey, eds, *The Limits of Ancient Christianity: Essays presented to Robert Markus* (Ann Arbor, Michigan, 1999), pp. 7–25.
133. *Inst.* VII, 24, 6, has God as the founder of the city, Lactantius' *Epitome of the Divine Institutes (Epit.)* 67, 3, has it founded by 'rex ille justus et victor', who will have won the 'fourth battle'.
134. Argued at length in *Inst.*, II, 8–9.
135. Lactantius *Inst.*, VII, 15, 13 lists the four empires; cf. 'Broadening the Roman Mind: Foreign Prophets in the Apologetic of Lactantius', *Studia Patristica* 36 (2001), 364–74 at 374. Garth Fowden, *Empire to Commonwealth: Consequences of Monotheism in Late Antiquity* (Princeton, N J , 1993) considers the problems of connecting monotheism and universal empire.
136. Plentiful examples of such regulation in Franciszek Sokolowski, *Lois sacrés des cités grecques* (Paris, 1969).
137. Philostorgius, *Historia ecclesiastica*, II, 9.
138. A D Nock, 'Conversion and Adolescence' in his *Essays on Religion and the Ancient World* ed. Z Stewart (Oxford, 1972) I, p. 474.
139. The only martyr securely attested during Licinius' rule in the East between 313 and 324 is Basil Bishop of Amasya: Jerome, *Chronicle*, 230g Helm, but for Christian fears see Eusebius *Vit. Con.*, I, 48–56.
140. Eusebius, *Vit. Con.*, II, 45, 1.
141. Except that Zosimus, V, 24, 6–8, thought that the presence of the statues of pagan gods assured the safety of the City.

Chapter 3. Communities of the Living and the Dead in Late Antiquity and the Early Medieval West

1. Henry Chadwick, 'The Church of the Third Century in the West', in Anthony King and Martin Henig, eds, *The Roman West in the Third Century*, BAR International Series 109 (Oxford, 1981), pp. 5–13; reprinted in id., *Heresy and Orthodoxy in the Early Church*, Collected Studies series, CS 342 (Aldershot, Hampshire and Brookfield, Vermont, 1991).
2. It was precisely the location of the house (and the buildings of the Jews and followers of Mithras) against the outer wall that led to the astonishing degree of its preservation. In preparation for the Persian attack, the occupants of the city built an embankment to strengthen the walls, filling in the buildings in the process. See Susan B Matheson, *Dura-Europos* (New Haven, 1982), p. 35; and Carl H Kraeling, *The Christian Building*, The Excavations at Dura-Europos, Final report VIII, 2 (New Haven, 1967).
3. Matheson, *Dura-Europos*, pp. 25–30; Kraeling, *The Christian Building*, pp. 3–39. The assembly hall could accommodate a group of some seventy people (ibid., p. 109).
4. Victor Saxer, 'Hagiographie et archéologie des martyrs', in M Lamberigts and P Van Deun, eds, *Martyrdom in Multidisciplinary Perspective* (Leuven, 1995), pp. 11–28, esp. p. 17; Clark Hopkins, *The Discovery of Dura-Europos* (New Haven, 1979), p. 93, citing Kraeling, *The Christian Building*, pp. 140–1; Pierre du Bourguet, *Early Christian Painting* (New York, 1965), p. 7.

5. Wilhelm Schneemelcher, *Neutestamentliche Apokryphen*, fifth ed., 2 vols (Tübingen, 1989).
6. Elaine Pagels, *The Gnostic Gospels* (New York, 1979); Michael Williams, *Rethinking 'Gnosticism': an argument for dismantling a dubious category* (Princeton, 1996); W H C Frend, 'Christianity in the second century: Orthodoxy and diversity', *Journal of Ecclesiastical History*, 48 (1997), pp. 302–12, esp. pp. 309–10.
7. R A Markus, *The End of Ancient Christianity* (Cambridge, 1990), p. 21, where he refers as well to the 'vast community' of which 'the congregation in the church was an outlying colony, its prayer a faint imitation of the perfect praise unceasingly offered to God by the angels and the saints in heaven'.
8. Caroline Walker Bynum, *The Resurrection of the Body in Western Christianity, 200–1336* (New York, 1995), pp. 22–58.
9. Patrick J Geary, *Living with the Dead in the Middle Ages* (Ithaca and London, 1994), pp. 36, 78. I suspect, however, that the elders among the dead to whom he is referring were in fact familial ancestors and relations of the living, and thus not entirely different from the dead in pre-Christian antiquity, with whom their descendants interacted in a variety of ways; see J M C Toynbee, *Death and Burial in the Roman World* (Ithaca, 1971), pp. 43–64.
10. Membership in the School of Historical Studies at the Institute for Advanced Study for the 1998–9 academic year allowed me to catch up on recent scholarship, take stock of the field and pursue new lines of inquiry in a truly incomparable setting, and I gratefully acknowledge the Institute's support. Research for this essay was supported also in part by the Nancy Batson Nisbet Rash Research Scholar Award from Connecticut College. I would like to thank Oliver Nicholson, Brian Golding, Paul Rorem and Peter Brown for their helpful responses to earlier versions.
11. François Dolbeau, 'Nouveaux Sermons d'Augustin pour les conversions des païens et des donatistes (II)', *Revue des études augustiniennes*, 37 (1991), pp. 261–306, at p. 294: 'catechumenorum defunctorum corpora inter fidelium corpora, ubi etiam fidelium sacramenta celebrantur, sepelire non debere nec cuidam posse concedi'. I thank Peter Brown for bringing this newly discovered sermon to my attention.
12. On Novatian and the origins of the split between Africa and Rome, see W H C Frend, *The Rise of Christianity* (London, 1984), pp. 351–7.
13. A D Nock, 'Tertullian and the ahori', *Vigiliae christianae*, 4 (1950), pp. 129–41. See also P-A Février, 'La tombe chrétienne et l'au-delà', *Le Temps chrétien de la fin de l'antiquité au moyen âge, IIIe–XIIIe siècles* (Paris, 1984), pp. 163–83, esp. 174ff.; Jean-Claude Schmitt, *Les Revenants: les vivants et les morts dans la société médiévale* (Paris, 1994), tr. Teresa Lavender Fagan, *Ghosts in the Middle Ages: The living and the dead in medieval society* (Chicago, 1998), p. 29; and Nancy Caciola, 'Wraiths, revenants and ritual in medieval culture', *Past and Present*, 152 (August 1996), pp. 3–45.
14. Frend, *Rise of Christianity*, pp. 355–6; and for the status of the Donatist church in the fourth century, see id., 'Donatus "paene totam Africam decepit". How?', *Journal of Ecclesiastical History*, 48 (1997), pp. 611–27.
15. John Van Engen, 'Christening the Romans', *Traditio*, 53 (1998), pp. 1–45, esp. p. 2.
16. Ambrose, *De sacramentis*, ed. Otto Faller, CSEL, 73 (Vienna, 1955), pp. 33–4, bk. II, 6, 19: 'Audi ergo: Nam ut in hoc quoque saeculo nexus diaboli solveretur, inventum est, quomodo homo vivus moreretur et vivus resurgeret... Ideo fons quasi sepultura est'.
17. A Khatchatrian, *Les Baptistères péleochrétiens* (Paris, 1962), pp. 49, 108; cf. J G Davies, *The Architectural Setting of Baptism* (London, 1962), pp. 13–19.
18. Kraeling, *The Christian Building*, pp. 3–39; see above note 2.
19. Kraeling, *The Christian Building*, p. 145, and notes 2–3 for references to the opinions of H Lietzmann, M Aubert and O Eissfeldt. The necropolis at Dura was full of catacombs, but most are undecorated and no Christian graves have been identified. A few tombs have arcosolia, but most are deep and narrow rather than shallow and wide.

There may be a hint of change in the late tombs at Dura such as tomb four, which has double-width loculi and semicircular ceilings, and was fully plastered. See N P Toll, *The Necropolis*, The Excavations at Dura-Europos, Preliminary report of the ninth season of work, 1935–6, part 2 (New Haven, 1946); and, in general, Toynbee, *Death and Burial*, pp. 219–23.

20. P-A Février, 'Baptistères, martyrs et reliques', *Rivista di archeologia cristiana*, 62 (1986), pp. 109–38.

21. Ibid., pp. 136–8. Février says that multiplications of liturgical sites in basilicas as well as baptisteries 'traduisent un besoin qui est ressenti de plus en plus fortement dans la conscience chrétienne', but does not explicitly identify that need.

22. Kraeling, *The Christian Building*, pp. 141–51, 200–3.

23. C de Clercq, ed., *Concilia Galliae a. 511–a. 695*, CCL 148A (Turnhout, 1963), p. 267, c. 14. Howard Colvin (*Architecture and the After-life* (New Haven and London, 1991), p. 52) mentions a 'wealthy Christian politician Flavius Rufinus', who 'built himself a private *martyrium*-cummausoleum…and had himself baptised on the day of its dedication', around the year 394.

24. Mario Mirabella Roberti, 'Il battistero antico de Milano', *Atti del VI Congresso Internazionale di Archeologia Cristiana*, Studi de antichità cristiana, 26 (Vatican City, 1965), pp. 703–7; Colvin, *Architecture and the After-life*, pp. 50–52, 106–7. Colvin (p. 52, note) suggests Diocletian's co-emperor Maximian as the possible builder of the mausoleum in Milan.

25. Richard Krautheimer, *Early Christian and Byzantine Architecture* (Harmondsworth, Middlesex, 1965), p. 70; Colvin, *Architecture*, p. 107.

26. The bishop's reference recalled the words of Paul's letter to the Romans 6:3–4 (RSV): 'Do you not know that all of us who have been baptized into Christ Jesus were baptized into his death? We were buried therefore with him by baptism into death, so that as Christ was raised from the dead by the glory of the Father, we too might walk in newness of life.' Cf. Colossians: 2.12: 'and you were buried with him in baptism, in which you were also raised with him through faith in the working of God, who raised him from the dead.' An understanding of baptism in the spirit of these texts was standard among Catholic Christians in Ambrose's time. The dating of the *De sacramentis* to ca. 391 (*De sacramentis*, ed. Faller, p. 270), and the building of the baptistery of Santo Giovanni next to the cathedral of Santa Tecla in Milan to 390–97 (Roberti, 'Battistero', p. 705), suggest an even closer connection between Ambrose's architecture and theology.

27. Frederick S Paxton, *Christianizing Death: The creation of a ritual process in early medieval Europe* (Ithaca and London, 1990), pp. 34–5: see also Dolbeau, 'Nouveaux sermons', p. 292, for references to African canons and other texts prohibiting baptism to the dead.

28. Joseph D Alchermes, '*Cura pro mortuis* and *Cultus martyrum*: Commemoration in Rome from the second to the sixth century', PhD dissertation (NYU 1989), chapter 1, pp. 32–3, has emphasized the fact that death and burial were family affairs in early Christian Rome. Cf. Paxton, *Christianizing Death*, pp. 19–27.

29. Bynum, *Resurrection of the Body*, pp. 21–58.

30. Alchermes, '*Cura pro mortuis*', chapter 4, pp. 70, 108, and P-A Fevrier, 'Vie et mort dans les "Epigrammata Damasiana"', *Saeculum Damasiana*, Studi di antichità cristiana, 39 (Rome, 1986), p. 98, note that epigraphical evidence from the fourth century shows that the ordinary dead, and not just martyrs, could intercede in heaven for the living.

31. Colossians 1:18.

32. Markus, *End of Ancient Christianity*, pp. 27–30; Peter Brown, *Authority and the Sacred: Aspects of the christianisation of the Roman world* (Cambridge, 1995), pp. 38–54. Chadwick, 'Church in the third century', pp. 11–12, shows how far assimilation to the dominant culture had gone even before Constantine.

33. William Tronzo, *The Via Latina Catacomb: Imitation and discontinuity in fourth-century Roman painting* (University Park and London, 1986), p. 71, thinks that it may have been a 'commercial endeavor'.

34. Ramsay MacMullen, *Christianity and Paganism in the Fourth to Eighth Centuries* (New Haven and London, 1997), pp. 109–17; Brown, *Authority and the Sacred*, pp. 23–4.

35. See Augustine, *Confessions*, 6.2, and the comments on it by Markus, *End of ancient Christianity*, pp. 33–4. I will return to episcopal efforts to control the cult of the dead below.

36. Eric Rebillard, *In hora mortis: Evolution de la pastorale chrétienne de la mort aux ivᵉ et vᵉ siècles*, Bibliothèque des écoles françaises d'Athènes et de Rome, 283 (Rome, 1994), pp. 11–28.

37. Markus, *End of Ancient Christianity*, p. 54.

38. Rebillard, *In hora mortis*, pp. 29–92.

39. Markus, *End of Ancient Christianity*, p. 19.

40. Ibid., pp. 27–83. Cf. Kate Cooper, *The Virgin and the Bride: Idealized womanhood in Late Antiquity* (Cambridge, Mass. and London, 1996), esp. pp. 119–27.

41. Brown, *Authority and the Sacred*, pp. 20–6.

42. Rebillard, *In hora mortis*, pp. 199–227.

43. Rebillard, *In hora mortis*, p. 227, n. 4.

44. Damien Sicard, *La Liturgie de la mort dans l'église latine des origines à la réforme carolingienne* (Münster, 1978), pp. 1–257; Paxton, *Christianizing Death*, pp. 37–44.

45. Ibid., p. 38: 'defensor et adiutor in resurrectione iustorum'.

46. Ibid.; the *ordo* says that the communion 'eum resuscitabit'.

47. But cf. note 91, below.

48. Paxton, *Christianizing Death*, pp. 47–91.

49. Peter Brown, *The Cult of the Saints: Its rise and function in Latin Christianity* (Chicago, 1982).

50. The last point has now been fully developed by Caroline Bynum, *Resurrection of the Body*.

51. Charles Pietri, 'Les Origines du culte des martyrs (d'après un ouvrage récent)', in id., *Christiana respublica: Eléments d'une enquête sur le christianisme antique*, 3 vols, Collection de l'École Française de Rome, 234 (Rome, 1997), 2.1207–33; originally printed in *Rivista di archeologia cristiana*, 3–4 (1984), pp. 293–319. I thank Peter Brown for directing my attention to this critique.

52. J Stevenson, *The Catacombs: Rediscovered monuments of early Christianity* (London, 1978), p. 15.

53. Leonard von Matt, *Early Christian Art in Rome* (New York, 1961), plate 23, but see the other examples therein and in Manuel Sotomayor, *Sarcofagos romanos-cristianos de España, Estudio iconográfico*, Biblioteca teologica granadina 16 (Granada, 1975).

54. Brown, *Authority and the Sacred*, pp. 38–54.

55. Even Pietri, 'Origines', pp. 1223–4, points out how aristocratic elites in Rome in the late fifth and early sixth centuries opposed papal claims to control and distribution of alms.

56. Brown, *Cult of the Saints*, pp. 23–35.

57. Brown, *Cult of the Saints*, pp. 32–49; Fred Paxton, '*Oblationes defunctorum*: The Poor and the Dead in Late Antiquity and the Early Medieval West', in K Pennington, S Chodorow and K H Kendall, eds, *Proceedings of the Tenth International Congress of Medieval Canon Law*, Monumenta iuris canonici, series C Subsidia, 11 (Vatican City, 2001), pp. 245–67.

58. Joseph Alchermes, 'Petrine politics: Pope Symmachus and the rotunda of St Andrew in old St Peter's', *The Catholic Historical Review*, 81 (1995), pp. 1–39; Kate Cooper, 'The martyr, the *matrona* and the bishop: networks of allegiance in early sixth-century Rome', unpublished paper.

59. Y Duval and J-Ch Picard, eds, *L'Inhumation privilégiée du IVᵉ au VIIIᵉ siècle en Occident* (Paris, 1986).

60. Frend, *Rise of Christianity*, p. 949.
61. Brown, *Cult of the Saints*, pp. 36–7.
62. Cod. Theod. VIII. 17.7 (386 Febr. 26), ed. Mommsen (Berlin, 1954), p. 463: 'Humatum corpus nemo ad alterum locum transferat; nemo martyrem distrahat; nemo mercetur'.
63. Giampaolo Ropa, 'Momenti e questioni del culto tardo-antico e medievale dei martiri Vitale e Agricola', *Vitale e Agricola: Il culto dei protomartiri de Bologna attraverso i secoli* (Bologna, 1993), pp. 27–46.
64. Victricius of Rouen, *De laude sanctorum*, ed. R Demeulenaere, CCL, 64 (Turnhout 1985), pp. 67–93; partial translation by J N Hillgarth, *Christianity and Paganism, 350–750: The Conversion of Western Europe*, rev. ed. (Philadelphia, 1986), pp. 23–8, quotation p. 23.
65. On time, Markus, *End of Ancient Christianity*, pp. 125–35; on time and space, Pietri, 'Origines', pp. 1215–16.
66. A point made by Philippe Ariès in *The Hour of our Death*, tr Helen Weaver (New York, 1981), p. 35 (originally published in French in 1978), and reiterated most recently by Cécile Treffort, *L'Eglise carolingienne et la mort*, Collection d'histoire et d'archéologie médiévales, 3 (Lyon, 1996), p. 134. On Africa, see Yvette Duval, *Auprès des saints corps et âme* (Paris, 1988), pp. 52–5; statements like Jean-Charles Picard's remark in *Les Souvenirs des évêques: Sépultures, listes épiscopales et culte des évêques en Italie du Nord des origines au xe siècle*, Bibliothèque des Écoles Françaises d'Athènes et de Rome, 268 (Rome, 1988), pp. 343–4: 'on constate qu'en Afrique on inhume massivement à l'intérieure des cités', should be tempered by Liliane Ennabli's more cautious remarks in *Les Inscriptions funéraires chrétiennes de Carthage III*, Carthage *intra et extra muros*, Collection de l'Ecole Française de Rome, 151 (Rome, 1991), p. 43. For church burials in rural Numidia, see Frend, 'Donatus', p. 613.
67. Duval, *Auprès des saints corps*, pp. 55–6.
68. *Romains et Barbares entre Loire et Gironde, ive–xe siècles: exposition au musée Sainte-Croix* (Poitiers, 1990), pp. 101–2; cited by Treffort, *Eglise*, p. 134.
69. *Romains et Barbares*, p. 102. Whether or not there is any connection with the erection, shortly thereafter, of the baptistery of St John a few meters to the southeast (the text at ibid. says '40m. à l'ouest', but the map on page 163 shows it to the southeast) remains to be seen, but is an intriguing possibility.
70. Donald Bullough, 'Burial, Community and Belief in the Early Medieval West', in *Ideal and Reality in Frankish and Anglo-Saxon society*, ed. P Wormald (Oxford, 1983), pp. 175–201.
71. Picard, *Souvenir des évêques*, p. 344 note 42; Treffort, *Eglise*, p. 134.
72. Picard, *Souvenir des évêques*, pp. 347–55.
73. Edward James, 'Merovingian cemetery studies and some implications for Anglo-Saxon England', *Anglo-Saxon Cemeteries 1979*, eds Philip Rahtz, Tania Dickinson and Lorna Watts, BAR British Series, 82 (Oxford, 1980), pp. 35–55.
74. In one of those hard-to-explain changes in burial practice, the interment of grave goods almost died out in Gaul in the fifth century among Gallo-Romans and barbarians, to be revived at the end of the century by Frankish kings; James, 'Merovingian Cemetery Studies', p. 38.
75. Bailey K Young, 'Exemple aristocratique et mode funéraire dans la Gaule mérovingienne', *Annales ESC*, 41 (1986), pp. 379–407, and 'The barbarian funerary tradition in Gaul in the light of the archaeological record: Considerations and reconsiderations', *Minorities and Barbarians in Medieval Life and Thought*, eds Susan J Ridyard and Robert G Benson (Sewanee, 1996), pp. 197–222.
76. Edward James, *The Franks* (Oxford, 1988); Patrick J Geary, *Before France and Germany: The creation and transformation of the Merovingian world* (New York and Oxford, 1988), pp. 73–5, 103–5, 173–5; Young, 'Exemple aristocratique'; Bonnie

Effros, 'From grave goods to Christian epitaphs: Evolution in burial tradition and the expression of social status in Merovingian society', PhD dissertation, UCLA, 1994, pp. 205–27; Treffort, *Eglise*, pp. 134–7. A number of the essays in *The Age of Sutton Hoo: The seventh century in north-western Europe*, ed. M O H Carver (Woodbridge, Suffolk, 1992) report on similar changes and levels of diversity in contemporary Anglo-Saxon England.

77. Effros, 'From grave goods', pp. 196–9, 303–7.
78. Young, 'Exemple aristocratique'.
79. Effros, 'From grave goods', pp. 196–99; 'Symbolic expressions of sanctity: Gertrude of Nivelles in the context of Merovingian mortuary custom', *Viator*, 27 (1996), pp. 1–10. This point is supported by Treffort's conclusion, *Eglise*, p. 132, that prayer was much more important in Carolingian commemoration than proximity to the relics of the saints. Effros ('Symbolic expressions', p. 10) wrongly cites Guy Halsall, 'Social Change around AD 600: an Austrasian perspective', *The Age of Sutton Hoo*, pp. 265–78, in support of the first point; the change to above-ground markers that he discusses occurred around 600, not 700. Such markers had moreover always been important: pagan barrows preceded Christian mortuary chapels.
80. Treffort, *Eglise*, p. 123.
81. Paxton, *Christianizing Death*, pp. 192–200.
82. James, *Franks*, pp. 160–1; Effros, 'From grave goods', p. 223.
83. Patrick J Geary, 'Exchange and interaction between the living and the dead in early medieval society', *Living with the Dead*, pp. 77–92. In agreeing with Geary, I disagree somewhat with Bonnie Effros in 'Beyond cemetery walls: Early medieval funerary topography and Christian salvation', *Early Medieval Europe*, 6 (1997), pp. 1–23, who, I think, overemphasizes the clerical side of the equation and misunderstands Geary's argument (ibid., p. 8, note 33).
84. Peter Brown, The Tanner Lectures, October 1996; one has been published in French as 'Vers la naissance du purgatoire: Amnestie et pénitence dans le christianisme occidental de l'antiquité tardive au haut moyen âge', *Annales*, 52 (1997), pp. 1247–61; and the other as '*Gloriosus obitus*: The end of the ancient other world', in William E Klingshirn and Mark Vessey, eds, *The limits of ancient Christianity: Essays on late antique thought culture in honor of R A Markus* (Ann Arbor, 1999), pp. 289–314.
85. Brown, 'Vers la naissance', p. 1260: 'la réduction finale de la somme de l'expérience humaine, de l'histoire, de la politique, de l'ordre social et enfin de la destinée de l'âme humaine en fonction de deux principes universels d'explication: le péché, la pénitence'.
86. Brown, 'End of the ancient other world', unpublished typescript, pp. 1–2.
87. Treffort, *Eglise*, p. 34.
88. Paxton, *Christianizing Death*, pp. 47–91.
89. Paul Corby Finney, *The Invisible God: The early Christians on art* (New York and Oxford, 1994), makes a strikingly similar case for the emergence of specifically Christian themes in the otherwise traditional tomb paintings in the catacomb of Callistus outside Rome in the early third century, whose purpose was 'to lift the minds and hearts of the survivors, to provide meaning in a place filled with death' (p. 285).
90. Effros, 'From grave goods', pp. 283–303; for images, see James, *Franks*, pp. 132, 135, 142–3.
91. Dorothy Hoogland VerKerk ('Job and Sitis: Curious figures in early Christian funerary art', *Mitteilungen zur christlichen archäologie*, 3 (1997), pp. 20–9) finds the scene on one of the panels of the sarcophagus of Junius Bassus, together with the presence of antiphons taken from the book of Job in the Roman *ordo*, as evidence for a deep consciousness of original sin among fourth-century Roman Christians. While she also notes the positive force of the antiphons, which stress resurrection and the happy outcome of the story, she does not comment on the heroic classicism of the iconogra-

phy of the sarcophagus itself, which must also have mitigated some of the negative force of the images. Still, her analysis supports the notion that while triumphalism or penitence may be dominant at particular times and places, the other is always present in some form.
92. Treffort, *Église*, pp. 123–32 (on penitential themes in epitaphs) and Effros, 'From grave goods', p. 299, n. 234; and 'Beyond cemetery walls' (on clerical control).
93. Michel Aubun, *La Paroisse en France des origines au xv⁵ siècle* (Paris, 1986), p. 57.

Chapter 4. The Gothic Intellectual Community: The Theology of the *Skeireins*

1. Massmann, H F, *Skeireins aiwaggeljons þairh Iohannen. Auslegung des Evangelii Johannis in gothischer Sprache*, Munich, 1834. Figure I shows my own reconstitution of this text. This is not meant to function as a facsimile; it is merely to indicate how the original looked. The methods used in the reconstitution are discussed in Marchand, James W, 'The Uses of the Personal Computer in the Humanities', *Ideal*, 2 (1987), pp. 17–32. For a picture representing the present state of the manuscript, see the facsimile at the beginning of Dietrich's 'Prolegomena'. For a (mostly failed) attempt to deal with the leaves using high-contrast printing and ultra-violet radiation, see Bennett, William H, *The Gothic Commentary on the Gospel of John: Skeireins Aiwaggeljns þairh Johannen* (New York, 1960), who also has excellent plates. On the problem of the photography of the manuscript, see Marchand's review of Bennett, *Journal of English and Germanic Philology*, 63 (1964), pp. 268–73.
2. Massmann, XIV ff.: 'Hier zugleich Rechtfertigung des gothischen Titels: Theodorus von Heraklea nannte sein Werk thatsächlich *Hermeneia eis to Euaggelion kata Iwannhn*... Das von mir schon früher gewählte *skeireins* (von *skeirjan* 'interpretari') übersetzt nun wirklich (Here at the same time is justification for the gothic title: Theodorus of Heraclea called his work in fact 'Interpretation of the Gospel according to John...'; the title I had earlier selected, *Skeireins* (from 'skeirjan, to interpret'), is now in fact translated), 1.C. 12, 10. 14, 26 *Hermeneia*.
3. E.g. Heather, Peter and John Matthews, *The Goths in the Fourth Century* (Liverpool, 1991), p. 157: 'known since its publication in 1834 as 'Skeireins', or 'elucidation' (*skeinan* is 'to shine, gleam') of the *Gospel of St John*'. *Skeireins* has nothing to do with *skeinan*, except that they both go back to the same Indo-European root.
4. This is 'Maj's wild angewandte Galläpfeltinctur' (Maj's wildly used nut-gall tincture), as Massmann called it.
5. Though Waitz said of his similar treatment of the Auxentius letter with blue vitriol: 'Ich habe die Überzeugung, dass meine Behandlung dem Codex keinen Schaden zugefügt hat; dass die Tinctur das Pergament blau färbt, ist bekannt und kann dem der sie anwendet nicht zum Vorwurf gemacht werden' (I am convinced that my treatment of the Codex caused it no harm; it is well known that the tincture turns the parchment blue, and this cannot be a cause for reproach to the one who uses it): Waitz, Georg, *Das Leben und die Lehre des Ulfila* (Hannover, 1840), p. 4. Sancta simplicitas!
6. Bennett, *The Gothic Commentary on the Gospel of John*, p. 1.
7. Cromhout, E H A, *Skeireins aivaggeljons þairh Iohannen* (Delft, 1900). Originally diss. Leiden.
8. Dietrich, Ernst Gustav, *Die Bruchstücke der Skerireins* (Strassburg, 1903).
9. Berkowitz, Luci, and Karl A Squitier, *Thesaurus Linguae Graecae. Canon of Greek*

Authors and Works, 2nd ed. (New York, 1986). A list of works contained in the *TLG* database.

10. Landow, George P, 'Moses Striking the Rock: Typological Symbolism in Victorian Poetry', in *Literary Uses of Typology: From the Late Middle Ages to the Present*, ed. Earl Miner (Princeton, 1977), p. 315.

11. Haslag, Josef, *'Gothic' im 17. und 18. Jahrhundert*, Cologne, 1963.

12. Scardigli, Piergiuseppe, 'La conversione dei Goti al cristianesimo' in *La conversione al cristianesimo nell'Europa dell'alto medioevo*, Settimane di Studio del Centro Italiano di Studi sull'Alto Medioevo, 14 (Spoleto, 1967): 'Inventario', 49–57, which Professor Fontaine (p. 482) found so useful.

13. Cf. in particular the sarcastic remark by Steubing, H, 'Miscellen zur gotischen Bibelübersetzung des Ulfilas', *Zeitschrift für Kirschengeschichte*, 64 (1952–3), pp. 137–65 (esp. p. 139): 'Ulfilas ist kein Bibelübersetzer von Gottes Gnaden gewesen (...Ulfilas was no Bible translator graced by God...)'.

14. Oxenstierna, Eric C G Graf, *Die Urheimat der Goten*, Mannus Bücherei, Band 73 (Leipzig, 1945).

15. The authorities on whom *Das alte Germanien* bases itself are: Agathias (531–580), Ambrose (339–397), Ammianus Marcellinus (330–395), Anonymus Valesianus (sixth century), Appian (fl. 125), Arnobius (Adversus Nationes, c. 300), Arrian (second century), Ausonius (d. c. 395), Aurelius Victor (c. 360), Caesar (BG and BC, before 50 BC), Cassius Dio (fl. 200–230), Cicero, Consolatio ad Liviam (c. 9 BC), Dexippus (fl. 250–275), Dionysius Periegetes (second century), Epitome de Caesaribus, Eunapius (345–420), Eusebius (260–340), Eutropius (fl. 365), Florus (c. 122), Fredegar, Frontinus (30–104), George Syncellus (fl. c. 800), Granius Licinianus (second century), Gregory of Tours (540–594), Herodian (third century), Horace, Irenaeus (130–202), Jerome (348–420), John of Antioch, Jordanes (fl. 550), Josephus (first century), Julian (332–363), Justin (100–165), Libanius (314–393), Livy (59 BC–17 AD), Lucan 39–65), Manilius (first century), Marcus Aurelius, Martial (40–104), Monumentum Ancyranum (c.15 AD), Obsequens (Julius, fourth century), Orosius (fifth century), Panegyrici Latini (n.d.), Paulus Festi, Petrus Patricius, Pliny (*Naturalis Historia*, 23–79), Pliny the Younger (61–112), Plutarch (50–120), Polemius Silvius, Pomponius Mela (fl. 35–50), Posidonius (135–50 BC), Ptolemy (fl. 127–148), Pytheas (c. 310–306 BC), Sallust (86–35 BC), *Scriptores Historiae Augustae* (c. 300), Seneca (first century), Sokrates (380–450), Sozomen (d. c. 450), Statius (Silvae, 92–96), Suetonius c. 69–130), Symmachus (340–402), Tacitus (first century), Themistius (fourth century), Timagenes (first century BC), Valerius Maximus (first century), Varro (116–27 BC), Velleius Paterculus (19 BC–30 AD), Xiphilinus, Zonatas, Zosimus (fifth century). All of these are reasonably well known and available in modern editions and translations.

16. For a large, but incomplete, list of the sources on Christianity among the Goths, see the list by Piergiuseppe Scardigli in 'La conversione dei Goti al cristianesimo' p. 49–57.

17. Salaville, S, 'Un ancien bourg de Cappadoce: Sadagolthina', *Echos d'Orient*, 15 (1912), 61–3.

18. These are gathered in Streitberg, Wilhelm, *Die Gotische Bibel*, 3rd ed. (Heidelberg, 1960), pp. 13–25, and translated in Heather and Matthews.

19. Massmann, *Skeireins aiwaggeljons þairh Iohannen*, p. 76. On p. 77, he excludes Latin fathers for much the same reasons. In defense of Massmann, it should be noted that he *did* note some parallels; cf. p. 77, f.n. 2.

20. Reuss, Joseph, ed., *Johannes-Kommentare aus der griechischen Kirche, aus Katenenhandschriften gesammelt und herausgegeben*, Texte und Untersuchungen, vol. 89 (Berlin, 1966).

21. 'Dagegen mußte auf die von Dietrich in reicher Fülle zusammengestellten biblischen "Quellennachweise" verzichtet werden, weil sie im besten Falle nur die Herkunft einzelner Gedanken oder Worte dartun, für die charakteristische Form der Skeireins

jedoch ohne jede Bedeutung sind' (We had to omit the list of biblical sources so richly collected by Dietrich, because, at best, they only explain the origin of unrelated words or thoughts, which are of no importance for explaining the characteristic form of the Skeireins.) Streitberg, *Die Gotische Bibel*, p. xxx.

22. As he pointed out long ago, the *Skeireins* can be understood 'nur von dem genauen Kenner der Patristik, welcher der Germanist doch immer nur als Laie gegenüber steht, voll gewürdigt werden; weshalb es sehr zu wünschen wäre, daβ die Theologen dem Werk mehr, als bisher geschehen ist, ihr Interesse zuwendeten, da es ihnen doch leichter fallen wird, gotisch zu lernen, als dem Germanisten, sich in das ungeheure Gebiet der Exegese, Dogmen-und Kirchengeschichte einzuarbeiten' (Can only be appreciated by true expert in Patristics, a subject which the Germanist naturally only approaches as a layman. Therefore it is to be desired that the theologians might turn their interest to the work more than has previously happened, since it would naturally be easier for them to learn Gothic, than for the Germanist to work himself into the monstrous field of theology): Jellinek, Max Hermann, review of HG van der Waals' edition of the *Skeireins, AfdA*, 20 (1894), 148–62 (esp. pp. 148 ff.).

23. Though he made bold to say: 'Dass also der Skeireinist den Irenaeus benützt hat, scheint mir höchst wahrscheinlich' (it seems most likely to me that the Skeireinist relied on Irenaeus): Jellinek, *Zur Skeireins, PBB* 15 (1891), pp. 438–40.

24. Bennett, *The Gothic Commentary on the Gospel of John*, p. 4.

25. Mossé, Fernand. 'Bibliographia gotica', *Medieval Studies*, 12 (1950), pp. 237–324. Supplements: 15 (1953), pp. 169–83; 19 (1957), pp. 174–96 (by Marchand); 29 (1967), pp. 328–43 (by E A Ebbinghaus); 36 (1974), pp. 199–214 (by E A Ebbinghaus); 59 (1997), pp. 301–56 (by C T Petersen).

26. Bennett, William H, 'The Troublesome Passages of the *Skeireins*', *Annales Universitatis Saraviensis*, 4 (1955), p. 80, n. 13.

27. Bonsirven, Joseph, 'La Vache rousse', *Textes rabbiniques des deux premiers siècles chrétiens*, Pontificio Istituto Biblico (Rome, 1955), p. 688–92; Maimonides, Moses, 'The Red Heifer' in *The Code of Maïmonides*, Book 10, 'The Book of Cleanness', tr. Herbert Danby, Jr. (New Haven, 1954), pp. 96–145.

28. Theodoret, *Dialogues*, p. 226.

29. Rashdall, Hastings, *The Idea of the Atonement in Christian Theology* (London, 1920); Rivière, Jean, many books bearing the title of *Le Dogme de la rédemption*... The one which deals best with our period is *Le Dogme de la rédemption, Essai d'étude historique* (Paris, 1905).

30. Russell, J B, *Satan. The Early Christian Tradition* (Ithaca, 1981), p. 193.

31. Leo the Great (390–461) *Sermon XXII*, 'On the Nativity,' *APNF*, 2nd series, 12.130.

32. Zellinger, Johannes, 'Der geköderte Leviathan im Hortus Deliciarum der Herrad von Landsberg', *Historisches Jahrbuch*, 45 (1925), pp. 161–77.

33. Ambrose on Luke 4:1–12

34. Augustine, *De trinitate*, 57.

35. Jellinek, *Zur Skeireins*, p. 439.

Chapter 5. 'Seed-sowers of Peace': The Uses of Love and Friendship at Court and in the Kingdom of Charlemagne

1. Foucault, *History of Sexuality: vol. 2: The Use of Pleasure*, tr. Robert Hurley (New

York, 1990). The insight into the political force of emotion is extensively studied in the collection of essays, Barbara H Rosenwein, ed., *Anger's Past: The Social Uses of an Emotion in the Middle Ages*, (Ithaca and London, 1998).

2. Georges Duby, *France in the Middle Ages, 987–1460: From Hugh Capet to Joan of Arc*, tr. Juliet Vale (Oxford and Cambridge, Mass, 1996), p. 180.

3. See D W Robertson, 'The Concept of Courtly Love as an Impediment to the Understanding of Medieval Texts' in F X Newman, ed., *The Meaning of Courtly Love* (Albany, 1968), pp. 1–18, and in the same volume, John Benton, 'Clio and Venus: An Historical View of Medieval Love', pp. 19–42. More recently, Joachim Bumke, *Höfische Kultur: Literatur und Gesellschaft im hohen Mittelalter* (Munich, 1986), esp. pp. 503–82.

4. Gerd Althoff, *Amicitiae et Pacta: Bündnis, Einung, Politik und Gebetsgedenken im beginnenden 10. Jahrhundert*, MGH Schriften, 37 (Hannover, 1992).

5. Klaus van Eickels, '*Homagium* and *Amicitia*: Rituals of Peace and their Significance in the Anglo–French Negotiations of the Twelfth Century', *Francia*, 24 (1997), pp. 133–140, and 'Two Princes in One Bed: A Neglected Ritual of Peace-making in the Middle Ages', forthcoming.

6. See note 1.

7. See my study, *Ennobling Love: In Search of a Lost Sensibility* (Philadelphia, 1999).

8. Anglo-Saxon Chronicle for year 790. Alcuin considered the destruction of Lindisfarne in 793 as God's punishment on the land for its 'violence, contempt of justice, and the evil lives of its rulers'. See F M Stenton, *Anglo-Saxon England* (Oxford, 1971), p. 93. See also Alcuin's poem on the destruction of Lindisfarne, Carmen 9, pp. 229–35, and his letters in the aftermath (Epist. 19, 20, 21, 22). Alcuin's poems are quoted from the edition in MGH Poetae Latini Aevi Carolini, vol. 1, pp. 160–351, his letters from the edition by Ernst Dümmler in MGH Epistolae vol. 4, Epist. Karolini Aevi vol. 2.

9. See Stenton, *Anglo-Saxon England*, p. 93.

10. Epist. 8, p. 33, l. 16.

11. Alcuin, Epist. 16 to King Aethelred, p. 44, l. 1.

12. Epist. 8, pp. 34–5.

13. Archbishop Aethelhard of Canterbury no doubt among them. Alcuin's Epist. 17 reminds the prelate that the historian Gildas had blamed the 'laziness and cowardice' of the clergy partly for the decline of the kingdom in an earlier generation and urges him in no uncertain terms to preach to the populace against the current evils of the land, lest the sins of the people be laid to his own charge (p. 47, 1.17–; p. 48, l. 11).

14. Epist. 9, p. 35, ll. 20–1.

15. Alcuin, Epist. 16, 18.

16. Epist. 16, p. 42, 'Memor dulcissime dilectionis vestre, viri fratres et patres etiam et honorabiles in Christo domini … idcirco sepius vos, karissimi commilitones … ammonere non cesso, que ad sospitatem patriae terrene atque ad beatitudinem perpetuae pertinere noscuntur… Quae est enim karitas in amicum, si utilia tacet amico?'

17. Epist. 16, p. 44: 'Sit una pax et caritas inter vos… Super omnia autem karitatem Dei habete in cordibus vestris, et eandam caritatem in observatione mandatorum eius ostendite. Amate eum ut patrem ut ille vos defendat quasi filios.'

18. Epist. 18, p. 49: 'Excellentissimo filio Aethelredo regi et amicis dulcissimis Osbaldo Patricio et Osberhto duci et omnibus fraternae dilectionis amicis Alchuinus aeternae beatitudinis salutem… Suavitas sancti amoris saepius me cogit de antiqua ammonere amicitia, de animarum vestrarum salute et de fidei veritate et de pacis concordia, quam habere debetis inter vos. Quia amicitia, quae deseri potest, numquam vera fuit. Amicus fidelis diu quaeritur, vix invenitur, difficile servatur. Vos quaerens inveni amicos, servabo amicos nec dimittam, quos amare coepi.'

19. Epist. 275, p. 432: 'Quos fida semper sequitur caritas, saepius litterarum sequatur et series, quia quoddam est amantis refrigerium aestuantis animi fervorem verbis vel

litteris explicare. Quia verba data sunt ad veritatis demonstrationem, uti quod cor veraciter concipit, lingua non fallaciter proferat; et suum cor frater alterius infundat cordi, et fiat unanimitas animorum, in quibus est communio caritatis.' The letter is dated 804. Other letters admonishing peace and fraternal harmony in love: Epist. 166, 187, 278.

20. Epist. 149, pp. 241–5.
21. Epist. 149, p. 242, ll. 9–14: 'Et dulcem versificationis melodiam inter horribiles armorum strepitus et inter raucos tubarum sonitus ammonuit miscere, quatenus truces animorum motus aliqua musicae suavitatis melodia mulcerentur...ut puerorum saevitia vestrorum cuiuslibet carminis dulcedine mitigaretur, voluistis.'
22. Epist. 149, p. 242, 30–243, 6: 'Igitur amicus dicitur quasi animi custos, id est qui animum amici sui cum omni sollicitudine fidei studet custodire integrum, quatenus nullatenus sacrum amicitiae ius alicubi violetur. Et hoc rari sunt qui intellegunt. Pene unusquisque secundum animi sui qualitatem, non alterius animi, qui amicus est suus, satisfactionem amicitiam [var.: amicitiae] custodire quaerit. Et si hoc in amico et coaequali diligenter observari debet, ut inviolata animi integritas permaneat illius, quanto magis in domino et in tali persona, qui suos subditos omni honore exaltare et gubernare amat? Veterum itaque proverbialis fulget sententia: "Amicus diu quaeritur, vix invenitur, difficile servatur"; et in sancta scriptura: "Amico fideli nulla est comparatio".' The etymology, *amicus* from *animi custos* comes from Isidore, who took it from Gregory the Great. See Brian Patrick McGuire, *Friendship and Community: The Monastic Experience, 350–1250* (Kalamazoo: Cistercian Publications, 1988), pp. xiv–xv.
23. See the study by Jan Ziolkowski, 'Twelfth-century Understandings and Adaptations of Ancient Friendship' in Andries Welkenhuysen, Herman Braet and Werner Verbeke, eds, *Mediaeval Antiquity*, Mediaevalia Lovaniensia Series, 2, *Studia*, 24 (Louvain Press, 1995), pp. 59–81. Ziolkowski points to the strong connection of friendship and music.
24. Epist. 149, p. 242, ll. 19–21: 'Quod militantibus virtutis genus maxime necessarium esse in antiquis historiarum libris legimus, ut cuncta sapiens temperantia, quae agenda sint, regat atque gubernet.' The source of this idea in 'ancient books of history' escapes me.
25. Ibid., 1. 25.
26. See my study, *The Envy of Angels: Cathedral Schools and Social Ideals in Medieval Europe, 950–1200* (Philadelphia, 1994), pp. 143–57.
27. See McGuire, *Friendship and Community*, pp. 91–7.
28. See Aristotle, *Nichomachean Ethics*, books 8, 9. On friendship and justice, 8.11, 1161a–b.
29. *Leges Heinrici Primi*, chapter 49, 5a, ed. L J Downer (Oxford, 1972), p. 164: 'Pactum legem vincit et amor iudicium.' The passage is the central text in Michael Clanchy's study, 'Law and Love in the Middle Ages', in John Bossy, ed., *Disputes and Settlements: Law and Human Relations in the Medieval West* (Cambridge, England, 1983), pp. 47–68.
30. See Judith W George, *Venantius Fortunatus: A Latin Poet in Merovingian Gaul* (Oxford, 1992), pp. 35–61; Peter Godman, *Poets and Emperors: Frankish Politics and Carolingian Poetry* (Oxford, 1987), pp. 1–37; and Jaeger, *Ennobling Love*, pp. 33–5. See also George's translations and annotations of selected poems: *Venantius Fortunatus: Personal and Political Poems* (Liverpool, 1995).
31. 1a, ll. 3–4, Friedrich Leo, ed., MGH Auctores Antiquissimi, 4, p. 129: 'me...non trahit ingenium, sed tuus urguet amor'. On Fortunatus and King Sigibert, see George, *Venantius Fortunatus* (1992), pp. 28–32, pp. 40–3.
32. 7.1, 37, 43, ed. Leo, p. 154.
33. 7.16, ll. 5–6, 33–4, 39, 49; ed. Leo, pp. 170–1.
34. 7.8, 33–8; ed. Leo, p. 162. Lupus was a member of Sigibert's court and a friend of Fortunatus. See George, *Venantius Fortunatus: A Latin Poet*, pp. 79–82. There are many other such references in the context of royal courts.

35. See Jaeger, *Ennobling Love*, pp. 38–50; McGuire, *Friendship and Community*, pp. 116–27.
36. I argue the aristocratic, courtly provenance of the cult of friendship in *Ennobling Love*, chapters 2 and 3. McGuire's idea of friendship as specifically 'monastic experience' has limited relevance prior to Anselm of Canterbury in the late eleventh century.
37. Smaragd, *Via Regia*, chapter 1, PL 102, 937B: 'Vere enim haec…regalis est virtus, quae…dulcia cunctis oscula tribuit, et diligens omnes ulnis extensis amplectit [sic].' It is hard to agree with Peter Dinzelbacher that the Carolingian expressions of friendship were 'restricted narrowly to monastic circles' ('Gefühl und Gesellschaft', p. 220).
38. Quoted here from Peter Godman, ed. and tr., *Poetry of the Carolingian Renaissance* (London, 1985), nr. 6, pp. 112–19. For commentary see Godman, *Poets and Emperors*, pp. 64–8; Dieter Schaller, 'Vortrags – und Zirkulardichtung am Hof Karls des Grossen', *Mittellateinisches Jahrbuch*, 6 (1970), pp. 29ff.
39. *Die Gedichte des Paulus Diaconus*, ed. Neff, Carmen 22, p. 103 (MGH Poetae 1, 51, Carm. 14, ll. 9–16): 'Non opus est claustris nec me compescere vinclis:/Vinctus sum domini regis amore mei … /Ut sacer inmenso Christi Petrus arsit amore … / Sic …/ Inflammat validus cor mihi vester amor.'
40. Carm. 45; Poetae 1.257, l. 1: 'Carmina dilecto faciat mea fistula David'; 'Te mea mens sequitur, sequitur quoque carmen amoris' (1. 17).
41. Godman, *Poetry of the Carolingian Renaissance*, nr. 25, p. 198 (MGH Poetae 1, p. 367, ll. 30–1): 'Ille duces magno et comites inlustrat amore;/Blandus adest iustis, hilarem se praebet ad omnes…' Godman's translation: 'He bathes his dukes and counts in the brilliance of his great love,/he is gentle to the righteous and displays good humour to everyone'. The poem, 'Karolus Magnus et Leo Papa', was undoubtedly composed by a member of the court circle. Dümmler edited it among the works of Angilbert. On this work see Dieter Schaller, 'Das Aachener Epos für Karl den Grossen', *Frühmittelalterliche Studien*, 10 (1976), pp. 134–68. On the question of authorship, pp. 163–8. Schaller revives Einhard's candidacy.
42. 1.26; MGH Poetae 1.396: 'Versibus incomptis, summo sed mentis amore,/Haec tibi conficiens, Caesar: dignare superne/Munera, quaeso, tui devoti sumere servi.'
43. Theodulf, Carm. 35, ll. 9–10; MGH Poetae, 1. 527: 'Te nimium capitis sitiunt duo lumina nostri/Cernere teque cupit pectoris altus amor.'
44. See Otto Eberhardt, *Via Regia: Der Fürstenspiegel Smaragds von St. Mihiel und seine literarische Gattung*, Münstersche Mittelalter–Schriften 28 (Munich: Fink, 1977) esp. on the letter of dedication, pp. 104ff. On Charlemagne as recipient and the dating, pp. 262–3.
45. These lines in the Migne edition were rejected as 'efféminé et absurde' by Donatien De Bruyne in favor of the older but less reliable ms. M, which omits the mentions of 'sweet kisses' and 'embraces' and speaks a language 'qui soit digne de l'abbé et de la majesté royale'. Friedel Rädle rescued the sentiments, if not the priority, of ms. G by reference to *Via Regia*, chapters 1 and 19, which speak the same language of royal love, kisses and embraces. See the summary of the debate in Eberhardt, *Via Regia*, pp. 106–7.
46. MGH Epistolae 4, Epist. Karol. Aev. 2, p. 533.
47. Chapter 19.
48. *Vita Carol.*, chapter 16.
49. 'Seniori tuo K[arolo], quisquis ille est…' A 'Charles' had become a generic term for emperor.
50. Dhuoda, *Manuel*, ed. Riché, pp. 166–8. See Peter Dronke, 'Dhuoda' in *Women Writers of the Middle Ages*, pp. 36–54. Manitius, 1.442–44. Also *Manuel*, 3.9, p. 170: 'Love [*ama*], cherish [*dilige*] and serve constantly the dignitaries of the royal court and their counselors … and any who shine with distinction at the court…'
51. See McGuire, *Friendship and Community*, pp. 38–72; Jaeger, *Ennobling Love*, pp. 30–3.
52. Carmen 55, pp. 266ff.

53. Epist. 39, p. 82, ll. 8ff.: 'O si ... in tuo pectore spiritus esset prophetiae, ut ... crederes ... quam suavissimo sapore tui amoris pectus meum impleretur... Hos parvos apices magnae indices caritatis tibi dirigo, ut per hos intellegas quod vix intellegi potest. Sicut flamma potest videri, tangi autem non potest: ita caritas in litteris cerni potest, sed vix in animo scribentis sentiri valet. Quasi scintillae de igne sparguntur, ita dilectio litterarum officio volat.' Cf. Epist. 19, p. 53, ll. 11–15; Epist. 209, p. 348, l. ll; Epist. 83, p. 126, ll. 2–7; Epist. 139, p. 220, ll. 15–17; Epist. 191, p. 318, ll. 7–8; Epist. 212, p. 352, l. 39; p. 353, l. 3. References from Adele Fiske, 'Alcuin and Mystical Friendship', *Studi Medievali* (1961), p. 571.
54. Epist. 86, p. 129, ll. 14–15: 'mellifluo caritatis iaculo vulnera omni favo dulciora in corde...'
55. Epist. 78, p. 119, ll. 15–17: 'familiari quadam flamma in corde meo efficacius haec eadem ardebat, ita ut mens mea respondebat mihi: "Caritate vulnerata ego sum".' Cf. Epist. 59, p. 102, l. 30; Epist. 78, p. 119, ll. 16–17; Epist. 159, p. 257, l. 29. References from Fiske, 'Mystical Friendship', p. 573. 'Caritate vulnerata ego sum'. Cf. Song of Songs 4.9: 'caritate/amore languescor.' (Var: 'caritate vulnerata sum'.)
56. He imagines a kingdom and a court where friendship remains unchangeable:

> Happy is the court of heaven, which never abandons a friend,
> The heart which burns with love always possesses the object of its love.
> (Felix aula poli nunquam disiungit amicum;
> Semper habet, quod amat, pectus amore calens.) (Carmen 11, ll. 17–18)

Heaven is a place 'where our love will never suffer separation (Qua noster nunquam dissociatur amor)' (Carmen 11, l. 20). It is a vision of lovers meeting in the beyond to fulfil a love that was thwarted in earthly life. The motif is anticipated in Paulinus of Nola and Venantius Fortunatus. Cf. Fortunatus, ed. Leo, MGH AA 4.1, p. 284 (Appendix 16, ll. 5–7): 'quam locus ille pius qui numquam abrumpit amantes,/ quo capiunt oculis quos sua vota petunt/in medio posito bonitatis principe Christo...'
57. Epist. 275, p. 432, ll. 30–1.
58. Joseph Fleckenstein, 'Karl der Grosse und sein Hof' in *Karl der Grosse: Lebenswerk und Nachleben, vol. 1: Persönlichkeit und Geschichte* (Düsseldorf, 1965), pp. 24–50.
59. *Friendship and Community*, pp. 116–27.
60. Wolfram von den Steinen, 'Karl und die Dichter', *Karl der Grosse: Lebenswerk und Nachleben*, vol. 1, pp. 75–6).
61. John Boswell, *Christianity, Social Tolerance and Homosexuality: Gay People in Western Europe from the Beginning of the Christian Era to the Fourteenth Century* (Chicago, 1980), pp. 188–92.

Chapter 6. Scaldic Poetry and Early Christianity

1. *Njáls saga. The Complete Sagas of Icelanders*, ed. Viðar Hreinsson (Reykjavík 1997), vol. 3, p. 123.
2. *Njáls saga*, p. 124.
3. *Njáls saga*, p. 124.
4. Translation according to *Hrafns saga Sveinbjarnarsonar*, ed. Guðrún P Helgadóttir (Oxford 1987), p. 101.
5. *Njáls saga*, p. 125.

6. *Njáls saga*, p. 125. Keeper of bells: priest (Þangbrandr); Slayer of the son of the giantess: Þór; Seagull's rest: sea; Sea's horse: ship; Gylfi: a sea-king; Gylfi's reindeer: ship; Thvinnil (þvinnill): a sea-king; Thvinnil's beast: ship; Atal: a sea-king; Oak of his field: ship. The account of Steinunn and her verses are also in *Kristni saga*, ed. B Kahle, *Altnordische Saga-Bibliothek*, 11 (Halle a.d. Saale, 1905), pp. 27–8.

7. Foote, Peter, *On the Conversion of the Icelanders*. *Aurvandilstá*, Norse Studies, ed. Michael Barnes et al., Viking Collection, 2 (Odense, 1984), pp. 56–64; Jón Hnefill Aðalsteinsson, *Under the Cloak. The Acceptance of Christianity in Iceland*, Acta Universitatis Upsaliensis (Uppsala 1978); Strömbäck, Dag, *The Conversion of Iceland. A Survey*, tr. and annot. Peter Foote, Viking Society for Northern Research, text series, 6 (London, 1975).

8. Ari Þorgilsson, *The Book of the Icelanders*, ed. and tr. with an introductory essay and notes by Halldór Hermannsson (1930), p. 60.

9. *The Book of Settlements. Landnámabók*, tr. with an introduction and notes by Hermann Pálsson and Paul Edwards (Winnipeg, 192), p. 23.

10. A good basic introduction to scaldic poetry is to be found in Frank, Roberta, *Old Norse Court Poetry. The Dróttkvætt Stanza, Islandica*, 42 (Ithaca and London, 1978); Frank, Roberta, *Skaldic Poetry. Old Norse-Icelandic Literature. A Critical Guide*, ed. Carol J Clover and John Lindow, *Islandica*, 45 (Ithaca and London 1985), pp. 157–96; Turville-Petre, E O G, *Scaldic Poetry* (Oxford, 1976).

11. Turville-Petre, E O G, *Myth and Religion of the North*. London 1964, pp. 185–6.

12. A good example is the poem *Vellekla* by Einar Skálaglamm, in Finnur Jónsson, ed., *Den norsk-islandske skjaldedigtning* (Copenhagen and Christiania, 1912–15), IA (tekst efter handskrifterne), pp. 122–31, IB (rettet tekst), pp. 117–24.

13. On women poets, see Straubhaar, Sandra Ballif, *Critical Notes on the Old Icelandic 'Skaldkonur'* (Ann Arbor, 1986).

14. Fidjestøl, Bjarne, *Pagan Beliefs and Christian Impact. Two Contributions of Scaldic Studies. Viking Revaluations*, Viking Society Centenary Symposium, 1992, ed. Anthony Faulkes and Anthony Perkins (London, 1993), pp. 106–10.

15. Clunies Ross, Margaret, *Prolonged Echoes. Old Norse Myth in Medieval Northern Society*, vol. 2: *The Reception of Norse Myths in Medieval Iceland* (Odense, 1998), pp. 173–83.

16. The best source on Hallfreðr's life and poetry is his saga: *Íslenzk fornrit*, 8, ed. Einar Ól. Sveinsson (Reykjavík, 1939); *Hallfreðar saga*, eds Bjarni Einarsson, Stofnun Árna Magnússonar, *Rit*, 15 (Reykjavík, 1977). See also: Bjarni Einarsson, *To skjaldesagaer. En analyse af Kormáks saga og Hallfreðar saga* (Bergen, 1976). Margaret Clunies Ross has convincingly argued that the relationship between poet and royal patron imitated that of the poet with Óðinn, the god of poetry. *Prolonged Echoes*, vol. 2, p. 177.

17. Einarsson, *Hallfreðr saga*, pp. cxxviii–cxxix.

18. Marold, Edith, *Das Gottesbild der christlichen Skaldik*, The Sixth International Saga Conference (Copenhagen, 1985), Vorkshop Papers, II, pp. 717–49. On Christian scaldic poetry, see mainly: Lange, Wolfgang, *Studien zur christlichen Dichtung der Nordgermanen 1000–1200, Palaestra*, 222 (Göttingen, 1958). See, Klaus von, *Christliche Skaldendichtung. Göttingsche gelehrte Anzeigen 213* (1959), pp. 81–7. Paasche, Fredrik, *Kristendom og kvad. En studie in norrøn middelalder* (Oslo, 1914, repr. in *Hedenskap og kristendom. Studier i norrøn middelalder*, Oslo, 1949), pp. 29–212.

19. *Den norsk-islandske skjaldedigtning*, A I, p. 291, B I, p. 314.

20. *Den norsk-islandske skjaldedigtning*, A I, p. 318, B I, p. 294.

21. *Den norsk-islandske skjaldedigtning*, A I, p. 452, B I, p. 420.

22. *Den norsk-islandske skjaldedigtning*, A I, p. 353, B I, p. 326.

23. *Íslenzk fornrit*, 8, p. 178.

24. Sources on Sighvatr are the various versions of *Ólafs saga helga* (*The Saga of St Olaf*), especially Heimskringla.
25. *Den norsk-islandske skjaldedigtning*: A I, p. 270.
26. *Den norsk-islandske skjaldedigtning*: A I, p. 331, B I, p. 305.
27. *Den norsk-islandske skjaldedigtning*: A I, pp. 459–73, B I, pp. 427–45.
28. *Den norsk-islandske skjaldedigtning*: A I, pp. 562–72, B I, pp. 548–65.
29. Translation of *kenning*, according to Frank, *Old Norse Court Poetry*, p. 99.

Chapter 7. Heloise and the Abbey of the Paraclete

1. For a select bibliography of editions, translations and studies of Abælard and his works up to 1967, see Eligius Butaert, *Petri Abælardi Opera Theologica*, vol. I, CCM 11 (Turnhout, 1969), pp. xxix–xxxvii; for a select bibliography for the period 1967–86, see Constant Mews, *Petri Abælardi Opera Theologica*, vol. III, CCM 13 (Turnhout, 1987), pp. 23–37. See also Julia Barrow, Charles Burnett and David Luscombe, 'A Checklist of the Manuscripts Containing Writings of Peter Abelard and Heloise and Other Works Closely Associated with Abelard and His School', *Revue d'histoire des textes*, 14–15 (1984–5), 183–302. The most important recent addition to these publications is Constant Mews, *The Lost Love Letters of Heloise and Abelard. Perceptions of Dialogue in Twelfth-century France* (New York, 1999).
2. Charlotte Charrier's *Héloïse dans l'histoire et dans la légende* (Paris 1933) is a notable exception.
3. Heloise died in 1164; Abælard, on 21 April 1142 (or 1143 according to a few chronicles).
4. See above, note 1.
5. *Epistolae duorum amantium. Briefe Abælards und Heloises?* Mitellateinische Studien und Texte, 8 (Leiden, 1974). The 113 letters and letter-fragments have been translated into Italian by Graziella Ballanti, *Un Epistolario d'Amore del XII secolo (Abelardo e Eloisa?)* (Rome, 1988). The French translation by Etienne Wolff includes only a sampling of the complete letter-collection: *La Lettre d'amour au moyen âge: Boncampagno da Signa, La Roue de Vénus; Baudri de Bourgueil, Poésies; Manuscrit de Tegernsee, Lettres d'amour; Manuscrit de Troyes, Lettres de deux amants (Héloïse et Abélard)* (Paris, 1996), pp. 117–51. The recent edition by C Mews reproduces the Latin text established by Könsgen, but with an English translation by himself in collaboration with Neville Chiavaroli.
6. Conference given 20 October 1998 at the University of Virginia, Charlottesville.
7. Page 3 of the unpublished conference-text.
8. Peter Dronke, *Abelard and Heloise in Medieval Testimonies*. W P Ker Lecture 26 (Glasgow, 1976), pp. 24–6; reprinted in *Intellectuals and Poets in Medieval Europe* (Rome, 1992), pp. 270–2.
9. Ibid., p. 25.
10. Personal letter dated 21 October 1998.
11. The best account of the proceedings is by Thomas G Waldman, 'Abbot Suger and the Nuns of Argenteuil', *Traditio*, 41 (1985), pp. 239–72.
12. *Epistola* II, PL, 178:183C; Letter I in the edition by J T Muckle, *The Personal Letters, Medieval Studies*, 15 (1953), p. 69.
13. Abælard's distancing of himself from Heloise and the early Paraclete community is a recurring theme in Heloise's letter referred to in the preceding note.
14. *PL*, vol. 178, col. 213 B-C; J T Muckle, op. cit., p. 242.

15. R W Southern, 'The Letters of Abelard and Heloise' in *Medieval Humanism and Other Studies* (New York and Evanston, 1970), p. 101.
16. Ibid.
17. Betty Radice, *The Letters of Abelard and Heloise*. Penguin Classics (Harmondsworth, 1970), p. 180. Letter VII is numbered Letter 6 in this edition.
18. Pascale Bourgain, in *Abélard en son temps* (Paris, 1981), pp. 218–20.
19. Chrysogonus Waddell, *The Paraclete Statutes 'Institutiones nostrae'*. Introduction, Edition, Commentary. Cistercian Liturgy Series, 20 (Trappist KY, 1987), pp. 42–56.
20. See David Knowles' edition of Lanfranc's *Epistola Henrico priori cantuariensi missa*, in *Corpus Consuetudinum Monasticarum* 3/4 (Sieburg, 1967), pp. 3–4. For the Latin text with English translation by the same scholar, see David Knowles, *The Monastic Constitutions of Lanfranc* (London, 1951), pp. 1–3. See also the *Apologetica hoc est satisfactionalis praefatio*, which introduces the occasional statutes assembled by Peter the Venerable, edited by Giles Constable in the same series, vol. 6 (Sieburg, 1975), pp. 39–40.
21. Thomas Symons, *The Monastic Agreement of the Monks and Nuns of the English Nation* (New York: Oxford University Press 1953).
22. Most recently edited by Chrysogonus Waddell, *Narrative and Legislative Texts from Early Cîteaux* (*Cîteaux – Commentarii cistercienses*, 1999).
23. Page 43 of the edition of *Institutiones nostræ* indicated above, n. 19.
24. Ibid., pp. 55–6.
25. Yvo of Chartres, *Panormia*, Lib. III, Canons 187–215, 'De virginibus, viduis et abbatissis'; *PL*, 161:1175A–1182A.
26. Identified and edited by John F Benton, 'The Paraclete and the Council of Rouen of 1231', *Bulletin of Medieval Canon Law*, n.s. 4 (1974) [publ. 1975], pp. 33–8. Benton suggests that the link between the Rouen canons and the Paraclete text may be found in the reformer archbishop of Rouen, Eudes Rigaud, who was at the Paraclete on 10–12 June 1249 – the same year that Eudes' sister Marie took office as abbess of the Paraclete.
27. See D Van Den Eynde, 'En marge des écrits d'Abélard. Les Excerpta ex regulis Paracletensis monasterii', *Analecta Premonstratensia*, 38 (1962), pp. 70–84, with particular reference to pp. 76–84.
28. *MGH: Concilia Ævi Karolini* II (1906), pp. 422–56.
29. *PL*, 178:731–84; Victor Cousin, *Petri Abaelardi Opera* I, pp. 625–79. Both these editions merely reproduce the edition by E Martène and U Durand, *Thesaurus novus anecdotorum* V (Paris 1717), cols. 1361–1416.
30. First printed in Duchesne-Damboise, *Petri Abaelardi... Opera* (Parisiis, 1616), pp. 384–451; reproduced without substantial change, first in Victor Cousin, *Petri Abaelardi Opera* I, pp. 237–95; and then in *PL*, 178:677–730.
31. See Chrysogonus Waddell, 'Peter Abelard as Creator of Liturgical Texts' in Rudolf Thomas, in collaboration with J Jolivet, D E Luscombe, L M de Rijk, *Petrus Abaelardus (1079–1142). Person, Werk und Wirkung*. Trierer Theologische Studien 38 (Trier 1980), pp. 267–85. See also vols 3–7 of the *Cistercian Liturgy Series*: Paraclete Old French Ordinary and Paraclete Breviary, with commentary.
32. For the entire Paraclete hymn repertory, including Abelard's cycle of Sacred Triduum hymns and occasional hymns, see vols 8–9 of the same series referred to in note 31. Of three sequences recently identified by Waddell, the first of these, the Easter sequence *Epithalamica*, was edited and commented on by the same author, '*Epithalamica*: An Easter Sequence by Peter Abelard', *The Musical Quarterly*, 72 (1986), pp. 239–71. An edition and detailed study of these three sequences by Thomas J Bell, *Peter Abelard after Marriage: The Spiritual Direction of Heloise and Her Nuns through Liturgical Song*, will soon appear under the imprint of Cistercian Publications (Kalamazoo, Michigan).

33. Bruxelles, Bibliothèque royale de Belgique, ms 10147–10158, ff. 81–95; late twelfth/ early thirteenth century; provenance uncertain (probably in the region around Liège).
34. Individual hymns are found in Chaumont, Bibliothèque municipale, ms 31 (breviary for Day Hours, late fifteenth/early sixteenth century); Paris, Bibliothèque nationale de France, ms lat. 1209A (early fourteenth-century breviary from St Maur de Verdun); ibid., ms Lat. 2040 (late twelfth/early thirteenth century; provenance unknown); Épinal, Bibliothèque municipale, ms. 235 (97) (thirteenth-century breviary from St Maur de Verdun); Sankt Gallen, Stiftsbibliothek, Codex 528 (fourteenth/fifteenth-century psalter from Grossmünster, Zürich); there are also four mss from Zürich, Zentralbibkliothek: ms Rh. 18 (thirteenth/fourteenth-century summer-season Night Office lectionary from Rheinau); ms Rh. 21 (fifteenth-century psalter-tonary-hymnal from Rheinau); ms Rh. 27 (fourteenth-century psalter-hymnary from Rheinau); ms Rh. 28 (thirteenth-century monastic breviary of unknown provenance, but with fourteenth-century additions from Rheinau).
35. Chaumont, Bibliothèque municipale, ms 31. The ms has been edited by Chrysogonus Waddell in the Cistercian Liturgy Series, 5–7: (Trappist, KY, 1985): *The Paraclete Breviary*: IIIA *Kalendar and Temporal Cycle*; IIIB *The Sanctoral Cycle*; IIIC *Common of Saints, Varia, Indices.*
36. Paris, Bibliothèque nationale de France, ms français 14410; *The Old French Paraclete Ordinary*, ed. Chrysogonus Waddell, Cistercian Liturgy Series, 4 (Trappist, KY, 1985), with a companion volume, *The Old French Paraclete Ordinary and the Paraclete Breviary* I. *Introduction and Commentary* (Trappist, KY, 1985).
37. Edited in *The Paraclete Breviary* IIIA Edition, pp. 185–9 (see Note 35, above).
38. First edited by Duchesne, pp. 244–51 of the edition indicated above, Note 30; reprinted in Cousin, pp. 618–25 (see Note 30, above) and *PL*, 178:335–340. E R Smits followed the Duchesne edition controlled by Paris, Bibliothèque nationale de France, ms lat. 13057 for his edition, *Peter Abelard. Letter IX–XIV* (Groningen, 1983), pp. 239–47. Letter 10 was printed with detailed commentary, Chrysogonus Waddell, 'Peter Abelard's *Letter 10* and Cistercian Liturgical Reform', in John R Sommerfeldt (ed.), *Studies in Medieval Cistercian History* II (Kalamazoo, 1976), pp. 75–86.
39. Both the 'primitive' Cistercian hymnal, based on Milanese sources, and the Bernardine revision have been edited with commentary by Chrysogonus Waddell, *The Twelfth-Century Cistercian Hymnal*. Cistercian Liturgy Series 1–2 (Trappist, KY, 1984). For a detailed description of the two versions, see the Introduction in vol. I, pp. 18–105, with special reference to pp. 47–51 for a discussion of the early Cistercian hymns at the Paraclete.
40. See the article by Chrysogonus Waddell, 'The Origin and Early Evolution of the Cistercian Antiphonary: Relections on Two Cistercian Chant Reforms' in M Basil Pennington, ed., *The Cistercian Spirit* (Spencer, Mass. 1973), pp. 190–223.
41. See the detailed analysis of the Paraclete Kalendar in 'Excursus II', pp. 319–36-of the Introduction to the Paraclete Old French Ordinary and Breviary indicated above, n. 36.
42. Besides the deacon-saints already in the universal kalendar (Stephen, Lawrence, Vincent) there are, among the 'first seven deacons', Nicanor (10 February), Prochorus (9 April), Timon (19 April), Philip (6 June – a twelve-lesson feast). The prestigious deacon-martyr Lawrence draws into his orbit not only Romanus but Secundianus as well (9 August), Quiriace (23 August – twelve lessons), and Cyrilla (29 October – twelve lessons).
43. The Congregation included six priories: Sainte-Madeleine-de-Trainel (Aube), founded at the latest by 1142; La Pommeraye (Yonne), founded in or shortly after 1147, and later raised to the rank of an abbey; Laval (Seine-et-Marne), founded before 1154; Noëfort (Seine-et-Marne), founded before 1157; St-Flavit (Aube),

also founded before 1157; Boran or St-Martin-aux-Nonnettes (Oise), founded before 6 April 1163.

44. There was regularly a procession each Sunday. On Wednesdays and Fridays, a small-scale procession through the cloister was accompanied by the chanting of the seven penitential psalms. In addition there were a few ample processions of a more particular nature (Palm Sunday, Low Sunday, Rogation Days, Vigil of the Ascension, St John the Baptist, All Souls). For further details see Excursus III 'On the Paraclete Processions', pp. 337–44 of the work referred to above, n. 41.

45. Conventual life at the Paraclete had been interrupted for a number of years when the Lady Abbess, Jeanne III de Chabot (1560–93) and the majority of her nuns joined the Huguenot reform. When the community was reassembled, only three of the former members returned to resume monastic life at the Paraclete. Since Abælard's orthodoxy had become a matter of concern for the early seventeenth-century ecclesiastical establishment, and since the Paraclete's Huguenot sympathies had brought the community under a cloud, the new régime at the Paraclete became remarkable for its super-orthodoxy. The result was a calculated break with a past in which the memory of Abaelard had been kept alive in part by his many contributions to the Paraclete liturgy. From now on the Paraclete breviary was the post-Tridentine Roman Breviary. For further details, see Constant Mews, 'La bibliothèque du Paraclet du XIIIᵉ siècle à la Révolution', in *Studia Monastica*, 27 (1985), pp. 31–60, with special reference to pp. 40–41, 59.

46. 'Ad hæc perniciosam et detestabilem consuetudinem quarumdam mulierum, quæ licet neque secundum regulam beati Benedicti, neque Basilii, aut Augustini vivent, sanctimoniales tamen vulgo censeri desiderant, aboleri decernimus'... The text may be found in any of the several editions of the canons of the Second Lateran Council, as in Mansi, *Sacrorum Conciliorum nova et amplissima collectio*, vol. XXI (Venice edition, 1776), cols. 532–3.

47. Jacque Dubois, 'Les Ordres religieux au XIIᵉ siècle selon la Curie romaine', *Revue bénédictine*, 78 (1968), p. 308.

48. 'Unam quippe nunc Regulam beati Benedicti apud Latinos feminæ profitentur æque ut viri. Quam sicut viris solummodo constat scriptum esse, ita ab ipsis tantum impleri posse...' *Epistola* VI; *PL* 178:213CD; J T Muckle, 'The Letter of Heloise on Religious Life and Abelard's First Reply', Letter V, *Mediaeval Studies*, 17 (1955), p. 242.

49. See pp. 292 and 293 of the article referred to above, note 47; but similar formulas are to be found throughout this study.

50. Ibid., p. 308.

51. See above, n. 19.

52. For a detailed analysis of the structure of this opening section of *Institutiones nostræ*, see pp. 66–177 of the edition referred to above, n. 19.

53. Ibid., p. 9 (for the text). pp. 77–85 (commentary).

54. Ibid., pp. 78–80 (sketch map of the priories, p. 79), with special reference to p. 79 for La Pommeraye.

55. The so-called *Capitula*; critical edition in Chrysogonus Waddell, *Narrative and Legislative Texts from Early Cîteaux* (Cîteaux – Commentarii cistercienses 1999), pp. 186–91, preceded by an Introduction, pp. 167–75; Latin text with English translation and commentary, ibid., pp. 408–13.

56. For the Cistercian background of Paragraph VII of *Institutiones nostrae* (p. 11 of the edition), see pp. 104–9 (ibid.).

57. For a discussion of work at the Paraclete, see the edition of *Institutiones nostrae*, pp. 194–6.

58. Page 284 of the collection of studies referred to above, n. 31.

Chapter 8. Communities of Reform in the Province of Reims: The Benedictine 'Chapter General' of 1131

1. Orderic Vitalis, *Historia Ecclesiastica*, ed. M Chibnall, Oxford Medieval Texts (Oxford, 1969–80), XIII. 11, pp. 418–19 and 424–5): 13 archbishops, 263 bishops and a great multitude of abbots and monks and secular clerks were present at the council. Jaffé and Potthast, *Regesta pontificum romanorum*, 1:860, has more modest figures: 'Concilium episcoporum 50 et abbatum 300'. See also *Anselmi Gemblacensis Continuatio* of *Sigeberti Gemblacensis Chronographea*, ed. L C Bethman; *Monumenta Germaniae Historiae. Scriptores* 6, pp. 383–4: '…cum episcopis et abbatibus 300'.
2. Canon 6, see Mansi, Giovanni Dominico, *Sacrorum conciliorum, nova et amplissima collectio*, 53 vols in 59 (repr. Graz 1961), 21, pp. 457, 459, 461.
3. Suger, *Vita Ludovici grossi regis* xxxii, ed. H Waquet (Paris, 1929), pp. 266–8. Cf. Vitalis, *Historia Ecclesiastica,* ed. Chibnall, XIII. 11, pp. 418–19, 424–5.
4. In view of the liturgical focus of the agreement, we may note that the treatise of pseudo-Bernard on Cistercian chant, attributed to Guy of Cherlieu, singles out the province of Reims as a hopeless hodgepodge: '…take the antiphonary of Reims and compare it to Beauvais or Amiens or Soissons, which lie almost on its doorstep; if you find any similarity, thank God for it…' (*Cîteaux: Documents primitifs*, p. 158)
5. For *Acta primi capituli provincialis ordinis S. Benedictii*, see pp. 51–64, esp. p. 58, in Ceglar, Stanislaus, 'William of St Thierry and his Leading Role at the First Chapters of the Benedictine Abbots' (Reims, 1131, Soissons, 1132), *William, Abbot of Saint Thierry*, pp. 34–112 (French edition, pp. 299–350). Also, see below, note 57.
6. 312 lines compared to 71 lines in the Ceglar edition.
7. 307 lines in the Ceglar edition.
8. A mere 46 lines in the *Sancti Bernardi Opera*, eds. Jean Leclercq, H M Rochais, C H Talbot (Rome, 1957–77), vol. 7, pp. 239–41.
9. Edited in Mansi, Giovanni Domenico, *Sacrorum conciliorum, nova et amplissima collectio* (Rept. Graz. 1960–1), vol. 21, pp. 430–1; Martène and Durand, *Thesaurus novus anecdotorum* (Paris 1717, repr. New York, 1968), vol. 1, pp. 389–90; *Patrologia cursus completa*, L 179:253.
10. Letter of Innocent II dated Nov. 17, Pisa (in Jaffé and Potthast, *Regesta pontificum romanorum*, 1:868; 7738 (5519): 1133–1136) granted permission to the following abbots to hold an annual 'meeting together': N Resbacensi, R Latiniacensi, S Cassiacensi, H S Theodorici, A S Amandi (Elnonensis), Io Aquicinctensi, W Letiensi, Se Lobiensi, Pa S Sepulchri Cameracensis, S Luciani Bellovacensis, S Eligii Noviomensis, I S Nicolai de Saltu abbatibus permittit, ut singuli annis congressum faciant (Martène and Durand, *Thesaurus*, 1:389; Bouquet, *Rec* 15:388; Mansi, *Sacrorum conciliorum*, 21:430; Migne, 179:253). Ceglar ('William of Saint-Thierry. The chronology of his life, with a study of his treatise *On the Nature of Love;* his authorship of the *Brevis Commenatio'*, Dissertation: Catholic University of America, 1971, p. 409, n. 25) points out that the pope's letter must be dated after 1135, as H S Theodorici refers to Hellin, who succeeded William only in 1135. Adriaan H Bredero ('William of Saint Thierry at the Crossroads of the Monastic Currents of His Time', in *William, Abbot of St Thierry*, Cistercian Studies Series, 94 (Kalamazoo, 1987), pp. 126, 136 n. 61)) argues for an 1131 date, on the grounds that 'five abbots are wrong' (Rebais, Anchin, Lobbes, St Eloi, St Nicolas). In this assertion he is mistaken. Three of the abbots are clearly Natalis/Noel of Rebais, who likely became abbot only c. 1133; Goswin/Joswin of Anchin (1130–65); Gilbert/Jilbert of St Nicolas

(1134–56); H S Theodorici places the document after 1135, the year William retired to Signy and Helluin succeeded him. The only problematic abbots are St Eloi, where a careless copyist may have mistaken the abbreviation for Sancti for the abbot's initial, and Se for Lobbes, whose abbot from until 1129 was Walter and from 1137–49 Lambert (Berlière, *Monasticon Belge*, p. 214, citing *Gesta* 329 and *Patrologia cursus completa*, L 182, pp. 713–15). The 'Se' may conceivably have originally been 'Le'.

11. Most of the houses dated back to the sixth, seventh or ninth centuries, and many had been refounded or reformed after Viking or Hungarian devastation; St Eloi (986), St Thierry (993), St Michel (tenth), St Vincent (tenth). Hasnon (1065), Hautmont (1016), Lagny (late tenth), Liessies (1095), Lobbes (eleventh), St Lucien (c. 1100).

12. Anchin, St Nicolas-aux-Bois, and St Sépulcre were eleventh-century foundations.

13. H E J Cowdrey, 'Abbot Pontius of Cluny (1109–22/6)' in *Studii Gregoriani per la storia della "libertas ecclesiae"*, II (Rome, 1978), pp. 266.'

14. See below, note 43 (Matthew of Albano). See also Peter the Venerable, letter 79 (Constable 1:213 = ep 2.43; *Patrologia cursus completa*, 189:265), where Geoffrey of St Médard was praised for being 'the first to disseminate, promote and advance the divine Order of Cluny throughout the whole of France' and to have driven 'the devil from his lair in many a monastic dormitory' Cf. W Williams, *Saint Bernard of Clairvaux*, p. 227. According to H Platelle (*Le Temporel de l'abbaye de saint Amand* (Paris, 1962) p. 178), the only Flemish abbey to be incorporated into Cluny was St Bertin, and that lasted only from 1099–1143; but in the space of 30 years Cluniac customs were adopted by all the monasteries in Flanders. Roger Gaussin (La rayonnement de la Chaise Dieu (Brionde, 1981), p. 342) claims – without giving supporting evidence – that St John Laon followed the customary view of la Chaise Dieu, a possibility which, in view of my conclusions, needs to be explored carefully.

15. Peter the Venerable, Letter 28 provides the handiest example of Cluniac criticism and defense. See also, Bernard, *Apologia to Abbot William*.

16. Ep. 91: rascor occupationibus meis, quibus impedior conventui vestro... Intendite saluti parvulorum, non murmuri malevolorum (*Sancti Bernardi Opera*, 7:239, 9 and 240, 25)

17. Berlière's assumption that Geoffrey was a moving force behind the Benedictine Chapters rests entirely on the basis of Bernard's letter 91, declining the abbots' invitation to meet with them. The letter is, however, addressed simply to 'The Abbot of St Médard' and, if Ceglar is correct, when it was written in 1132, the abbot of St Médard was no longer Geoffrey but his successor, Odo.

18. Geoffrey was consecrated on 10 Aug 1131 (M J Gut, 'Liste critique des évêques de Châlons-sur-Marne aux XIᵉ et XIIᵉ siècles', *Bulletin philologique et historique*, 1958 (Paris 1959), pp. 117–27, esp. 122–3; 'before October 1131', according to Stanislaus Ceglar ('The Chapter of Soissons and the Authorship of the Reply of the Benedictine Abbots to Cardinal Matthew', in J R Sommerfeldt, ed., *Studies in Medieval Cistercian History 2*, Cistercian Studies Series, 24 (Kalamazoo, 1976), pp. 92–105 (p. 102)) and continued as bishop until his death on 21 June 1143.

19. Platelle, *Le Temporel de l'abbaye de saint Amand*, pp. 192–3, citing a 1246 privilege of Innocent IV, 12 H 1, fol. 59), and five years later Serlo of St Lucien had dealings with Beaupré (*Gallia Christiana*, 9:781, 835).

20. Something which Mansi doubted; see Mansi, *Sacrorum conciliorum*, vol. 21, pp. 467–8.

21. Mansi, *Sacrorum conciliorum*, vol. 21, pp. 467–72.

22. *Sancti Bernardi Opera*, vol. 3, pp. 3–4, l. 63. See also Introduction to *Bernard of Clairvaux: Treatises 1* (Cistercian Publications, 1970), now published as Bernard of Clairvaux, *Cistercians and Cluniacs: Apologia to Abbot William*, Cistercian Fathers Series 1A, pp. 5, 7

23. C J Holdsworth, 'The Early Writings of St Bernard', *Cîteaux: Commentarii cistercienses*, 45 (1994), pp. 21–61 at pp. 47, 59.

24. Bernard, ep. 84 *bis* to William: *Sancti Bernardi Opera*, vol. 7, p. 219.

25. Apo I 3 (*Sancti Bernardi Opera*, vol. 3, p. 83, ll. 15–21) '...ex me habeatis, unde quod de me certissime scitis, eis pro me verissime persuadeatis'.

26. Foigny 1121, Igny 1126, Ourscamp 1129. Within four years of the synod, the Claravallian family in the immediate area had increased to eight; from Clairvaux itself: Longpont 1131, Vaucelles 1132, Vauclair 1134, and two granddaughters, Signy (from Igny) and Beaupré (from Ourscamp) in 1135.

27. Ep 48.2 to Haimeric; *Sancti Bernardi Opera*, vol. 7, p. 138.

28. There is no evidence to identify who attended, besides William (Geoffrey, Frag. 31, *Ana Boll* [1932] 106) and perhaps Drogo of St John Laon. See below.

29. See below, anno 1131.

30. *Monumenta Germaniae Historiae Scriptores*, vol. 21, p. 324.

31. Ceglar, 'William of Saint Thierry', p. 37 n. 40. Annual Chapters General would be mandated by IV Lateran Council in 1215. Matthew of Albano: '...abbatibus illius qui condixere singulis annis Remis convenire...' (Berlière, *Doc. inéd.* 1:94; Ceglar, 'William of Saint Thierry', p. 65; see also Ceglar, 'The Chapter of Soissons', p. 102 n. 31). Cf. Innocent II, ep (*Patrologia cursus completa* 179:253 et par.); Chronicle of Lobbes (*Monumenta Germaniae Historiae Scriptores*, vol. 21, p. 324, ll. 44–50). Ceglar, 'William of Saint Thierry', pp. 37–8) traces the subsequent chapters: autumn 1134, end October 1135.

32. Dissertation, Chapter XI, and articles in Ceglar, 'The Chapter of Soissons', p. 95.

33. Berlière, R Ben, 'Les chapitres généraux de l'ordre de S. Benoît avant le IVᵉ Concile de Latran (1215)', *Revue Bénédictine*, 8 (1891), pp. 255–64 (p. 257).

34. Bredero, 'William of Saint Thierry', pp. 123, 121–2. Bredero sees ties between Peter the Venerable's 'defense of the usages of Cluny' and 'defense of the old customs' (Bredero, 'William of Saint Thierry', p. 120) and 'the conservative reaction which took place after Pons' fall' (p. 123). Cowdrey, on the other hand, opposes Abbot Pontius party 'which, like the Anacletans at Rome, represented the by now obsolescent traditionalism of the eleventh-century reform...and that associated with Peter the Venerable which, like to Innocentians, championed the vigorous spiritual and ascetic tendences of more recent decades' (Cowdrey, 'Abbot Pontius of Cluny', p. 263).

35. Bredero, 'William of Saint Thierry', p. 115 et passim.

36. Bredero, 'William of Saint Thierry', pp. 120ff.

37. Some thirty other Benedictine houses existed in the province at the time.

38. Peter the Venerable, *De miraculis* 2. 14 (*Patrologia cursus completa*, 189:926): 'Nihil de officiis, nihil de cantibus, nihil de prolixa Cluniacensi psalmodia...reliquit'.

39. Ceglar, 'William of Saint Thierry', ll. 11–16: '...in ruinosa monastici ordinis fabrica in frigidis illis regionibus ...'

40. Ceglar, 'William of Saint Thierry', l. 25: 'gloriosa Christi ovilia (delectabiliaque praesepia) reparastis...' Matthew also addresses them in Ciceronian fashion as conscript fathers and senators of the celestial curia. He may have been indulging in sarcasm on both points.

41. Ceglar, 'William of Saint Thierry', l. 23: '...in claustris vestris, quae prius tamquam delubra voluptatum exstiterant, in quibus habitabat ericius, ululae morabantur, sirenae cantabant, saltabant pilosi ...'

42. Ceglar, 'William of Saint Thierry', ll. 151–61.

43. Ceglar, 'William of Saint Thierry', ll. 152–3.

44. Ceglar, 'William of Saint Thierry', l. 180: 'semper inutilis...'

45. Ceglar, 'William of Saint Thierry', ll. 202–4: '...cum eisdem bubulcis vel bubulcorum magistris saepe, et mane et vespere, loqui summis necessitatibus compellimur'.

46. Ph. Grierson, *Les annales de Saint-Pierre de Gaudet et de Saint-Amand* (Brussels, 1937), pp. 163–4, records the following:
    1123 hyemps facta est asperrima
    1125 fames valida fit
    1126 Clades vehemens.
47. *pauci in numero*: ll. 287–90. See Evergates, *Homblières*, #41 (p. 94), a grant of land to Ourscamp signed by sixteen monks, not including the abbot.
48. Ceglar, Stanislaus (CS 94), l. 190.
49. Ceglar (CS 94) ll. 33, '...consuetudines statuimus', 283, 'Nos enim Cluniacenses consuetudines...non abicimus'.
50. Ceglar (CS 94) ll. 103–4, 'appetendam potius esse rei veritatem quam nominis huius claritatem'.
51. Not identified on the agreement. See below, n. 57.
52. Not identified on the agreement.
53. H Sproemberg, 'Die Grundung des Bistums Arras im Jahre 1094', *Anciens Pays et assemblées d'Etat*, 24 (1962) 1–50, cited by Benoit-Michel Tock, *Les Chartes des évêques d'Arras (1093–1203)* (Paris: CTHS, 1991), p. xxxi.
54. Not identified on the agreement.
55. Michel Bur, *La Formation du comté de Champagne* (Nancy, 1977), p. 317. Chezy was also a comital abbey, as St Médard Soissons and St Nicaise Reims had once been.
56. Orebais and Homblières, for which documents dated exactly to 1131 have not yet been found.
57. *Gallia Christiana* 9:600 dates the beginning of his abbacy to c. 1124; this is supported by Ceglar, Diss, 'William of Saint-Thierry', p. 82, who corrects it to the modern calendar and sets its beginning in March 1125.
58. Ivo of Chartres refers to abuses at Lagny (ep. 65; *PL* 162:82).
59. Although there is some doubt about the identity of the abbot of Rebais, I have included him among here in the probable rank.
60. See Ceglar, CS 94:58, note. Ceglar cites in support Luc d'Achery, *Spicilegium* (Paris, 1723) 2:751–3, and 2:889; Berlière, R Ben, 'Les chapitres généraux', p. 260.
61. Sonon, cardinal bishop of Prenesta. This was the synod which originally condemned Peter Abælard – which suggests that William had been present and witnessed this condemnation.
62. Paris BN Picardie 249, f. 235. Cf. AD Somme H16 (001) (Stein 2015). It concerned a house, land, farm and dependencies in Artois.
63. A charter of Bartholomew of Laon [Dufour, item 93: orig lost; copy BN coll. Picardie, vol. 267, f. 24; le Paige, *Bibliotheca Praem. ordinis*, p. 373; and Dufour, item 94: Archives nationales K 22, n° l, pièce n° 1 *et al.*].
64. Ep 83; SBOp 7:216.
65. Bernard, Ep 83 (Leclercq-Rochais date it 'paulo post 1121;' Cf VdE 365–379). Hermann of Tournai/Laon, *De miraculis* 3. 18, wrote that the community had become 'just a bit tepid in religious observance' and refers to Simon as 'a very strenuous monk of St Nicaise Reims'.
66. Dufour #99: AD Aisne H325 f. 124, a 16th c copy of a cartulary-chronicle of Nogent.
67. According to the Annales de Saint-Amand (ed. Grierson, p. 1123) was 'a very harsh winter', and 1125 saw 'severe famine' and 'virulent pestilence'. Cf. Herman of Tournai, *Restoration of the Church of St Martin*, Epilogue (ET Nelson p. 129):

> The years 1125–1126 saw another of those periodic famines that began to afflict Flanders more frequently as its population grew and its arable land did not. The poor suffered terribly during such times, and the monks struggled vainly to sustain them until the new harvest. Communities went on short rations themselves, and

abbots, such as Siger of St Martin's, sold the church ornaments and vessels to buy more grain for charity although prices rose so high that even extreme sacrifices seemed ineffectual. The monks had to balance the needs of the moment to feed the hungry against the equally pressing necessity of holding back sufficient seed grain to plant the new crops. It was not possible to strike a happy medium; paupers starved at the abbey door, and the monks inside were constantly haunted by the words of twenty-fifth chapter of Matthew.

Similarly, 1124–25 saw severe famine in neighboring Burgundy; see MGH 4:449 and *Vita quarta Bernardi* 2.6.

68. A Dufour, item 105: D Aisne H 871, f. 3, a 17th copy of the Cartulary of St Martin Laon.
69. *Gallia christiana* 9:111.
70. J Cossé-Durlin, *Cartulaire de Saint-Nicaise de Reims* (Paris: CNRS 1991) #24.
71. In a document dated 1126, but corrected by Pechenard (1883) to 1127: it was signed by entire chapter of Reims and by Abbots Odo of St Rémy, Joran of St Nicaise, William of St Thierry, Urso of St Denis Reims, and Suger of St Denis Paris. It was confirmed by the king 1128; and by Reynald of Reims in 1130.
72. Stanley Ceglar, 'The Date of William's Convalesence at Clairvaux', *Cistercian Studies Quarterly* 30:1 (1995), pp. 27–33, esp. 31. Cf. C J Holdsworth, 'The Early Writings of Bernard of Clairvaux', *Citeaux: Commentarii cistercienses* 45 (1994), p. 59.
73. Mansi 21:371E.
74. Geoffrey, Fragmenta 31, *Analecta Bollandiana* (1932), p. 106.
75. An action confirmed by Innocent II on 4 Nov 1130 (Potthast, Regestra 1:844).
76. Bernard, Ep 48 to Haimeric: 'his sanctuary was restored to the Lord after being a brothel of Venus... Why am I blamed for the actions of others? Or supposing they were mine, why am I blamed for them as if they were evil...? Let [people] praise, if they choose, or blame me if they dare, first of all my Lord of Albano, and secondly my Lord of Reims, and thirdly the same archbishops together with the bishop of Laon, the king, and many other respected persons. None of them will deny responsibility for these affairs or that they were the chief persons concerned... I was present, I cannot deny it. But I was summoned and dragged there... I am vexed at having been embroiled in these disputes, especially as I knew that I was not concerned with them personally. I am vexed, but I was dragged there'. (*Sancti Bernardi Opera* dates c. 1130).
77. Matthew, line 23, in the Ceglar edition, '*Acta primi capituli*', in *William, Abbot of St Thierry*, CS 94:58.
78. Ep 34 to Drogo, *dilectissime* (*Sancti Bernardi Opera* 7:90–91).
79. Ep 32 (SBOp 7:86–88, dated *Paulo ante novembrem 1124*).
80. Ep 33 to Hugh of Pontigny (*Sancti Bernardi Opera* 7:88–89).
81. Ep 34 (above, n. 76).
82. Bernard to Haimeric, Ep. 48 (Sancti Bernardi Opera 7:137–140, dated c. 1130).
83. Mabillon (PL 182:137n), *Gallia Christiana* 9:594, and Leclercq, 'Drogo et saint Bernard' (*Recueil* 1:96–97).
84. Beauvais, Archives départementales G 1984, ff. 64v–65v.
85. Whose death Wyard, *Histoire de l'abbaye de saint Vincent de Laon* (St Quentin, 1858) 337, sets at 7 March 1128.
86. Dufour #117 (Copie BM Laon, ms 532, f.83 *et al.*)
87. Reims BM 1602, f. 209v; Mabillon, *Annales OSB* 6:149.
88. Vitalis, *Historia Ecclesiastica*, ed. Chibnall 6.10; Orderic places Warin of St Evroul with Natalis.
89. Gallia 9:611, citing Herman of Tournai 3.18.
90. *Saint Bernard of Clairvaux* 105–106. On this, see the recent study of Martha Newman,

The Boundaries of Charity: Cistercian Culture and Ecclesiastical Reform, 1098–1180 (Stanford University Press, 1996) esp. 195ff.

91. *Orderic Vitalis, Historia Ecclesiastica*, ed. Chibnall, 418/19-424/5: 'Gregory Innocent' [II] was entertained at Cluny, where he consecrated the church at Cluny on 24/25 Oct 1130 (see Conant: *Cluny: les églises et la maison du chef d'ordre'*, Medieval Academy 77 [Macon 1968] 75ff): 'Afterwards the pope traveled through France for the whole of that year and seriously burdened the churches of Gaul, because he had Roman officials and many dependents in his company and was unable to draw anything from the revenues of the Holy See in Italy' (p. 421). According to Watkin Williams (*St Bernard of Clairvaux*, pp. 105–6), Innocent went from Cluny 'by Roanne to Clermont in Auvergne, where he held his first council. Although, as Duchesne remarks, his itinerary is a little doubtful, he proceeded first to Orleans...then to Chartres...'.

92. By January 1131 (Williams continues), Innocent had visited the Abbey of Maurigny, not far from Étampes. After a visit to Rome, Innocent 'returned to France and spent Holy Week and Easter at St Denis' (Williams, 110, citing Suger's *Vita Ludovici Grossi*; PL 186: 1331). On 1 April 1131, the pope was at Liège where he held another council attended by Lothair and his queen, some twenty-five to thirty-two archbishops and bishops and fifty-three abbots, among them Bernard (Williams 109, using *Annaes Magdaburg. An. 1131*; *Historia Ecclesiastica Vitalis*, ed. Chibnall, 418/19-424/5. On 9 May he was at Rouen, as was Bernard. 'A few days later the Pope was at Beauvais' (Innocent II, Epp. et Privil. PL 179:99ff); and not long afterwards we find him at Compiègne and then at Crépy-en-Valois on his way to Auxerre, where he remains for some two months; the first document given at Auxerre during these months bears date 26th July and the last 24th September. From this place undoubtedly it was that he set forth to pay his memorable visit to Clairvaux (Williams 110). When Innocent left Clairvaux for Reims and the council Bernard accompanied him. For this itinerary (*in both notes*) Williams relied also on the *Liber Pontificalis* (ed. Duchesne 2:380 ff and on the *Chronicon Mauriniacensis II* (PL 180: 157ff) Cf. RHGF 12:80.

93. Vacandard, *Vie de saint Bernard* 1:307.

94. *Monasticon Belge* 1, fasc. 2: Province de Hainault (Maredsous, 1890; rpt Liège) 213; *Gesta continuata* (ed Arndt, MGH SS 21:308-333) 21:323; *Annales Laubienses*, ad annum 689 (ed. Pertz MGH SS) 4.22; Jaffé-Loewenfeld, *Regesta pontificum Romanorum* (Leipzig 1885–1888) 1:847, n° 7468. Cf. Joseph Warichez, *L'Abbaye de Lobbes depuis les Origines jusqu'en 1200* (Louvain-Paris, 1909) xvii.

95. *Annal.*, 4.22, *Gesta*, 21:325, Jaffe, 1:847.

96. BN nal 1386, ff 7v-8 (Stein 1682) IRHT 10339, ff. 7v-8. Cf. BN Coll. Picardie 249, Chapitre 6: Hautmont: f.323-359v (AD 1688), which does not name the abbot.

97. Jacquin, PM (OP) *Etude sur l'abbaye de Liessies 1095–1147, Compte-rendu des séances de la commission royale d'histoire* LXXI. Brussels 1903, p. 97.

98. Innocent II, Epp et Privil. PL 179:99ff.

99. Dufour #129 (AD Aisne, H 235 *et al*, including *AA SS OSB* 6:665), gives several sources: the lands were the village of Erlon and the manse of St Lambert usurped by the late Thomas de Marle. See also Dufour #135 (AD Aisne H. 235 *et al*, including *AA SS OSB* 6:656.

100. 10 August 1131.

101. Jaffe 1:850.

102. Dufour, item 134 (*olim* 129): 13th c Cart St Thierry, Reims BM 1602, f. lxxxi; – 18th c copy BN Coll Picardie 235, f. 30; – Mabillon, *Annales* 6 (1739) p. 654; – Varin, *Archives* adm. 1:283 '...*contradicente abbate Guillelmo et rusticis ejusdem ville. Cumque dominus papa Innocentius Lauduni esse, presentie ejus se distulit et me presente, presentibus etiam aliis episcopis et cardinalibus et abbate Sancti Theoderici'*.

103. Herman, *De miraculis* 18–20; Marcel Pacaut, *Louis VII*, 114.
104. Bernardi Ep. 66, referring to Abbot Alvisius of Anchin, who became bishop of Arras in 1130.
105. DGHE 20 (1984). pp. 538–9.
106. Foigny: Cartulary BN 18373 (Stein 1369) Bartholomew (in synod) gave to Clairvaux the allod of Foigny which he received from abbot 'Elbert' and the monks of St Michel–en–Thiérache.
107. See A Dimier, 'L'Eglise de l'abbaye de Foigny', *Bulletin monumental* 118 (1960) 191–205; Idem. 'L'Eglise de Foigny', *La Thiérache 1873–1973*, Société archéologique de Vervins et de la Thiérache (1973) 71–77.
108. An exodus dated to 1124, November, by van den Eynde, and Holdsworth ('The Early Writings of St Bernard', *Cîteaux: Commentarii cistercienses* 45 [1994] p. 25); and to 1124–1128 by Jean Leclercq, 'Drogo et saint Bernard' (*Recueil*, 1:96–97), Mabillon (PL 182:137n), and *Gallia Christiana* 9:594.
109. Ep 34 to Drogo *dilectissime*: '...the whole city was buzzing about your holiness and very religious way of life (very observant; *religiossisimum*)...'
110. Hermann of Laon 3. 18; Bernard, Ep 83 (SBOp dates *Paulo post 1121*; VdE 365–379). *Histoire littéraire de la France* 9:96. Ceglar, Diss., 82, suggests that, in light of his zeal at abbot of St Nicolas for recovering the altars assiduously alienated by Simon, Gilbert may, in fact, have led the opposition to his predecessor.
111. Herman of Laon 3.18: 'Count Theobald of Champagne, on the advice of Dom Norbert, accepted from the aforesaid abbot [Simon] a certain monk of [St Nicolas-aux-Bois], Ralph by name, and appointed him abbot of the enormously wealthy monastery of Lagny'. See also G Marlot, *Metropolis Remensis historia* (1666) 1:632, n. 26, lettre 231, vers 1140; PL 182:417–419.
112. Absalon, Gilbert and Thierry are listed as being among the 'great men who emerged from St Nicaise...our guarantee that good studies there were not neglected', in the *Hist. litt.* 9:96, citing Mabillon, *Annales OSB* 1:73, n. 136; *Card. Fr.* 1:116–117.
113. Ep 33.1; SBOp 7:88, 21–89, 1.
114. Ep 33.2; SBOp 7:89,14.
115. F Poirier-Coustansais: *Gallia monastica* 1:25; J Cossé-Durlin, *Cartulaire de Saint Nicaise de Reims* (Paris: CNRS 1991), 39ff. This is noted in passing by Bredero, Crossroads, CS 94: 116, 123–citing P G Gaussin, *L'Abbaye de la Chaise-Dieu* (Paris 1962) 310–311.
116. Bernard, Ep. 83.

Chapter 9. When Jesus Did the Dishes: The Transformation of Late Medieval Spirituality

1. As in R W Southern, *Western Society and the Church*, Penguin History of the Church (Harmondsworth, 1970).
2. Some medievalists simply subsume the Italian Renaissance into their treatment of the period, without considering how some of their historian colleagues traditionally have separated the Renaissance from the Middle Ages. See, for example, Daniel Waley, *Later Medieval Europe from Saint Louis to Luther* (Harlow 1989), as in Chapter 8, 'The Early Renaissance'. Elsewhere treatments of the period simply ignore the term 'Renaissance', as in Francis Oakley, *The Western Church in the Later Middle Ages* (Ithaca and London, 1979).

3. As in the by now classic textbook treatment by Maurice Keen, *The Pelican History of Medieval Europe* (Harmondsworth, 1968). See p. 299: 'the unity of Christendom was dead. The universal authority of the Church was no longer a living force...'

4. *Herfsttij der Middeleeuwen* was translated into English by F Hopman in 1924 under Huizinga's guidance and published by Pelican Books in 1955. Still available today in Penguin paperback editions.

5. *The Autumn of the Middle Ages*, tr. Rodney J Payton and Ulrich Mammitzsch (Chicago, 1996), with a helpful translators' introduction.

6. The central work on sainthood in this period is André Vauchez, *La Sainteté en Occident aux derniers siècles du moyen âge* (Rome, 1988), now available from Cambridge University Press (1997) as *Sainthood in the Later Middle Ages*. Vauchez is mainly interested in institutional aspects of sainthood as manifestations of the exercise of church authority. I try to go beyond this understanding in order to see sainthood in a larger cultural context.

7. The past decades have brought a great swell of studies on female life and spirituality in the Middle Ages, while male spirituality has been neglected. One of the few contributions has been the article collection edited by Clare A Lees, *Medieval Masculinities: Regarding Men in the Middle Ages* (Minneapolis and London, 1994).

8. For a summary of the cult of St Joseph through the centuries, a good point of departure is the article signed by 'D C A', 'Le développement historique du culte de saint Joseph', *Revue Bénédictine*, 14 (1897), pp. 104–14, 145–55 and 203–9. The *Cahiers de Joséphologie*, published at the Oratory of St Joseph in Montreal, sometimes offers careful studies of historical development but is mainly interested in contemporary manifestations of devotion to the saint.

9. *The Waning of the Middle Ages* (n. 4 above), p. 150.

10. See Kathleen Ashley and Pamela Sheingorn, *Interpreting Cultural Symbols: St Anne in Late Medieval Society* (Athens, Georgia, 1990), especially the long and thoughtful introductory article.

11. See André Vauchez, *The Spirituality of the Medieval West* (originally, *La Spiritualité du moyen âge occidental*, Les Presses Universitaires de la France, 1975), tr. Colette Friedlander (Kalamazoo, 1993), with a good definition (p. 9) of spirituality as 'the dynamic unity between the content of a faith and the way in which it is lived'.

12. In the standard edition of *Legenda Aurea* (ed. Th Graesse, Leipzig, 1850), there is a chapter (225, pp. 938–9) dedicated to 'St Joseph the spouse of the Virgin Mary', but this is a late medieval addition to the original text. No day is given for celebrating St Joseph.

13. David Hugh Farmer, *The Oxford Dictionary of Saints* (Oxford, 1978), pp. 222–3.

14. As in the description of the Nativity, where Joseph is hardly mentioned. It is said, however, that he had taken with him in leaving for Bethlehem an ox and a donkey: an ox to sell to pay the census; a donkey to bear Mary. See *The Golden Legend*, tr. Granger Ryan and Helmut Ripperger (New York, 1948), pp. 49–50.

15. See the *Ludus Coventriae*, 12, in *English Mystery Plays. A Selection*, ed. Peter Happé (Harmondsworth, 1975), pp. 221–9.

16. *Ludus Coventriae*, ed. Peter Happé, p. 223.

17. *Saint Joseph durant les quinze premiers siècles de l'église*, special issue of *Cahiers de Joséphologie*, 19 (Montréal, 1971). See, in the back of the volume, figure 57, from Tudela in Navarre.

18. As at Tuse parish church to the west of Holbæk on the Danish island of Sjælland, from about 1450. The tired Joseph, with hand to chin and already dressed for travelling to Egypt, is seen nearby at Mørkøv church, from the same period and the same workshop, the Master of the Ice Fjord.

19. For Augustine's views, see Elizabeth A Clark, "Adam's Only Companion': Augustine and the early Christian Debate on Marriage' in *The Olde Daunce: Love, Friendship,*

Sex and Marriage in the Medieval World, ed. Robert R Edwards and Stephen Spector (Albany, 1991), pp. 15–31.

20. *De perpetua virginitate beatae Mariae adversus Helvidium*, in J P Migne, *Patrologia Latina*, vol. 23:193–216.

21. Penny S Gold, 'The Marriage of Mary and Joseph in the Twelfth-Century Ideology of Marriage' in *Sexual Practices and the Medieval Church*, ed. Vern L Bullough and James Brundage (Buffalo, New York, 1982), pp. 102–17.

22. It is interesting to note that Vauchez's work on medieval spirituality, which is supposed to stop in the twelfth century but also considers the thirteenth, does not include a single mention of the cult of St Joseph (n. 11 above).

23. I am grateful to my Byzantinist colleague Christian Troelsgaard at the Institute for Greek and Latin, Copenhagen University, for this information. See *Mit der Seele Augen sah er deines Lichtes Zeichen Herr: Hymnes des orthodoxen Kirchenjahres von Romanos dem Meloden*, trans. Johannes Koder (Wien, 1996). Here in verse 12 we find a Joseph who understands what he sees at the Nativity: 'Deutlich kündet er alles, was er vernahm,/meldet klar alles, war er schaute/im Himmel und auf Erden'. This is a far cry from the fool of the Coventry cycle!

24. For details about Gerson's life and source references, see the introduction in Brian Patrick McGuire, *Jean Gerson: Early Writings*, Classics of Western Spirituality (Mahwah, 1998).

25. See Palemon Glorieux, 'La Vie et les œuvres de Gerson', *Archives d'histoire doctrinale et littéraire du moyen âge*, 25–6 (1950–1), pp. 149–92, esp. pp. 160–1.

26. As in most of the mentions in Francis Oakley (n. 2 above).

27. See the article on Gerson by L Salembier in the *Dictionnaire de Théologie catholique*, 6 (Paris, 1915), pp. 1315–30, where, in the light of the First Vatican Council's assertion of papal infallibility, it is said: 'Il est trop certain que le chancelier a soutenu à propos du pape et du concile des théories erronées, condamnables et plus tard condamnées' (p. 1318).

28. See Glorieux, 'La Vie' (note 25 above), p. 176: 'La maison de Gerson a été pillée; lui-même s'est réfugié sous les hautes voûtes de Notre-Dame'.

29. *Jean Gerson. Œuvres Complètes*, ed. P Glorieux, vol. 2 (Paris, 1960), p. 156: 'qui feust gouuerneur dudit enfant Jhesus, le porta souuent, le baisa souuent … plus familierement quaultre homme quelconques'. Further references to Glorieux's edition of Gerson will be to 'Gl' with the volume and page number.

30. Gl. 2.157: '… et auoit souuent esprouue son secours es necessites de soy et daultruy comme par miracle'.

31. Max Lieberman, 'Henri Chicot et le culte de saint Joseph', *Cahiers de Joséphologie*, 19 (1971), pp. 409–13 (n. 17 above).

32. For an overview of Gerson's prolific writings in 1413 in order to plead for a feast day for the marriage of Mary and Joseph, see Gl. 10.590–91. For a brief presentation of these works, see Glorieux's article, 'Saint Joseph dans l'œuvre de Gerson', *Cahiers de Joséphologie*, 19 (1971), pp. 414–28, esp. pp. 414–16.

33. Gl. 8.61–66: Here Gerson indicated that he knew there was resistance to the description of the betrothal of Joseph and Mary as a real marriage: 'Nemo propterea deputet arrogantiae, nemo curiositati, nemo superstitioni' (p. 62). It is almost uncanny how Gerson anticipated Huizinga's later charge of excessive curiosity on this matter!

34. Gl. 2.156: 'par icelluy doulz et bening enfant Jhesus qui en ce mariage sacre de nostre Dame et saint Joseph vot estre nez et nourris'.

35. Blaine Burkey, 'The Feast of Saint Joseph: A Franciscan Bequest', *Cahiers de Josephologie*, 19 (1971), pp. 647–80, esp. p. 651.

36. Gl. 7.63–94, dated August 17–September 26, 1413.

37. Gl. 7.66: 'Considerons encorez, quant a l'enfant Jhesus, que Joseph le nourry, le porta, le conduisi en Egipte, le ramena, le mena puis chascun an ou temple, l'enseigna et

disciplina seldon paternele auctorité, et a brief dire il accompli toute la cure que bon et loyal et saige pere peut et doit faire a son vray fils'.

38. Gl. 7.72: 'Et peut estre que pour ceste consideracion les paintres au commencement paignoient St Joseph comme un moult vieillart homme, a la barbe florie ...'

39. Gl. 7.75.

40. Gl. 7.81. Also Gl. 7.83: 'Considérons que par telle considération la Vierge pucelle estoit moult loée et honorée, et moult plaisoit a saint Joseph de plus en plus, sans quelconque vilaine pensée ou mauvaise concupiscence; mais en toute honesteté; non por quant eussent leurs chambres séparées et secrètes'.

41. Contained in Gl. 4.31–100. For a careful review of the evidence for the stages in which the poem was composed, see Max Lieberman, 'Chronologie Gersonienne. IV Gerson poète', *Romania*, 76 (1955), 289–333.

42. See Gilbert Ouy, 'Humanism and Nationalism in France at the Turn of the Fifteenth Century' in Brian Patrick McGuire, ed., *The Birth of Identities. Denmark and Europe in the Middle Ages* (Copenhagen, 1996), pp. 107–25, esp. pp. 114–15.

43. Gl. 4.34.

44. Gl. 4.35.

45. Gl. 4.36.

46. Gl. 4.36: 'Donec dormiat is cujus semper vigilat cor'. The phrase is taken from the Song of Songs 5:2 and provides a link between the everyday scenery and the mystical context.

47. As in his letter from Constance on January 1, 1417 to his brother Jean le Célestin (Gl. 2.199): 'quatenus ego peregrinus et advena – sic enim Gerson interpretatum significat – assidua meditatione recordarer verbi coelestis peregrini Pauli: nostra conversatio in coelis est' (cf. Philippians, 3.20).

48. Gl. 4.37.

49. Gl. 4.39–40.

50. Gl. 4.37.

51. Gl. 4.40.

52. Gl. 4.41.

53. Gl. 4.43.

54. Gl. 4.44.

55. Gl. 4.44: 'Creverat ipse Jesus, binos evaserat annos;/Mater ei tunicam polimitam neverat et jam/Stare licet tremulo poterat pede verbaque grato/Nondum perfecta balbutit lingua susurro/Suavior hinc multo blanditur utrique parenti/Arridet, ruit in ulnas gremioque vocatur/Brachiola attollens vult nectere colla parentum./Amplexu tenero vult oscula figere casta/Inserit atque manum manu tibi Virgo Josephque/Perque domum seuitur hunc et te dispare passu./Quaeque videt mirans sciscitatur ut omnia noscat/Forte interturbat quandoque laborem/Pensa, colum, calathos, serras parvasque secures/Contrectans ultrove petens sese bajular.'

56. *L'enfant et la vie familiale sous l'Ancien Régime* (Paris, 1973).

57. Gl. 4.44: 'Dixerit hoc aliquis totum puerile relatu/Nullo sed risu dignum; puerile fatemur/Sed puerile Dei ...'

58. Gl. 4.45.

59. Gl. 4.46.

60. Gl. 4.46: 'Hinc sperat, metuit, gaudet, dolet iste beatus/Infans ...'

61. Gl. 4.47.

62. Romans 12.15.

63. Genesis 37–41.

64. Gl. 4.48.

65. Gl. 4.49: 'Quis dederit peregre tales vidisse viantes/Alloquioque frui facundia quem satiasset/Grata Jesu?'

66. Gl. 4.49.
67. For this development, based on the *Protoevangelium of James*, known in its Latin version as Pseudo-Matthew, see Kathleen Ashley and Pamela Sheingorn's introduction to their book on St Anne (n. 10 above), pp. 6–17.
68. There is a wonderful wooden sculpture of the Holy Kinship at the National Museum in Copenhagen, taken from the demolished church of Rodsted in central Jutland. See the cover illustration in Niels-Knud Liebgott, *Hellige mænd og kvinder* (Arhus, Denmark, 1982).
69. Gl. 4.51.
70. Gl. 4.51: 'Nil super ignotis igitur meditatio nostra/Affirmet temere, sola suffecerit uti/Conjecturarum topica ratione modeste/Ex scriptis inferre potest non scripta pio mens/Cum studio, sic certa fides incerta revelat/Qualia sunt acta vel fieri potuere.'
71. Luke 2.51.
72. Gl. 4.51-2: 'Si subjectus erat, ut erat tibi Virgo Josephque/Christus, quid sibi vult, oro, subjectio talis? Obsequium nonne vobis praestabat eratque/In medio vestrum sicut qui rite ministrat?/Saepe focum crebroque cibum parat officiosus;/Vasa lavat, bajulat undam de fonte propinquo/Nuncque domum scopit, paleas vel aquam dat asello./Vicinis fert matris opus quod texuit ipsa./Exercenda datur ars crebro paterna fabrilis/In ligno vario; fuit hinc faber ipse vocatus.'
73. As has been pointed out to me by Gilbert Ouy, the dean of Gersonian studies, who several years ago encouraged me to look at the *Josephina* as an exhibition of Gerson's gentler side. I am most grateful.
74. Gl. 7.74: 'Et c'est contre ceulz ou celles qui ne veulent ouvrer, et reputent a honte ou a servage.'
75. Gl. 4.52.
76. Gl. 4.61: 'Filius atque pater numquid non grandis amoris/Nomina sunt et praecipuae pietatis imago.'
77. Gl. 4.61.
78. Gl. 4.95: '… complexans membra, pudicis/Oscula dat labiis: mi vir conclamat, abisne/Deseris et viduam passuram dira relinquis.'
79. Gl. 4.96.
80. Gl. 4.97.
81. Gl. 4.94.
82. See Gerson's letters to his brothers, which I have translated in *Jean Gerson: Early Writings* (n. 24 above).
83. Gl. 4.95.
84. For the technique of meditation in the rosary, see the helpful remarks in *Catechism of the Catholic Church* (New York, 1995), section 2708: 'Christian prayer tries above all to meditate on the mysteries of Christ, as in lectio divina or the rosary.'
85. See fig. 62 in *Cahiers de Joséphologie*, 19 (1971) (n. 17 above), from the provincial museum of Valencia, a detail from a scene of the Last Judgment. Here Jesus is clearly a boy. His father Joseph is twice as tall as he is and rests his right hand squarely on the youth's shoulder.
86. Quoted in Kathleen Ashley, 'Image and Ideology: St Anne in late Medieval Drama and Narrative', *Interpreting Cultural Symbols* (n. 10 above), p. 115.
87. See D Catherine Brown, *Pastor and Laity in the Theology of Jean Gerson* (Cambridge, 1987), pp. 238–51.
88. See *De parvulis ad Christum trahendis* (Gl. 9.681): 'Quod autem superadditur meam occupationem in majoribus esse debere.'
89. A less attractive side of Gerson's concern with education and upbringing – his near obsession with sexual matters – is not relevant here in his description of Jesus but certainly is important in his considerations about other children. See Brian McGuire, 'Education, Confession and Pious Fraud: Jean Gerson and a Late Medieval Change', *American Benedictine Review*, 47 (1996), pp. 310–38.

90. See McGuire, 'Sexual Control and Spiritual Growth in the Late Middle Ages: The Case of Jean Gerson', in *Tradition and Ecstasy: The Agony of the Fourteenth Century*, ed. Nancy van Deusen (Ottawa, 1997), pp. 123–52.

91. 'Late Medieval Care and Control of Women: Jean Gerson and his Sisters', *Revue d'histoire ecclésiastique*, 92 (1997), pp. 5–37.

92. See R N Swanson, *Religion and Devotion in Europe, c. 1215–c.1515* (Cambridge, 1995), p. 308: 'As men claimed a greater stake in religion, and one which was almost necessarily patriarchal if women's place was to be wrested from them, so the tensions increased. The developments are complex; but two features of the period perhaps show the changes. The first is the gradual development of the cult of St Joseph, advocated by Gerson in the late fourteenth century, but only slowly brought out of the shadows.'

93. Steven Ozment, *When Fathers Ruled: Family Life in Reformation Europe* (Cambridge, Mass., 1985).

94. As in Barbara Newman, 'Possessed by the Spirit: Devout Women, Demoniacs, and the Apostolic Life in the Thirteenth Century', *Speculum*, 73 (1998), pp. 733–70, p. 769: 'Jean Gerson, who was notoriously skeptical of devout women's visions.'

95. I have translated Gerson's *On Distinguishing True from False Revelations* in *Jean Gerson. Early Writings* (n. 24 above).

96. This change in Southern European attitudes to Joseph can be seen, for example, in the writings of Theresa of Avila, who is known for a great devotion to St Joseph. See Chapter 32 ff of her Autobiography.

97. 'Twelfth-century Spirituality and the Late Middle Ages', *Medieval and Renaissance Studies*, 5, ed. O B Hardison Jr. (Chapel Hill, 1971), pp. 27–60, and 'The Popularity of Twelfth-Century Spiritual Writers in the Late Middle Ages', *Renaissance Studies in Honor of Hans Baron*, ed. Anthony Molho and John A Tedeschi (Dekalb, 1971), pp. 5–28.